PERGAMON INTERNATIONAL LIBRARY
of Science, Technology, Engineering and Social Studies

*The 1000-volume original paperback library in aid of education,
industrial training and the enjoyment of leisure*

Publisher: Robert Maxwell, M.C.

Congress,
the Presidency and
American Foreign Policy

THE PERGAMON TEXTBOOK
INSPECTION COPY SERVICE

An inspection copy of any book published in the Pergamon International Library
will gladly be sent to academic staff without obligation for their consideration for
course adoption or recommendation. Copies may be retained for a period of 60 days
from receipt and returned if not suitable. When a particular title is adopted or
recommended for adoption for class use and the recommendation results in a sale
of 12 or more copies, the inspection copy may be retained with our compliments.
The Publishers will be pleased to receive suggestions for revised editions and new
titles to be published in this important International Library.

Pergamon Titles of Related Interest

Fitzgerald COMPARING POLITICAL THINKERS
Foreign Affairs AMERICA AND THE WORLD 1980
Khoshkish THE SOCIO-POLITICAL COMPLEX
Nogee/Donaldson SOVIET FOREIGN POLICY SINCE WORLD
WAR II
Talmor MIND AND POLITICAL CONCEPTS

Related Journals*

FUTURICS
HABITAT INTERNATIONAL
HISTORY OF EUROPEAN IDEAS
TECHNOLOGY IN SOCIETY
WORLD DEVELOPMENT

*Free specimen copies available upon request.

PERGAMON POLICY STUDIES ON INTERNATIONAL POLITICS

Congress, the Presidency and American Foreign Policy

Edited by
John Spanier
Joseph Nogee

Pergamon Press

NEW YORK • OXFORD • TORONTO • SYDNEY • PARIS • FRANKFURT

Pergamon Press Offices:

U.S.A.	Pergamon Press Inc., Maxwell House, Fairview Park, Elmsford, New York 10523, U.S.A.
U.K.	Pergamon Press Ltd., Headington Hill Hall, Oxford OX3 0BW, England
CANADA	Pergamon Press Canada Ltd., Suite 104, 150 Consumers Road, Willowdale, Ontario M2J 1P9, Canada
AUSTRALIA	Pergamon Press (Aust.) Pty. Ltd., P.O. Box 544, Potts Point, NSW 2011, Australia
FRANCE	Pergamon Press SARL, 24 rue des Ecoles, 75240 Paris, Cedex 05, France
FEDERAL REPUBLIC OF GERMANY	Pergamon Press GmbH, Hammerweg 6, Postfach 1305, 6242 Kronberg/Taunus, Federal Republic of Germany

Library of Congress Cataloging in Publication Data
Main entry under title:

Congress, the Presidency, and American foreign
   policy.

   (Pergamon policy studies on international
politics)
   Includes index.
   1. United States--Foreign relations--Law and
legislation--Addresses, essays, lectures.
2. Executive power--United States--Addresses,
essays, lectures. 3. Legislative power--United
States--Addresses, essays, lectures. I. Spanier,
John W. II. Nogee, Joseph L. III. Series.
KF4651.A5C58   1981   353.0089   80-28412
ISBN 0-08-025575-2
ISBN 0-08-025574-4 (pbk.)

Printed in the United States of America

Contents

Preface

As the 1980s begin, there are few problems confronting the United States which are of greater importance than the relationship between the Congress and the President in the conduct of the nation's foreign policy. The separation of powers between the legislative and executive branches was intended by the Founding Fathers to prevent an abuse of power and to preserve liberty. The war in Vietnam and Watergate have demonstrated for many Americans the wisdom of those who wrote the Constitution and the legitimacy of their concern. But did the Founding Fathers create a system which in its rightful preoccupation with preventing abuses of power cannot in the late twentieth century respond in an effective and timely manner to the many political, economic, and military challenges and changes abroad? At a time when the United States is a world power whose security and prosperity are affected by events in far away places, our concern cannot be limited to the preservation of freedom; America's political institutions must also be capable of making difficult decisions and making policy to ensure the nation's protection and fortunes—indeed, its economic viability.

The separation of powers is critical to the country's capacity to conduct an effective foreign policy. This problem—which, as often pointed out, is not really a problem of the separation of power as much as separate institutions sharing powers—was obviously not of major concern during America's long periods of isolationism. But as the United States emerged as one of the two super powers after World War II, this issue was perceived by many scholars and journalists, such as James McGregor Burns, George Galloway, Robert Dahl, and Walter Lippman, as the key impediment to a sound foreign policy. Ironically, the expectations that a Congressional-Presidential struggle would not allow the nation to act with authority, dispatch, continuity as well as flexibility, even with secrecy whenever necessary, were not realized as Congress increasingly subordinated itself to Presidential leadership in foreign policy during the cold war years.

Thus, it is only now, in the post-Vietnam era, that this problem has come to the fore. Since Presidents had led us into war, it was contended, the powers of the "imperial presidency" had to be cut back; above all, Congress had to be more assertive in foreign policy and hold the President more strictly accountable for his actions. Our case studies provide a critical look at the resulting executive-legislative relations in the conduct of American foreign policy. More fundamentally, they raise the question of the capacity of American political institutions to conduct a foreign policy which will meet the nation's many needs. As emphasized in the introductory chapter, the real test of the merit of our institutions, of their ability to work together in a responsible and effective fashion, comes now. Although the cold war, for reasons explained below, avoided the test, this test is no longer avoidable. The current relationship however, often appears more as a recipe for disaster than a way of ensuring a wise and thoughtful approach to the grave and immense problems the United States confronts in the world.

Finally, the editors wish to thank their colleagues for their cooperation and hard work, especially for sticking to our common framework for analyzing the executive-legislative relationship. Additionally we thank Dan Caldwell for his contribution to that framework; Bruce I. Oppenheimer for helpful comments on a portion of the text, and Robert A. Hoover for his assistance to the editors when this volume was conceived.

John Spanier
Joseph L. Nogee

Introduction
Congress and the Presidency: The Weakest Link in the Policy Process
John Spanier

Before Vietnam, the effective conduct of American foreign policy was associated with a strong presidency. The war, however, produced widespread disillusionment with the "imperial presidency." Presidential foreign policy was identified by the critics with a policy of "global policemanship," of widespread foreign commitments, an inability to distinguish between areas of primary and secondary interests, of needless involvements where vital interests were not at stake, and a general disposition to military and covert intervention. In turn, these characteristics were said to be symptomatic of a militarization of containment and, even more basically, of a confusion between the containment of Russia and the containment of communism. The result, in any event, was a costly anticommunist crusade which finally came to grief in Vietnam.

The conclusions drawn from these charges were: the need to constrain the presidency; and the need for Congress to be more assertive in fulfilling its foreign policy responsibilities, thereby ensuring presidential restraint and accountability. Franck and Wiesband have referred to the subsequent shift of power from the executive branch to the legislative branch as a revolution since it "radically redistributed" the powers of the presidency and the control over American foreign policy, long a presidential perquisite, to the Congress.[1]

Among the measures which Congress enacted and whose collective purpose was to restrain the President from involving the nation in another Vietnam were:

1. The War Powers Resolution, passed by the Senate and the House over President Nixon's veto, was intended to restrain Presidents from using their authority as commander-in-chief to involve the country in costly overseas "adventures," especially "presidential wars," and restore Congress' role in decisions involving the use of force.

2. Executive agreements, which Presidents had increasingly used to make foreign policy commitments in order to get around the difficulty of mobilizing two-thirds support in the Senate for treaties, were to be reported to Congress. Congress could then register its disapproval if it wished to do so. In addition, the Senate has increasingly insisted that "significant" agreements were to be submitted as treaties. No international obligations were to be undertaken without executive *and* legislative consent.

3. An increasing number of restrictions have been imposed on military assistance or arms transfers to other countries, including a congressional veto of specific arms transfers exceeding a few million dollars.

4. Intelligence operations—specifically, overt interventions in other countries and covert subversions against foreign regimes by the Central Intelligence Agency—were first to receive presidential approval and then to be reported to Senate and House committees involved with oversight of such operations. (At one time, this involved four committees in the Senate and four in the House; in 1980, the number was limited to the Senate and House intelligence committees, as congressional sentiment after the Iranian seizure of American hostages in Teheran and the Soviet invasion of Afghanistan in late 1979 moved toward relaxing the restrictions on the C.I.A.)

It is our contention that this relationship between the presidency and a more assertive Congress, while intended to produce a more responsible foreign policy, creates new difficulties for foreign policymaking and may well be the weak link, if not the weakest link, in the policy process. One need but look at some of our case studies. SALT II, the Strategic Arms Limitation treaty, which placed quantitative ceilings on the American–Soviet arms competition and attempted to stabilize the strategic balance, appeared doomed to defeat in the Senate when the President took advantage of the Soviet invasion of Afghanistan to withdraw the treaty from Senate consideration to save the nation and himself from a humiliating embarrassment. In the American government the legislature can repudiate its own chief executive who has negotiated an agreement with a foreign state on behalf of the country and undermine his prestige, thus raising questions for our friends and foes alike about the desirability of negotiating with a country whose Senate may, in the end, not give its consent to an agreement negotiated over a period of several years. The two Panama Canal treaties did squeak by in the end, but barely. To gain the two-thirds vote of the Senate needed for treaty approval, President Carter had to accept the De Concini amendment which, had the Senate not softened the interpretation of its own amendment, would have led Panama to reject the treaties, placed the United States in opposition to all of Latin America and the nationalism of the Third World, and been responsible for undoubted violence in Panama. Indeed, the Senate's Jackson-Vanik Amendment to the United States–Soviet trade agreement earlier in the decade had led the Russians to reject the agreement about

Jewish emigration as interference in Soviet domestic problems. The purpose of this agreement had been to use American trade and technology, both of which the Russians needed, as an incentive for the Soviets to restrain themselves politically and not unilaterally exploit all opportunities to expand their influence.

Formulating national policy to deal with the many difficult and complex problems the United States confronts in today's world is, in short, difficult because the executive and legislative branches all too often pull in opposite directions. As a Russian observer asked during the American SALT II debate:

> With whom in America can we have dealings? If the President needs to coordinate his actions and stand with the Congress, why isn't this done before any international agreement is concluded? Is it really so, [Soviet citizens] ask, that for more than six years of talks the U.S. authorities have been unable to decide among themselves what in SALT II they can agree to and what they cannot? . . . Opinions in our Government on this or that question may differ, too. But when our representative at negotiations agrees to something, he does so on behalf of the country. . . .
>
> In the case of the United States, however, it appears that agreement with the Administration even having a majority in the Congress often counts for little. It comes out that having reached agreement with the Administration, one ought then to enter into separate external relations with the American Congress, and renegotiate, as it were, the agreement reached.[2]

When the United States, after the 1973 Yom Kippur War between Israel and her Arab neighbors, attempted to play a more even-handed role in order to avoid an expansion of the war which might draw in the United States and the Soviet Union and/or lead to another oil embargo, the effectiveness of the Israeli lobby in Congress made playing this mediating role very difficult at times, for Congress set limits on the pressure that could be exerted on Israel to be more conciliatory in the peace negotiations with its Arab neighbors and less provocative, as on the settlements policy in the West Bank. In the dispute between Greece and Turkey, over the island of Cyprus the legislature and the executive also pulled in opposite directions—the former toward Greece, the latter to Turkey. The result, an arms embargo against Turkey, was heavily influenced by the Greek-American community; there are few Turkish-Americans. The same type of conflict arose over United States policy toward Rhodesia (now Zimbabwe) where a civil war and negotiations, conducted by this country and England, were going on in order to bring about a settlement through establishing minority rule and ending the governing of a vast majority of blacks by a tiny majority of whites. Again, President Carter and the Senate tended to pull in different directions, almost upsetting the delicate negotiations.

In all these instances, the influence of various ethnic and economic interest groups can be seen repeatedly. Nowhere is this more true than in the area in which inter(national) and (do)mestic policies overlap. In the area of "intermestic" policy, such as energy, Congress and interest groups are, as in most domestic policies, very active, thereby limiting even further presidential initiatives and leadership than on traditional foreign policies. Almost seven years after the Organization of Petroleum Exporting Countries (OPEC) first quadrupled oil prices and embargoed oil going to the United States, this nation still has no comprehensive energy policy. The meager results of years of executive-legislative conflict over this issue suggests the great difficulty of making policy in this intermestic area.

It was, significantly enough, the Treaty of Versailles ending World War I with Germany that first dramatized the damaging effect executive-legislative discord can have on foreign policy. America's participation in that war first signaled the end of the nation's long isolationist history and marked the beginning of its rise to superpower status and virtually global involvement during World War II with Germany and the subsequent cold war with Russia. It was, perhaps, a forecast of things to come that this initial participation in world affairs during 1917-18 and the peace treaty that followed that conflict, which provided for the United States to join the League of Nations to preserve the peace, should have fallen victim to the hostility between Democratic President Wilson and the Republican-controlled Senate.

After Germany's defeat of France in 1940, President Franklin Roosevelt wanted to strengthen Britain to keep her in the war. For over a century, the Royal Navy had guarded the approaches to this hemisphere and made America's isolationism possible. But Congress remained largely isolationist. Roosevelt, therefore, evaded Congress in the measures he undertook to help Britain. Versailles and the conflicts during the period 1940-41, until Pearl Harbor, led observers during and after this second world war to be concerned with the ability of the United States to conduct an effective foreign policy distinguished by such characteristics as continuity and consistency, as well as flexibility, responsibility, and moderation. Thomas Bailey, the distinguished diplomatic historian, wrote two volumes about the Versailles peace treaty, among other things attempting to show the mistakes the President and Senate needed to avoid in order not to repeat another Versailles.[3] (The cold war began, however, before the victors could get together and draw up a peace treaty with the defeated country.) Distinguished students of Congress such as James McGregor Burns and George Galloway wrote books with titles like *Congress on Trial* and *Congress at the Crossroads*.[4] There was considerable support among academics, journalists, and politicians themselves for "bipartisanship," or "nonpartisanship," as some preferred to call it. This was, in itself, a recognition of the difficulties that the separation of powers between the two branches of government and partisanship between the two parties posed for the conduct of foreign policy. It was suggested that politics should stop at the water's edge. Partisanship, it was feared, was likely to be acute when the two parties controlled the different ends of Pennsylvania Avenue but would occur even if the minority party, controlling neither end, attacked the administration's handling of foreign policy. Political considerations should not affect the management of the nation's affairs. The national interest was to be placed ahead of party interest. In protecting the nation against external threats the President deserved the support of both parties. "Bipartisanship" became the patriotic thing to do; partisanship was to be confined strictly to domestic affairs. Executive-legislative hostility and party controversy over foreign policy might undermine the stability and continuity of U.S. policy, make it impossible to speak with one national voice in world affairs, and erode the nation's credibility in its dealing with friends and foes.[5]

It was, therefore, somewhat of a surprise that, with the notable exception of America's Asian policy, Presidents and Congress were able to cooperate as well as they did during the cold war. The expected executive-legislative conflicts were largely avoided on policies toward the Soviet Union, Western Europe, the Middle East, and Latin America. (Sub-Sahara Africa drew little American attention until the 1970s.) The reasons for this willingness of Congress to accept presidential leadership in foreign policy, indeed, willingness to subordinate itself to the presidency in this area of policy, are worth brief consideration, if only to recognize that the conditions which gave rise to it have now disappeared and that this period was unique, an exception to normal executive-legislative relations.

THE COLD WAR AND CONGRESSIONAL SUBORDINATION

The most obvious reason why Congress followed the presidency in foreign policy was the constitutional primacy of the President in the conduct of foreign policies. The President was both the nation's chief diplomat and commander-in-chief. He had, for example, power to extend recognition to other countries' governments, to negotiate treaties with them (although he needed "the advice and consent" of the Senate to do so), as well as other agreements and, once Congress had appropriated the funds for the military and declared war, he directed the actual conduct of the war. But, since these powers are permanent, they only partially account for Congress' acceptance of its secondary role in foreign policy.

More important were other conditions which no longer exist today, at least to the same degree, and it is the absence of these conditions that brings executive-legislative relations to the fore.

1. The cold war was attended by the perception of a very high degree of threat. It was not called "cold war" for nothing. The United States was engaged in a war, even if it was not a hot one. But the adversary was as much, if not more, of a threat than Germany had been. Russia was the other "superpower," the

only nation in the world which could threaten our security—indeed, our survival. And the threat was not only because Russia was a great power but because *Soviet* Russia was also a totalitarian state which represented beliefs and values completely antithetical to those of American and Western democracy. The Soviet challenge was thus fundamental in terms of physical and political survival.

2. This perception of threat was reinforced by frequent high tensions. Each superpower watched the other carefully lest any shift of power would give his opponent an irreversible superiority. This had to be prevented to preserve the balance. Frequent confrontation and crises were the result: Greece and Turkey 1946-47, Berlin 1948-49, the Korean War 1950-53, Quemoy-Matsu 1954-55, the Suez War and Hungarian uprising 1956, Quemoy-Matsu 1958, Berlin 1958-1962, Cuba 1961-1962, and the deepening Vietnam involvement after 1961 and finally, war after 1965. Short time and the need to make rapid decisions often meant that Presidents spent most of their time consulting with their advisors; they then usually informed Congress of their decisions. When there was more time for consultation between the two branches of government, policy might be modified. Congress frequently put its imprint on the President's policy, but the essence of executive policy remained intact.

3. Congress recognized the executive's expertise in foreign policy. The President had at hand a large bureaucracy to help him. Senators and congressmen, therefore, relied upon executive officials for information and interpretation of events. Although there were notable exceptions, most members of Congress lacked the confidence they had on domestic matters. As citizens and representatives, they hold views on many of the problems their constituents experience, be it inflation or unemployment or busing or education or subsidies or health care; whatever their own professions, they presumably have wide acquaintanceship in their constituencies with individuals in other walks of life and their specific problems as doctors, farmers, or workmen. Moreover, they can call on a whole range of interest groups for other views of the facts and alternative policy views. But foreign problems—the question of Sino-Soviet relations, Soviet intentions, Third World nationalism, military strategy, force levels, and weapons systems—were, for most congressmen, just that, "foreign." This was also true for most interest groups; their expertise was essentially domestic. Deference to executive judgments followed logically. Congress tended to be not only supportive, therefore, but permissive in giving the executive a good deal of leeway.

4. Congressional subordination was the result of a consensus on foreign policy. For over two decades the President and Congress shared a common set of beliefs about the role and objectives of the United States in a world: the central conflict in international politics was the conflict between the communist world led by the Soviet Union and the "free world" led by the United States; any expansion of communist influence and power was a loss of influencce and power for the "free world"; the fundamental role for American and Western

policy, therefore, was to oppose such expansion; the United States, by far the strongest Western power, had the primary responsibility for containing communism; military power was a principal tool for preserving the strategic balance between the superpowers and deterring a Soviet first strike against the United States and her European allies, as well as for opposing any limited communist aggression around the Sino-Soviet periphery; firmness in negotiations was essential because concessions only whetted the unlimited ambitions of the totalitarian rulers of Russia and China and, therefore, would not resolve key issues but lead to further demands; other means for waging the struggle against communism—ranging from economic aid and arms sales to subversion—were legitimate in what was essentially a global competition between two giants whose rivalry would determine which of the two antithetical ways of life would dominate the world—freedom or despotism. Permeating this consensus was the feeling that this conflict between despotism and democracy was a struggle between the forces of good and evil. This set of "shared images" between the two branches of government meant that conflict between them largely revolved around the problems of means. The ends or objectives of American policy were agreed upon; controversy was focused on the implementation.

Since the Vietnam war and the end of the cold war, the era of presidential dominance in foreign policymaking has ended as well. Congress is no longer willing to be as permissive and supportive of presidential policy as before Vietnam. As Congress has become more assertive and determined to play a larger role in foreign policymaking, the result has been that the major issues have been drawn into the institutional quarrel between the executive and the legislature. The increasing role of the House, because of its responsibility for appropriations and the rising prominence of intermestic issues, ensures that this role is not likely to diminish as the memories of Vietnam fade. But the country cannot afford a relationship between the executive and legislative branches in which each speaks with different voices, confusing both friends and foes, and raising questions about the stability and continuity of American policy. The stakes for American security in a nuclear world, and for American prosperity and political stability in an economically interdependent world, are simply too high to allow an executive-legislative pattern in which, on the one hand, the President seeks to escape what he sees as congressional restraint and interference and attempts to establish a larger degree of discretion in order to deal effectively with foreign policy and, on the other hand, Congress in reaction attempts to tie the President's hands and becomes preoccupied with the details to ensure it does not lose control over policy. More specifically, closer cooperation is needed for four reasons.

First, the adversary relationship with the Soviet Union is still critical for American security, particularly now that Moscow has achieved strategic parity and the competitive relationship in the Third World, including Africa and the Persian Gulf-Indian Ocean area, has again intensified. Further, the division of the world between the rich and poor, persistent political instability in many non-Western regions, and the increasing dependence of the United States and the West for certain resources, especially oil, on some of the less developed nations in these areas spell further political troubles. Thus, the presidency must continue to exercise virtually emergency powers at times—e.g., the use or threat of force, wage and price controls, or rationing of gasoline. But the incumbents cannot wield these powers effectively without the support of Congress.

Second, and closely related, a president will on occasion face crises—usually unexpected, and perceived as a threat to major values (security abroad and/or prosperity domestically)—and the tendency will be to act quickly to prevent a bad situation from becoming worse. The situation may be one ranging from Soviet missiles in Cuba (as in 1962) to a threat, not necessarily from the Soviet Union, to the West's oil supplies in the Persian Gulf area. A President may then have to act with dispatch; it will be helpful for the unity of the country and his continued ability to act effectively during the duration of the crisis if he has the support of Congress.

Third, the United States in its security relationship remains leader of the Western world in NATO and has a key alliance with Japan in Asia. Because of the size of its market, the United States has also become economically and financially interdependent with the industrial democracies in Europe and Japan. Thus, crucial American decisions must be taken constantly which affect many nations whose security and prosperity is linked to ours. These decisions often require congressional legislation or other kinds of support. Given the central military and economic role of the United States, American leadership, stable policies, and mutual confidence among the nations concerned are essential. But these qualities may fall victim to the institutional executive-legislative conflict.

Fourth, foreign and intermestic policies all bear "price tags." The size of U.S. military forces, foreign aid, appropriations for MX missiles, surcharges (to pay for the cost of a war, as in Vietnam), and trade and tariff legislation, for example, have domestic impacts since they affect such things as taxation, federal spending, the national debt, military service, inflation, and employment. In intermestic policies the price tag is even more obvious. An OPEC oil embargo, drop in production, or rise in price affect inflation, recession, the value of the dollar, and standard of living. A large Soviet order for wheat, while good for the U.S. balance of payments, may tighten domestic supplies and send food prices upward. Given the demands for appropriations, the impact of foreign policy on domestic politics and vice versa, the President's need for congressional support is obvious.

If the case for closer executive-legislative relations is such a strong one, why has it so often been difficult to attain? Let us briefly look at some of the causes before turning to the individual case studies.

LACK OF CONSENSUS

If the cold war was characterized by a general consensus shared by the executive and legislative branches, about America's role in the world, the recent period has been notable for an absence of consensus. What should the U.S. role be? Should it continue to oppose the Soviets wherever they are involved, or should it be more aware of "the limits of American power"? How and to what degree should the United States exploit quarrels among communist states and use one communist state against another? What conditions should American-Soviet relations be based upon? Should Soviet expansionist behavior be tied to arms control negotiations? Indeed, should the emphasis not be on American arms build-up instead of arms control? What about conflicts in Third World areas—where, when, under what circumstances, and how, if at all, should the United States become involved? Indeed, how much attention should still be given to the super-power conflict, given the additional problems of Third World poverty, overpopulation, and lagging food production, as well as increasing shortages of resources and ecological damage? Even more fundamentally, what should be the priorities between foreign and domestic policies? These are but some of the many questions which required answers after the old consensus eroded. However, is a new consensus possible? And will the continued absence of consensus not mean that every major issue will become controversial and a matter for dispute within the executive and legislative branches, as well as between them?

It is not surprising that in this more complex world there should be disagreements on what the problems are, their significance and the priorities among them, and what to do about them, if anything. A "crusade against communism" can hardly be a rallying cry for a foreign policy which has to deal with a deeply divided communist world, whose divisions the United States is, in fact, seeking to exploit. Nor, at a time of growing dependence upon them, is opposition to communism an appropriate policy toward the underdeveloped countries, many of whom face problems of national cohesion, lack of economic growth, too many people, social dissatisfaction, political instability and, in general, a frustration which in foreign policy is often expressed in militant anti-Western rhetoric and alignment with Russia in international forums such as the United Nations and meetings of the non-aligned states, which most consider themselves still to be. In addition, consensus on the many domestic responsibilities which the federal government has assumed—economic growth, high employment, prosperity, welfare, social justice (including the redistribution of the wealth in the society to the disadvantaged and protection of the environment) is especially hard to attain as the ability to fulfill these tasks is growing increasingly difficult as America's society and economy are becoming more deeply caught in a web of interdependence which makes the United States more vulnerable to foreign events and forces. This country no longer controls its own economy to the degree it once did, and thus domestic problems are ever more enmeshed in foreign policy.

SEPARATE INSTITUTIONS, SHARED POWERS

The Constitution vests exclusive responsibility for the conduct of foreign policy in the federal government, and then divides this authority, as in the domestic area, between the President and Congress. The President can receive and send ambassadors—that is, deal with representatives of foreign powers—but the Senate has to give its consent to treaties by a two-thirds vote and confirm top diplomatic, military, and political appointments. The President was appointed commander-in-chief of the armed forces, but only Congress was empowered to declare war, appropriate funds for the maintenance of military forces, and regulate commerce with other nations. It can also investigate the operations of the various executive departments that participate in the formulation and implementation of the foreign policy of the United States.

Part of the reason for the resulting conflict is ambiguity of the Constitution itself. Treaties, for example, have historically constituted the most frequently used form of agreement between governments of different states. What, however, does the Constitution mean when it stipulates that the President shall make treaties with "the advice and consent of the Senate?" Does this Senate give its advice before or during the negotiations, or after the treaty has been signed? Is the President obligated to accept the Senate's advice, even if he does not like it and judges it harmful to the national interest? Once the Senate gives its consent, must it also play some role in the termination of a treaty or can a President terminate a treaty by himself? Indeed, since treaties are "the law of the land," can a treaty be rescinded without support from both houses of Congress or is this the responsibility of the Senate alone? The Constitution is not always clear on such issues and it may even be silent on them; and precedent may also be ambiguous.

Similarly, conflict exists over the control of the armed forces. Congress authorizes the size and composition of the armed forces and appropriates the funds to support them. It also declares war. But the President is the commander-in-chief of those forces. Does that mean, for example, that the President must be very careful in his diplomatic moves so that he does not provoke hostile action because he must respect the legislature's right to declare war? Or can he, as commander-in-chief, undertake actions he deems in the national interest even if they risk or result in hostilities? Neither Korea nor Vietnam were declared wars, although President Johnson asserted that, in the Gulf of Tonkin resolution, Congress had provided him with the functional equivalent of a declaration of war. This was quickly disputed and President Nixon supported its repeal by the Senate claiming, like Truman, that as commander-in-chief he had all the power he needed to wage the war anyway.

Precedent in the twentieth century suggests that Presidents, Democrat and Republican alike, have increasingly used their authority as commander-in-chief to undertake those actions they deemed would best realize America's vital interests. Thus, Wilson armed U.S. merchant ships in early 1917 after Germany had declared it would conduct an unrestricted submarine campaign against all ships bound for England even though the Senate had refused to grant him that authority. In order to help England against Nazi Germany, Franklin

Roosevelt sent the Marines to Iceland, helped convoy British and Canadian ships with American arms and munitions as far as Iceland, and finally declared a "shoot on sight" policy on German and Italian warships in the Western Atlantic; by the time of Pearl Harbor, the United States was already engaged in an undeclared, limited, naval war with Germany. It was only a matter of time until Germany would have sunk enough American ships and Roosevelt, like Wilson before him, would have gone to Congress to seek a declaration of war. In the period since 1940, the commander-in-chief power has been enormously expanded. Both the external situation and domestic consensus favored a broad interpretation of the Constitution by the President of the authority of his office.

INSTITUTIONAL RIVALRY

For Congress, its past subordinate role in foreign policymaking was not always easy to accept. Congress is a proud institution, jealous of its prerogatives; this has been especially true of the Senate whose Foreign Relations Committee has been one of its most prestigious. Before World War I and in the two decades between World Wars I and II, Congress was supreme. In these interwar years, it passed a series of Neutrality Laws intended to keep America out of future wars in Europe. When Roosevelt asked for some changes in the law on the eve of World War II, changes which the President felt might help deter Hitler, the chairman of the Senate Foreign Relations Committee informed the administration that *his* sources were more accurate than the State Department's and they told him that there would be no war. World War II and the cold war reversed this ascendancy and the presidency was now clearly in command. Indeed, foreign policy, more than domestic policy, has accounted primarily for the enormous growth of presidential power. Harold Laski once remarked that Congress is instinctively antipresidential because this allows it to exalt its own prestige.[6]

Thus postwar attempts from time to time by one or both legislative branches to rein in the presidency, to participate more actively in foreign policy and share the presidential limelight instead of being shunted aside rather humiliatingly to the periphery, is understandable. The Bricker amendment in the 1950s was one such attempt by the Senate to reassert itself and limit executive power; the presidency, weakened by Vietnam and discredited by Watergate, provided Congress with a golden opportunity to take advantage of the mood which rejected the "imperial presidency" in order to regain some of the power and status it had lost since Pearl Harbor. It has been said, not without reason, that the Constitution is an invitation for struggle between the executive and legislative branches for the control of American foreign policy.

It may also be true that while Democrat presidents have been in the forefront of expanding executive authority, it has been Republican presidents who, until President Carter, may have had an even greater vested interest in making foreign policy their strong suit. Because the Democrats were in power when the United States became involved in World Wars I and II, the Korean War, and the Vietnam War, they were sometimes accused of being the "war party." Democrats could, however, also run on their domestic record—the New Deal, the Fair Deal, the New Frontier, and the Great Society. By contrast, the Republicans (the party of Herbert Hoover and the depression) had no domestic record on which to run; they had to run on foreign policy and demonstrate to the nation that they could more effectively manage the country's foreign affairs. Thus, Eisenhower was urged to run by the eastern, moderate, internationalist wing of the Republican Party. Senator Taft, the leader of the dominant conservative, nationalist-isolationist, midwestern wing of the party, was favored as the party's presidential candidate. Eisenhower, elected after three years of the Korean War, was followed eight years later by Nixon, elected after three years of the Vietnam War. Nixon's only interest was foreign policy. Detente with Russia, with SALT I as its centerpiece, rapprochement with Communist China, a gradual disengagement from Vietnam which left the anti-communist Thieu regime in power in Saigon, was the record for which Nixon won every state except Massachusetts in 1972.

Thus, presidential interest in foreign policy is more than a matter of America's stakes in the world and more than a matter of personal interest; it is also a matter of political self-interest. It is their foreign policy role which has allowed them to establish the primacy of their office, their reputation for leadership and for the effective stewardship of the nation's affairs in this tumultuous world; this also obviously helps their party's reputation and fortunes. In contrast to domestic policy where, in the past, the more active congressional and interest group participation limited the possibilities of presidential leadership, and the multitude of "veto points" in the two houses of Congress often paralyzed the decision-making system, making it impossible to respond effectively to the nation's internal problems, foreign policy until Vietnam permitted the President to exercise a degree of initiative and possess a degree of autonomy he simply did not possess in domestic affairs. By and large, the President could count on public support and congressional deference on foreign policy issues. The temptation to be an activist in foreign policy is thus very great; so is the satisfaction derived from playing this role. "The fact of the matter is that the first casualty of any large-scale retreat on the part of the United States from international politics would be the presidency itself."[7] Thus, quite apart from legitimate security interests, no President is likely to want to preside over a retreat of American power that would diminish the stature of his office. The weakened presidency after Vietnam, coinciding with the weariness of America's "global policemanship" and calls for a more limited American role in the world, presented Congress with a chance to recover some of its powers.

This institutional friction and rivalry, it ought to be mentioned, is not limited to the President and Congress; it also extends to the two houses of Congress.

The House, because of its historic lesser role in the conduct of foreign affairs, has on occasions tried to upset what the Senate has accomplished as, for example, the Panama Canal treaties which the Senate had (barely) passed. Or, as in the case of Zimbabwe-Rhodesia, the House—and especially its Foreign Affairs Committee which has always been overshadowed by its prestigious counterpart in the Senate—came to the rescue of the President and saved him from the upper house's attempt to undermine presidential policy. The same thing happened during the Vietnam war when repeated Senate resolutions opposing the war died in the House.

PARTISANSHIP

Partisanship is also a major cause of discord and "disunity." While in a way an obvious reason, this runs contrary to the popular folklore that foreign policy issues should not be influenced by domestic politics. Whatever our differences at home, we should stand united when facing the outside world. The national interest should be above party rivalry and factionalism because partisanship may be harmful. Foreign policy requires bipartisan or nonpartisan support. Yet partisan considerations are bound to affect the conduct of foreign policy. The entire rationale of the American party system is that the out-party should hold the in-party accountable. If that is true for domestic issues, why not for more critical foreign affairs? In a democracy, should only the former but not the latter be subject to public debate? And is it at all surprising that each party should identify its position with the national interest, that it finds the in-party's policy wanting, or that it wishes to "improve" that policy by "Democratizing" or "Republicanizing" it? Bipartisanship or nonpartisanship has thus become increasingly identified with an uncritical acceptance of presidential policy, with a deliberate attempt by an administration to stifle debate and avoid hard questions and critical thinking.

The institutional and partisan causes for conflict between the two branches of government are often mixed. The precise mixture is hard to isolate since conflict between the President and Congress will, in all probability, affect party competition, just as partisan rivalry will affect institutional rivalry. Was the most famous of all the treaties rejected by the Senate because President Wilson did not take any leading Senators—let alone leading Republican Senators—with him to the Versailles Peace Conference after World War I, and the Republican majority in the Senate felt no need to put its stamp on the President's handiwork? Or was it due to the fact that the Republicans, anticipating the 1920 presidential election, did not feel compelled to place their brand on a Democratically-made peace after a successful Democratically-waged war? Did Versailles go down to defeat, then, because of institutional prerogatives and sensitivities, or because of Republican partisanship? And how much were such possible causes mixed with personal motives, the contempt and dislike Woodrow Wilson and Henry Cabot Lodge (the Republican majority leader in the Senate) felt for one another?

Partisanship is a problem, especially in the treaty ratification process. Few Presidents have such a sizeable majority that they can count on 67 votes from their party. Given the undisciplined nature of American parties, a President would not receive all of his party's support anyway, even if it held a majority. Thus, a President has to win support from the opposition. This is possible because the opposition is not cohesive either; but this task is made difficult because while members of the opposition may vote for the treaty, the President and his party reap the rewards that come from a successful policy. Opposition members may explain their pro-administration vote in terms of bipartisanship and patriotic duty, but the out-party as a whole cannot forget its role as the opposition and political future either. Thus, even before the SALT II negotiations were concluded, the Republican party declared that it would turn the SALT debate into a larger examination of American-Soviet political and military relations and Soviet intentions and policies. In short, bipartisanship would not apply. Howard Baker, Senate Minority Leader and Republican presidential aspirant, said that he would vote against the "fatally flawed" treaty unless certain amendments were added.[8] Baker could hardly do anything else if he wanted to win his party's presidential nomination. His rivals all opposed the unamended treaty negotiated by the President. Leading his 41 Republican senators into the treaty battle would focus the spotlight of publicity on Baker and give him the opportunity to establish his credentials among Republicans as a serious contender and, before the nation, his fitness to be President.[9] Baker had earlier supported the Panama Canal treaties for which he had been denounced as a virtual traitor to the party by Republican conservatives.

THE ELECTORAL SYSTEM

The electoral system by which the President and Congress are elected further hampers executive-legislative relations and the ability of the Congress to play a responsible foreign policy role. Congressmen are elected from and are responsible to specific constituencies. They represent local interests and, unlike the President, who is the only nationally elected figure in U.S. politics, do not usually take a long-term and national viewpoint on specific issues. A President may propose a tariff reduction to restrain the upward inflationary spiral by letting in more less expensive imported goods and win tariff concessions from other states thereby raising U.S. exports, employment, and balance of payments—a policy which, it is widely agreed, will be beneficial for the country. But a congressman, even if he should agree that this policy is worthwhile for the nation as a whole, will oppose the President's policy if it will have a negative affect on his part of the nation. As House Speaker Thomas "Tip" O'Neill has said, "All politics is local."[10] Representatives face almost constant reelection campaigns; senators hold office for six years. The electoral system thus places great stress on legislators who seek to please their constituents. In no other country are legislators as tied to local constituencies or as free from national party pressures as in the United States. Legislators can afford to be insensitive to national opinion of themselves or national preferences on policy; the nation does not elect them. They are sensitive only to the interests in their districts or states.

A senator, such as McIntyre (D.-N.H.), who voted for the Panama Canal treaties, or Clark (D.-Iowa), whose main interest was Africa—goes down to defeat if his vote is opposed by a vocal group of his constituents or he neglects local interests too much. Senator Baker (R.-Tenn.), by voting for the Panama Canal treaties, may be another example of a politician rising above many of his constituents' concerns. However, that vote was one reason he became unacceptable to the conservative wing of the Republican party, even as a vice-presidential running mate to presidential candidate Reagan in 1980, which helps to explain his anti-SALT II stance, for he had to make himself acceptable to Republicans in general as he was getting ready to make a bid for the presidential spot. In the House, which has historically not played the visible role the Senate has in foreign policy, representatives stand for election every two years. Local constituency interests are, therefore, of even more urgent and immediate concern to congressmen, although senators appear to be acting increasingly like them. By and large, then, Congress represents parochial interests and the sum of the parts does not equal the whole. It is the President rather than Congress who represents the national perspective. This difference in the electoral basis of the two branches of government, then, accentuates the conflict rather than drawing the two branches closer.

This congressional parochialism which has resulted from the electoral and weak party system has, if anything, intensified recently. Party loyalty, of course, has never been a strong point of American parties which have long been a collection of local parties who combine every four years to try and elect a President, and has declined even further. The decline of urban political machines, the lack of strong party organization to turn out the vote, the increasing emphasis of candidates on personality, the key role of television and the cost of a media campaign in the quest for reelection, the shift of pressure groups' funding to congressional election as presidential elections have been increasingly funded publicly, and the dramatic rise of well-organized, single-issue interest groups on such issues as abortion, gun control, or the Panama Canal and SALT II, all reemphasize local interests and deemphasize loyalty to the party. One of President Carter's staff members, Stuart Eizenstat, talked of the increasing "Balkanization" of American politics[11] in reference to the proliferation of interest groups, economic and otherwise, each interested only in its own program—protecting it, seeking more government money for it, and unwilling to modify it. All these groups contribute heavily to congressional election campaigns.

CONGRESSIONAL ORGANIZATION

The Congress is also highly decentralized. In each house, power is fragmented among committees which specialize in each of the major areas of government concern—e.g., foreign affairs, armed services, agriculture, commerce, education, labor, interior, banking, and appropriations. Congressional government is committee government.

> Farm state members want to deal with agriculture while city people do not, so the agricultural committees are rural and pro-agriculture in their composition. The military affairs committees are dominated by partisans of the military, urban affairs committees by members from the cities, interior committees by pro-reclamation westerners, and so on. By custom, the judiciary committees are made up exclusively of lawyers. Through logrolling, the advocates of various local interests form coalitions of mutual support.[12]

Membership on these committees, whose jurisdiction is of relevance to constituency interests, is obviously of great benefit for reelection purposes; the committee system, therefore, reinforces congressional parochialism. A measure designed to centralize congressional decisionmaking was that the Senate and House Budget Committees and Congressional Budget Office were to formulate an alternative budget to the President's and coordinate spending and revenue raising in the legislature. But success has been very limited. Thus, short of the presidency, there still is no place to gain an overall perspective on policy; to balance off foreign commitments against domestic claims; and to relate the economic, political, social, and military elements to one another. This fragmentation of congressional power and responsibility has grown since 1974, especially in the House, partly in response to the increasing need for greater specialization in an increasingly complex society; but, more importantly, the desire of more members to participate more actively in the legislature's work spawned this congressional birth rate. In fact, while justified in the name of democracy, this multiplication of a considerable number of subcommittees reflected the desire of more congressmen to gain greater prestige and power more quickly. In late 1978, there were 385 subcommittees in the House and Senate.[13]

Clearly, this dispersion of power benefited the many new subcommittee chairmen and their staffs; and, possessing their own funds to conduct their work, subcommittees became more independent of the full committees and their chairmen. The committee chairman's power, which until the 1960s had been so enormous that he was referred to as a feudal baron, has been gravely weakened by the reforms carried out by liberal Democrats seeking to reduce the hold of conservative Democratic chairmen who were against liberal social legislation and in favor of military spending. This proliferation of subcommittees, each jealously guarding its own "turf," was part of a general decentralization of authority and erosion of central direction and control; not only committee chairmen but the Majority Leader, Speaker, and their aides were all weakened. In short, the traditional leadership hierarchy has been weakened, but no alternate structure has taken its place. Thus, even a President who exercises leadership has a problem of mobilizing legislative support because he cannot be sure that his party's leaders in Congress can "deliver" the votes. The party system is so weakened that it cannot serve as a means of organizing its members in Congress and thus balance the forces of fragmentation in the legislature.

This decentralization of power means that every interest group—economic, ethnic, public interest, or whatever—gains access and can exercise influence at many different points as bills move through the legislative maze. While this is not new, the degree of the contemporary diffusion of power and the fact that well-financed lobbying has greatly expanded are recent. "Lobbying has reached new dimensions and is more effective than ever in history. It has become a big computerized operation in which Congress and the public are being bombarded by single issue groups.[14] These efforts have been estimated by David Abshire at $1 billion a year to influence opinion in Washington and probably the same amount to influence the general public.[15] Simultaneously, as the number and effectiveness of the lobbies has multiplied, so have the number of "veto points" in Congress where interest groups—each motivated only by its own interests, always seeking greater gain but unwilling to give up anything—can change legislation in their favor or emasculate it, if not delay or kill it outright. Thus, Congress, highly vulnerable to special interests, is the arena in which those who oppose presidential policies make their stand; for it is easier to stop changes in the legislature and preserve the status quo than to pass legislation to change the status quo.

There is only one place in the U.S. government where an overall perspective on policy and priority between foreign and domestic policy is possible: the presidency.

> If separate departments speak for the cities and the countryside, for the producer and the consumer, for employers and for labor, the White House and the executive office of the president command a broad view of the entire government and can discern from the clash of separate interests . . . where the national interest—defined by some as the 'greatest good for the greatest number' concept—lies.[16]

"ALL DELIBERATE SPEED"

Congress is also painfully slow in its work. Perhaps all democratic legislatures are slow because of the nature of their work, reconciling diverse and conflicting values and interests. Speed is secondary to its task of deliberation. But in the

United States Congress, this task is slowed down by the lack of party loyalty and discipline, the division into two houses, and the fragmentation of power within each. In the House, the Rules Committee assigns a bill to the committee and subcommittee under whose jurisdiction it falls; indeed, more accurately, a bill is usually referred to several committees since the jurisdictions of committees are not always clear-cut and the subject matter may straddle the competence of several committees. If it does not die somewhere in this maze, the bill goes to the floor. Then it goes to the Senate where, again, it is assigned to a specific committee and subcommittee, followed by the floor debate where it may be filibustered for days, weeks, even months, since a filibuster is hard to stop. Should a bill emerge, it then goes to a House-Senate conference committee to see if the differences that may exist can be compromised. After both houses approve the compromises it finally goes to the President for his approval; if he vetoes it, however, the bill is dead unless a two-thirds vote of both houses overrides the veto. Quite apart from the ability of any piece of legislation to survive these hurdles in reasonable shape—that is, not having been rendered ineffective—or even to survive at all, the slowness of this process is obvious. The concern for maximum participation, intensified in recent years, obviously slows down the legislative process even more and confers upon members of Congress and interest groups the opportunities to amend and/or block legislation. This, again, contrasts sharply Congress' ability compared to that of the President who in critical moments, if necessary, can act quickly and authoritatively.

Congress' awareness of its inability to act rapidly is, in fact, recognized even in such legislation as the War Powers Resolution, which was designed to prevent "presidential wars." Under this resolution, the President who uses force must inform the Congress within 48 hours, and if he does not gain the legislature's support within days he must withdraw U.S. forces within two months, or three months if such a withdrawal poses some special difficulties. Thus, in attempting to reassert its authority to participate in presidential actions which affect war and peace, Congress has changed the formal provision of the Constitution which says that the President cannot make war without a congressional declaration of war to say that a President can make war until Congress stops him. No act could have recognized more clearly the need for presidential leadership, initiative, flexibility, and capacity to move with dispatch in this day and age.

EXPERTISE

Finally, Congress cannot compete with the executive in expertise and information in the foreign policy area. Considering the vast resources the President can command in the Departments of State and Defense, the Central Intelligence Agency, and other executive departments and bureaus, it is not surprising that Congress has generally looked to the executive branch for information and interpretation of events. This dependence on the executive's greater capacity for collecting and evaluating information has been especially true in moments of tension and crisis.

But the war in Vietnam ended the legislators' general sense of deference toward the executive on foreign policy issues. To be sure, presidential wisdom had been questioned before in Congress, but the intervention in Southeast Asia and the lengthy, costly war of attrition that followed undermined executive claims to superior information and ability to analyze external problems. "The best and the brightest" had clearly failed; Congress could hardly do worse. It might not be able to match the bureaucracy in expertise, but could it not more effectively exercise the ability which the nonexpert is supposed to specialize in— the ability to ask questions of the experts, to bring out through cross-examination and debate what the assumptions are that underlie policy, its aims, and the feasibility of achieving these aims?

Moreover, in this area, Congress has tried hard to improve itself in recent years. It has vastly increased the number of staff assigned to committees and subcommittees, and greatly improved the quality of these staffs. The Senate Foreign Relations Committee in 1965 had 9 staff members; in 1979 there were 30. The House Foreign Affairs Committee staff for these years was 9 and 50, respectively. A lot more information is also available from the Office of Technology Assessment, Congressional Research Service, Congressional Budget Office, and the General Accounting Office (GAO). Their staffs have increased too; the GAO's International Division's professional staff increased from 160 in 1965 to 248 fifteen years later.[17] Furthermore, as has always been true, members of Congress who have served on a particular committee for many years have often gained considerable expertise relative to a newcomer to the office of the presidency or the Secretary of Defense or State; many members of Congress outlast these executive officials and see a number of Presidents and Secretaries come and go.

The irony is that, to the degree that Congress has enhanced its expertise, it has accentuated the fragmentation of power and made it even more difficult to arrive at an overall congressional position on key issues. The greater staff expertise, often supplied by former executive officials (e.g., Foreign Service Officers), makes it more possible to challenge the State or Defense Departments. It also enhances the power and independence of subcommittees, many of whom now have their own majority and minority staffs. But even with these enhanced staffs, the President retains incomparably greater informational capability, even though Congress has certainly acquired a greater ability to ask questions about the assumptions underlying policy.

PRESIDENTIAL LEADERSHIP

It should be clear by now that without presidential leadership there can be no effective foreign policy. Only he can establish the nation's aims, priorities, and direction. It is symbolic that the course of America's foreign policy throughout its history has been associated with presidential names, from Washington's Farewell Address through the Truman Doctrine to the Carter Doctrine. This is one reason why we are concerned that in the wake of Vietnam the efforts to constrain the "imperial presidency" may have swung too far in the opposite direction, toward an "imperiled presidency." A strong President is essential for the conduct of a foreign policy intended to protect the nation's security and welfare. A fragmented Congress, representing local and state interests, may as a representative of the American people help legitimate American foreign policy; but the President, who is nationally elected, remains the nation's chief diplomat and commander-in-chief.

The extensive, virtually global, involvement of the United States in the period since 1940 was significantly enough accompanied by a shift in the recruitment of presidential candidates. Before World War II, when America was still an isolationist country (from which she had emerged only briefly in 1917–18 during World War I), state houses had supplied most of the country's Presidents. While domestic experience was considered to be most important, governors had been prime candidates for the presidency. From 1865 to 1940 the list included Hayes, Cleveland, McKinley, Theodore Roosevelt, Wilson, Harding, Coolidge, and Franklin Roosevelt. After World War II, when foreign policy became important, most Presidents came from Washington. Until 1976, Eisenhower, the military officer with long experience in foreign policy and diplomacy, was the sole exception to Senators Truman, Kennedy, Johnson, and Nixon. "Washington experience" was considered critical and, in the nation's capital, it was the Senate which was more involved than the House with foreign policy issues; the upper chamber, therefore, became the launching platform for presidential candidates and most vice-presidential candidates. Indeed, those who were to be on their party's ticket after Truman were also members of the Foreign Relations or Armed Services Committees.

Governors were not generally successful in gaining their party's candidacy (Stevenson was the Democratic exception in 1952 and 1956), while foreign policy issues generally received priority over domestic issues. But after Vietnam and Watergate, with the reaction to the "imperial presidency," America's alleged over-involvement in the world, neglect of domestic problems, and a broad decline of trust in the federal government, governors were again more successful. Former Governor Jimmy Carter of Georgia ran successfully for the Democratic nomination in 1976 by running against the "Washington establishment." In 1980, ex-Governor Reagan of California captured the Republican party's nomination which had eluded him in earlier years when Washington experience was more highly prized. Foreign policy experience was not one of the benefits these governors brought with them. On-the-job training meant that they had first to acquire the deeper knowledge and experience needed to lead the country and Congress by articulating the administration's purposes and priorities.

Each of these men also benefited from the party reforms of the 1970s, which more than doubled the number of presidential primary elections, and the extensive use of television in these campaigns. The widespread public participation in the selection process has largely determined

> the kind of candidates you get. Carter and Reagan [are] men who are capable free-lance campaigners of somewhat idiosyncratic background and views, self-proclaimed outsiders, most remarkable for their dogged ambition and relentless energy, prepared to spend years of their lives seeking the presidential prize, but not viewed by their political peers—or by much of the public—as unusually gifted in governmental leadership.[18]

The nomination process, it was argued, favors temperaments and methods that, in fact, do not equip the candidate for political life in Washington. There is a contradiction between the requirements of getting the nomination and policymaking. As presidential candidates increasingly appeal to the party faithful in primaries, their world view or ideology may not only differ from the congressional party but it further weakens the political ties between the President and his party, which are the product of a shared background and mutual obligation. Michael Krasner has aptly noted that "The resources essential to capturing the nomination—a strong personal organization, an effective television image, and an appealing campaign theme—are not central to the conflict and bargaining that permeate national policymaking."[19] Once in power, why should the President change the habits which have brought him the highest secular political reward: "to go it alone, to keep his own counsel, to rely on his personal staff, to set himself apart from other politicians, to rely on persuasion and media appeals, to treat issues as separate problems"[20] without much sense of priorities?

But these qualities which make the candidate a formidable contender are likely to make him a poor political leader—to get things done, especially in mobilizing congressional support for his legislative proposals—because he has not learned to bargain and negotiate. He will come up with specific proposals on issues and he will expect these proposals to be accepted on the basis of their merit. Having not come up through the party, owing party leaders little, his views may not only differ significantly from the party mainstream, thus intensifying executive-legislative conflict, but his campaigning may not have prepared him for "the need to mend fences, solicit opinions, build support and compromise," and to do so on a continuing basis.[21] In these circumstances, the federal government's ability to deal with foreign policy and economic/energy/environment (which, as noted already, are often no longer solely domestic issues) may decline. Over and over again in the case studies which follow we shall note presidential inability to decide priorities, hastily put-together plans, poor understanding of specific problems, a lack of coordination among the executive bureaucracy, and especially amateurish handling of congressional liaison. While such problems afflict almost all Presidents to varying degrees, it seems to have especially afflicted the Carter administration. "Great Presidents have been rare in American history," says one political scientist, "The new nomination process ensures that in the future they will be rarer still."[22] If presidential leadership is characterized, among other qualities, by an understanding of political power and how to exercise it, the likelihood that this quality may be absent does not augur well for executive-legislative harmony. Nor does the fact that most governors will need more on-the-job training than most senators.

SUMMARY

The United States cannot be a responsible world power—particularly militarily or economically—without better executive-legislative relations. The case studies in this volume and the headlines in the news almost any day raise a serious question whether this is possible or what can be done to provide for a closer working relationship. One thing, however, is certain. The United States could "muddle along" during the cold war when only one major problem confronted the country; it was clear who the enemy was, and there was a consensus on what the problem was, and—with some exceptions—what to do about it. The "clear and present" external danger united the country. Today, the United States cannot muddle along as successfully any more. The relationship with the Soviet Union remains threatening, while America's relations with the communist world as a whole are more complex and ambiguous than before; but events and decisions other than those made in Moscow increasingly impinge on us, and some of the less pleasant and most discomforting of these come not from our acknowledged enemies but from our self-declared friends (e.g., Saudi Arabia). With no consensus on the role of the United States in the world on what ought to be—or can be—done about the many problems crowding the American political agenda, the continued executive-legislative distrust with its all too frequent adversary relationship is a recipe for disaster.

All nations contain a plurality of interests, but it is only in the United States that the organization of government has been established specifically to institutionalize that pluralism, divide power horizontally among the states and vertically within the federal and state governments, to multiply the number of veto points, and to grant even the smallest interest groups considerable influence, i.e., special interests over the broader public interest. In wartime, this diversity of interests is willing to subordinate itself to the nation for the purpose of winning the conflict. Even during the cold war, Congress, interest groups, and public opinion were willing to defer to the President's judgments on foreign policy. Today, even though detente seems dead and the country appears headed once more for vigorous competition with an increasingly powerful and energetic Soviet Union, the willingness of Congress and interest groups to subordinate themselves to the presidency as during the cold war does not exist. It is, therefore, a time, more than at any earlier period, in which America's democratic institutions will be tested and the results will be visible to all men.

The chapters which follow will deal with the issue of executive-legislative relations in more analytical and factual detail. The principal research technique employed is the case study. Each of the case studies in this volume is original. In terms of time, they span the post-Vietnam period from Nixon to Carter, although most of them occurred during the Carter administration. All but one comprise traditional foreign policy issues, including issues involving American-Soviet relations as well as regional issues, most of which do, however, impinge in some way upon the superpower relationship. One study focuses on oil and energy, an issue where foreign and domestic policies intersect. In selecting the case studies, we deliberately avoided only policies in which executive policy recommendations had come to a bad end in Congress. It was our intention to clarify the nature of the policy process with a focus on exploring the problems involved in making policy in an environment of frequent executive-legislative conflict.

In doing so, the contributing authors all tried to clarify what the major issues were in their case studies, who were the major actors in the executive and legislative branches, the interest groups involved and the extent of public concern, the stakes the various actors perceived on the issue, the means by which they pursued their aims (especially how the congressional actors asserted their powers), the compromises arranged, and the results of congressional actions. Each author then concludes with an evaluation of his case. In a final chapter, the material is summed up and some conclusions are drawn. In focusing as we do on this critical area of American foreign policy, we illuminate one of the important dilemmas of policy-making in a democracy.

NOTES

1. Thomas M. Franck and Edward Wiesband, *Foreign Policy By Congress* (New York: Oxford University Press, 1979), p. 3.
2. Genrik Trofimenko, "Too Many Negotiators," *New York Times,* July 17, 1979.
3. Thomas A. Bailey, *Woodrow Wilson and the Lost Peace;* and *Woodrow Wilson and the Great Betrayal* (New York: Macmillan, 1944 and 1945, respectively).
4. James McGregor Burns, *Congress on Trial* (New York: Harper & Bros., 1949); and George B. Galloway, *Congress at the Crossroads* (New York: Thomas Y. Crowell, 1946).

5. See, for example, Daniel S. Cheever and H. Field Haviland, Jr., *American Foreign Policy and the Separation of Powers* (Cambridge, Mass.: Harvard University Press, 1952); Cecil V. Crabb, Jr., *Bipartisan Foreign Policy* (New York: Row, Peterson & Co., 1957); and Robert A. Dahl, *Congress and Foreign Policy* (New York: Harcourt, Brace and Co., 1950).

6. Quoted by Burns, *Congress on Trial*, pp. 182-83.

7. Francis E. Rourke, "The Domestic Scene: The President Ascendent," in *Retreat From Empire?* edited by Robert E. Osgood, (Baltimore: The Johns Hopkins University, 1973), p. 104.

8. *New York Times,* June 27, 1979.

9. The Soviet invasion of Afghanistan in December 1979 and President Carter's "temporary" withdrawal of SALT II from Senate consideration undermined Senator Baker's strategy.

10. Thomas P. O'Neill, Jr., "The Man from Barry's Corner," *Yankee Magazine,* July 1978, p. 99.

11. *New York Times,* November 14, 1978.

12. James L. Sundquist, "Congress and the President: Enemies or Partners?" In *Congress Reconsidered,* edited by Lawrence C. Dodd and Bruce L. Oppenheimer, (New York: Praeger, 1977), pp. 230-31.

13. *New York Times,* November 13, 1978.

14. *Time,* August 7, 1978, pp. 15-21.

15. David Abshire, *Foreign Policy Makers* (Beverly Hills, Calif.: Sage Publications 1979), p. 6.

16. Sundquist, "Congress and the President," p. 231.

17. Clifford P. Hackett, *The Congressional Foreign Policy Role* (Muscatine, Iowa: The Stanley Foundation, 1979), pp. 14-15.

18. David S. Broder, "Would You Prefer a Mondale-Baker Race?" *Washington Post,* June 4, 1980.

19. Michael Krasner, "Why Great Presidents Will Become More Rare," *Presidential Studies Quarterly,* Fall 1979, p. 367.

20. Ibid., p. 373.

21. Ibid., p. 375.

22. Ibid.

Chapter 1
The Jackson-Vanik Amendment*
Dan Caldwell

INTRODUCTION

When Richard Nixon and Henry Kissinger entered office in 1969, they confronted an agonizing dilemma in foreign policy. On the one hand, the Vietnam war had led to widespread disillusionment with the United States' extensive overseas role. The American public and the Congress appeared weary and wary of U.S. involvement in world politics. The economic and human costs of this involvement had been substantial and seemed never-ending. Denunciations of the United States' role as a "global policeman" were common, and many stressed the limits of American power suggesting that it could not solve the world's problems and that it should accept fewer obligations.

On the other hand, the Soviet Union had steadily increased its power and, by the late 1960s, had achieved strategic parity thereby nullifying the strategic superiority that the United States had held since the end of World War II. In addition to its strategic nuclear forces, the Soviet Union also possessed substantial conventional forces, including a modern navy and airlift capacity. This meant that at the same time the Soviets' ability to neutralize the United States' nuclear power grew, their capacity to project Soviet influence beyond Eurasia was also increasing. Historically, Russia has been a Eurasian power, limiting its expansion to the areas surrounding Russia. Under Brezhnev and Kosygin, however, the Soviet Union grew more powerful in military terms than ever before

*The author would like to thank John Spanier for his comments on an earlier draft of this chapter.

1

and gained a capacity for global reach that only the United States had enjoyed until then.

Thus, at a time when the United States was unlikely to use military power in response to Soviet challenges as readily as in the past (due to greater risks and domestic constraints stemming from the painful memories of Vietnam), the Soviet Union had emerged from being a regional power and had become a global power. Under these circumstances, how could the United States provide the Soviets with incentives to exercise self-restraint? Among the principal means Nixon and Kissinger felt they could use was American economic power. Ever since the Bolshevik Revolution, the Soviet Union had lagged behind the West in the manufacture of advanced technology and, despite their military build-up, the Soviets at the beginning of the 1970s lagged far behind the West, particularly in their production of computers and petrochemicals. Nixon and Kissinger believed that the United States could use its economic resources to provide the Soviets with an incentive to contain themselves. Military threat could always be used if necessary as an instrument of final resort, but the offer of economic and technical assistance might be more rewarding and safer for the United States and, conversely, more costly for the Soviet Union if withdrawn in case of Soviet attempts to exploit detente on a unilateral basis, in an age of nuclear parity.

Although economic incentives were not offered to the Soviet Union immediately, negotiations on Soviet-American trade were begun in 1971 and, on October 18, 1972, President Nixon and Soviet Trade Minister Patolichev signed a comprehensive trade agreement which called for an expansion of Soviet-American trade and included the settlement by the USSR of its Lend Lease debt to the United States in exchange for the granting to the Soviet Union of most-favored-nation (MFN) status. This event marked the culmination of the negotiations between the Soviet and American governments and the beginning of another set of much more complex negotiations among a diverse collection of individual legislators and their staff members, domestic interest groups, transnational and transgovernmental actors, as well as the United States, the Soviet Union, and Israel.

Two weeks prior to the initialing of the Trade Agreement, Senator Henry Jackson introduced an amendment to block the extension of MFN status and credits to those nonmarket countries that restricted or taxed the emigration of their citizens. In January 1973, Congressman Charles Vanik introduced a similar bill in the House of Representatives. The debate over the Jackson-Vanik Amendment lasted for two and a half years and concerned a number of critical issues relating to the development and implementation of American foreign policy. In this chapter, I will analyze the most important issues raised by the Jackson-Vanik Amendment, describe the major actors and their stakes and strategies in the debate over the amendment, and note the lessons to be learned from this particular episode in American foreign policy.

SUBSTANTIVE ISSUES

The Jackson-Vanik Amendment concerned five major issues: U.S. human rights policies, the relationship between domestic electoral politics and foreign policy in the United States, the improvement of the general political relationship between the Soviet Union and the United States, the development of Soviet-American trade, and executive-legislative relations.

A number of political scientists have pointed out that Americans approach foreign policy from a moralistic perspective.[1] In fact, this approach is one of the principal features that distinguishes U.S. foreign policy from other states' foreign policies, for instance, the *realpolitik* approach of the European states.

At many points in its history, the United States government has sought to support the human rights of the citizens of other countries, including Russia. In 1869, when the Russian government announced that it planned to expel 20,000 Jews from Bessarabia, President Ulysses S. Grant's protests were successful in preventing the tsarist government from doing so. The U.S. House of Representatives passed resolutions concerning Russia's treatment of Jews in 1879 and 1883.[2] Responding to Russian persecution of Jews and the pressure from American Jewish leaders to do something about this situation, President Theodore Roosevelt, in 1911, unilaterally abrograted the Russo-American Commercial Treaty of 1832.[3] Echoing many of the speeches heard in 1911, Senator Hubert Humphrey, in 1972, pointed out: "What we are seeking to do [with the Jackson Amendment] is not to obstruct trade but to uphold the cause of human rights."[4]

The second major issue raised by the Jackson-Vanik Amendment concerns the relationship between domestic electoral politics and foreign policy in the United States. While Jews constitute only 2.7 percent of the American population, they have far greater influence than this figure would indicate, particularly in the states with the largest number of electoral votes including California, New York, New Jersey, Massachusetts, Florida, and Pennsylvania. These six states cast 30 percent of the votes in the electoral college. Further adding to its impact, the Jewish community tends to vote as a block and to have a high voter turnout. In addition, there are a number of Jewish organizations, many of which became very concerned about the question of Soviet Jewish emigration in the early 1970s. When asked why so many legislators agreed to cosponsor the Jackson-Vanik Amendment, Jackson replied bluntly: "Because there is no political advantage in not signing it. If you do sign, you don't offend anyone. If you don't sign, you might offend some Jews in your state."[5]

In 1972, the entire House of Representatives, one-third of the Senate, and President Richard Nixon were all up for reelection and, given its influence, the support of the Jewish constituency was important for many candidates. Indeed, in his memoirs William Safire, who served as one of Nixon's speech writers and political confidants, noted that in 1972 Nixon actively courted the Jewish vote.[6]

In the Ninety-third Congress (1973-74), almost one-third of the Senate was running either announced or informally for the presidency or vice-presidency including among others, Henry Jackson, Edmund Muskie, George McGovern, Hubert Humphrey, Walter Mondale, Birch Bayh, Edward Kennedy, Lloyd Bentsen.[7] By introducing his amendment linking MFN and Soviet emigration policies, Jackson simultaneously demonstrated his support for human rights and the Jewish cause as well as his anticommunist credentials. Other candidates for the presidency and vice-presidency felt the pressure to cosponsor Jackson's amendment giving him prestige among the American electorate in general and the Jewish constituency in particular. To a very great extent, the history of the Jackson-Vanik Amendment is explicable only by referring to the dynamics and demands of American domestic politics.

The third major issue affected by the Jackson-Vanik Amendment was the political relationship between the United States and the Soviet Union. Nixon and Kissinger sought to develop a new international order supported by the United States, the Soviet Union, and the People's Republic of China. By concluding mutually beneficial agreements in various issue areas, particularly in the limitation of strategic arms and in trade, the United States, Nixon and Kissinger believed, could encourage the active, cooperative involvement of the Soviet Union into the international system.[8] Nixon and Kissinger felt that increased Soviet-American trade was an essential component of their approach to the Soviet Union. In Kissinger's view, " . . . we regard mutually beneficial economic contact with the U.S.S.R. as an important element in our overall effort to develop incentives for responsible and restrained international conduct."[9] Increased trade thus provided the means to promote detente within the Soviet Union by providing goods and services that the Soviet leaders wanted and, within the United States, by providing U.S. corporations with expanded business opportunities. To some of its supporters, the Jackson Amendment provided a means to check the momentum that the Nixon-Kissinger policy of detente was gaining in the early 1970s; their motivation was primarily anticommunist and the amendment provided a means to register their antidetente sentiment.

The Jackson-Vanik Amendment clearly and directly concerned a fourth major issue: the expansion of Soviet-American economic relations. Some in the United States, particularly American business and labor leaders, saw the expansion of Soviet-U.S. trade as affecting their respective constituencies. Donald Kendall, the Chairman of the Board of Pepsico, testified:

> I think we have a tremendous opportunity because of the rising consumer demand in the Soviet Union. The people have money in the bank today and they have purchasing power. They need consumer goods to purchase and I think we can help supply those. . . . If you live in a country where life is harder, where the good things are fewer, a cold freshly-opened Pepsi can mean a great deal. I didn't come here to praise our product, but

I want you to understand why I think the opening of the Soviet market to a product like ours is very significant in terms of what the headline writers call detente.[10]

While many American businessmen supported passage of the provisions of the Trade Agreement without amendment, the AFL-CIO not surprisingly adopted just the opposite position. According to George Meany, "We don't want any part of it [the Trade Agreement]. We're not interested in seeing American workers displaced by slave labor."[11] The Jackson-Vanik Amendment thus provided an issue over which business and labor went to battle.

The fifth major issue raised by the Jackson-Vanik Amendment concerned executive-legislative relations.[12] The roles of the President and the Congress in the making of U.S. foreign policy were somewhat ambiguous when the Constitution was first signed. Article II grants the President the power to make treaties and to appoint ambassadors with the advice and consent of the Senate. The Constitution also makes the President the chief executive officer of the government and the commander-in-chief of the armed forces. The foreign affairs powers granted to the Congress, in addition to those mentioned above, include the regulation of commerce, the punishment of piracies and felonies committed on the high seas and offenses against the law of nations, and declarations of war. Through decades of practice, the President has become preeminent in the making of foreign policy and this development has been supported by the courts.[13]

Public and congressional opposition to American involvement in the Vietnam war led to an assertion of congressional involvement in the making and implementing of foreign policy, as evidenced by passage of the War Powers Act, various end-the-war resolutions, and limitations on the appropriations for military operations in Southeast Asia. The scandals that occurred in the Nixon administration further weakened the power and credibility of the executive branch and opened the door for the assertion of congressional power. As Henry Jackson pointed out, "It is important that the Russians understand they are dealing with not only the administration but also with Congress."[14] After the passage of the Jackson-Vanik Amendment, it was very unlikely that Soviet leaders would fail to pay attention to the Congress, a lesson underscored by the history of SALT II.[15] Clearly, the Jackson-Vanik Amendment demonstrated the power of Congress to influence the course of American foreign policy, but is this influence desirable? We will return to this prescriptive question in the conclusion.

THE MAJOR ACTORS AND THEIR STAKES AND STRATEGIES

Only rarely do issues become politically salient on their own merits; most prominent issues are politicized by interested individuals and organized groups.

Therefore, to understand the evolution of the Soviet Jewish emigration issue from the concern of a few Jewish organizations in the 1960s to an issue of major national attention in the 1970s requires an examination of the actors who became interested and involved with the issue.

Over time, a number of diverse actors became concerned about the Jackson-Vanik Amendment. On one level, the controversy created by the amendment was waged among a number of individuals—Richard Nixon, Leonid Brezhnev, Henry Kissinger, and Henry Jackson, to name the most prominent. On another level, the issues raised by this case concerned Soviet-American interstate relations. Somewhere between these two levels, domestic politics should be considered. A number of international relations theorists (such as Arnold Wolfers, James Rosenau, Robert Keohane, and Joseph Nye) have noted that nation-states are no longer the only actors in world politics; in fact, there are many transnational and transgovernmental actors that establish "contracts, coalitions, and interactions across state boundaries that are not controlled by the central foreign policy organs of governments."[16] A number of these actors were also involved in the debate over the amendment.

The history of the Jackson-Vanik Amendment illustrated the complexity of contemporary politics. It concerned neither purely domestic nor purely international issues; rather, it concerned both simultaneously. Because of this, many different individuals and groups were involved in the debate over the amendment. Despite the complexity of the debate and the number of actors involved, there was some pattern to their involvement. Prior to the introduction of the Jackson Amendment and the signing of the Trade Agreement in October 1972, within the American governmental bureaucracy Nixon and Kissinger controlled all important discussions of U.S.-Soviet trade. Since all revenue bills must originate in the House of Representatives, the Jackson-Vanik Amendment was referred to the House where it was considered and debated for most of 1973. In 1974, the Senate considered the bill and negotiations among Kissinger, Jackson, and the Soviets took place. Throughout the two-and-a-half-year debate on the amendment, there were a number of other groups that were actively lobbying. I will describe the activities, stakes, and strategies of the following actors: the executive branch of the U.S. government; the Congress; interest groups within the U.S. including business, labor, and Jewish groups; and transnational and transgovernmental groups.

The Executive Branch

When Richard Nixon and Henry Kissinger entered office in January 1969, they faced a number of complex international challenges and a domestic environment stretched to the breaking point by Vietnam. Due in large part to the post-1945 economic recovery of the European states and Japan, the American share of the world's gross national product had gone from 50 percent in 1945 to 30 percent in 1970, and the international monetary system that had been carefully planned at Bretton Woods in 1945 threatened to collapse. The Soviet Union had built a military force equal to that of the United States, and the People's Republic of China became increasingly involved in international affairs. On the home front, American public opinion was growing more and more critical of U.S. involvement in Vietnam, and Congress was reasserting its power over the development and conduct of American foreign policy.

Rather than attempting to deal with these substantive international problems on an issue-by-issue, ad hoc basis, Nixon and Kissinger sought to construct a framework for dealing with these diverse issues in a systematic, coherent fashion. In short, the two leaders sought to formulate a grand design of a new international system and a grand strategy for achieving this new order. Believing that bureaucratic and congressional involvement in the making of foreign policy made goals and objectives more difficult to achieve, Nixon and Kissinger sought to centralize foreign policymaking in the White House.[17]

In his inaugural address, President Nixon told "adversaries as well as friends" that negotiation and not confrontation would be the hallmark of his administration. True to this promise, Nixon emphasized the development of improved relations between the United States and the Soviet Union and between the United States and the People's Republic of China. Within a year of Nixon's inauguration, Soviet and American representatives had begun negotiations on the limitation of strategic arms, Berlin, and other matters; but negotiations on trade were not begun.

There were several reasons that Nixon and Kissinger did not seek to improve U.S.-Soviet economic relations during their first two and a half years in office. First, the United States faced significant economic problems, both domestically and within the Western international economic system. Secondly, Nixon and Kissinger chose to link the expansion of Soviet-American economic relations with the improvement of political relations.[18] In testimony before the Senate Finance Committee in 1974, Kissinger recalled:

> the first time we approved a commercial deal, which was on the order of some $30 million, was in May of 1971, following the first breakthrough in the SALT negotiations. . . . In other words, for a period of more than two years, we told the Soviet Union that restraint in its foreign conduct would lead to an expansion of trade relations with the United States.[19]

On June 1, the Department of Commerce approved export licenses for $85 million worth of vehicle manufacturing equipment to the Soviet Union and, nine days later, President Nixon removed grain from the list of U.S. exports requiring licenses. In retrospect, it seems that the timing of the first U.S. approval of a commercial deal was related to the announcement by Brezhnev at the Twenty-Fourth Party Congress that the Soviets would be seeking expanded trade with the West. A third reason for expanding U.S.-Soviet economic relations was the domestic political reason: the 1972 presidential campaign was approaching, and it was clear the U.S. businessmen wanted to increase trade with the Soviet Union.

The Nixon administration's effort to expand U.S.-Soviet trade was centralized in the White House where Henry Kissinger, at that time the President's Assistant for National Security Affairs, and Presidential Assistant Peter Flanigan, who was also in charge of the Council on International Economic Policy, oversaw the trade negotiations with the Soviets. The Special Trade Representative, William Eberle, was in charge of a comprehensive trade bill being negotiated in 1972-73 and had very little to do with the Soviet-American negotiations. After the Jackson-Vanik Amendment was introduced, George Shultz was appointed Secretary of the Treasury and the chief American representative on the U.S.-U.S.S.R. Joint Commercial Commission. In 1971-72, Kissinger and Flanigan played the most important roles in the economic negotiations with the Soviets; and, after his appointment in early 1973, George Shultz also played a key role.

There were differing perspectives on the question of Soviet-American trade within the governmental bureaucracy of the executive branch. For instance, in his memoirs, Henry Kissinger notes that, while the White House and the Department of Defense believed that increased trade should follow improvement in political relations, the State Department believed that expanded trade would improve political relations.[20] Peter Peterson, who was Secretary of Commerce until November 1972, authored a report that advocated a substantial increase in Soviet-American trade, a development that was supported by the Department of Commerce's primary constituents: businessmen.[21] To encourage and facilitate trade with Communist countries, the Department established a special East-West Trade Bureau. The Department of Treasury viewed increased trade as a means of reducing the growing U.S. balance of payments deficit; while Defense opposed increased trade, and particularly certain transfers in technology, on the grounds that such transfers would directly contribute to the Soviet defense effort by releasing resources to other aspects of defense sector production.

These differences in bureaucratic perspective did not block the successful signing of the U.S.-Soviet Trade Agreement due, no doubt in large part, to the high degree of centralization of foreign policymaking in the White House.

The Congress

Once the agreement was signed, it had to be referred to Congress; but Senator Henry Jackson had already indicated congressional interest in the issue of Soviet-American trade by introducing an amendment linking MFN and Soviet emigration policies. Jackson contended that he had introduced the amendment in response to the imposition by the Soviet government of an "education tax" ranging from $5,000 to $25,000 against potential emigrants.[22] Jews in both the

United States and the Soviet Union were upset by this action because they felt that the burden of the new emigration tax would fall most heavily on Soviet Jews. On August 15, 1974, a number of Soviet Jewish dissidents issued an appeal in which they expressed a fear of becoming "the slaves of the twentieth century."[23] On the same day in Washington, D.C., three prominent Jewish leaders paid a visit to Secretary of State Rogers in order to air their concerns about the new Soviet tax. Because of his close ties with the American Jewish community, Jackson was quick to see his opportunity. Here was an issue that would simultaneously help him attract Jewish support in his upcoming presidential campaign, attract more general electoral support because of the relevance of the issue to human rights and, finally, would allow him to attack the Nixon-Kissinger detente policies which, following the Moscow summit of May 1972, were very popular.

In order to gain support for his amendment, Jackson turned to one of his assistants, Richard Perle, who met with a number of other Senators' aides as well as several representatives of Jewish organizations. Eventually, Senators Jacob Javits from New York and Abraham Ribicoff from Connecticut, both Jewish and from states with relatively large and influential Jewish constituencies, became Jackson's closest allies in the Senate. But in the drafting of the Jackson Amendment and in organizing the coalition to support the amendment, "It was," according to Jackson, "the able staff of the three Senators who did the job. They were led largely by Mr. Richard Perle of my staff, Morris Amitay of Senator Ribicoff's staff, and Mr. Lakeland of Senator Javits' staff. . . . They provided the professional expertise that resulted in what we were able to do."[24] As a result of their combined efforts, Jackson, his sympathetic colleagues, and their staff assistants were able to obtain 73 cosponsors for the amendment when it was introduced in the closing days of the Ninety-second Congress on October 4, 1972.

All revenue bills must originate in the House of Representatives and, since tariffs are a means of raising revenue, legislation concerning MFN falls within the jurisdiction of the House and, more particularly, the House Ways and Means Committee. Thus, the House was the locus of battle during 1973 in the fight over MFN treatment for the Soviet Union.

Representative Charles Vanik, a third generation Czech, represented the Twenty-second Congressional District of Ohio, a district in suburban Cleveland that includes a large percentage of residents of Jewish or Eastern European extraction.[25] A member of the House Ways and Means Committee, Vanik introduced two measures relating to the emigration tax in the Ninety-second Congress. It was not unexpected, then, when Vanik introduced the Jackson Amendment in the House. As had been the case in the Senate, the staff aides of House members proved to be important. Vanik's assistant, Mark Talisman, met with Senate staffers to coordinate their legislative strategy.

During the first two weeks of January 1973, Talisman called the offices of all 435 members of the House. Talisman summarized his strategy for obtaining cosponsors:

> . . . my plan: to call every member in Congress, every office. I didn't send our "dear colleague" letter; this I did when I felt safe, to mop up. We were being pestered by the press and the State Department asking [how many sponsors we had lined up.] I didn't want any office to think it was a massive effort. I didn't want to stir up opposition. . . . No one knew how many cosponsors I had for the Vanik-Jackson Amendment. I had to call some offices fifteen times. [Representative Jonathan] Bingham [D.-N.Y.] and [Representative Sid] Yates [D.-Ill.] were trusted colleagues to help. . . . The first sixty members were easy to get because they were from large Jewish areas. . . . Sixty would go on as cosponsors just because they were anti-Communist and anything like that was alright [sic] with them. Forty or fifty couldn't be categorized; they were key. They had to be convinced.[26]

Talisman convinced a number of these uncommited congressmen by employing a variety of arguments. He pointed out that Nixon and Kissinger had not consulted with Congress prior to signing the Trade Agreement; the Holocaust should not be forgotten; and the wheat deal, the other major U.S.-Soviet economic deal already concluded, had hardly been in the interest of the United States. Eventually, 253 representatives cosponsored the Jackson-Vanik Amendment when it was formally introduced.

Despite the strong support for the amendment, the powerful chairman of the Ways and Means Committee, Wilbur Mills, had not agreed to cosponsor it. In early February, Mills announced his support and in mid-April he reversed himself. He again announced his support on May 2. The amendment was then approved by the Ways and Means Committee and passed by the entire House by an overwhelming vote of 319-80 on December 11, 1973. The bill was then sent to the Senate.

Throughout 1974, there were three principal negotiating parties working on the amendment: Kissinger, Jackson, and the Soviets. Jackson and his supporters in the Senate wanted the Soviet Union to give specific assurances concerning the number of Jews who would be allowed to emigrate. Nixon and Kissinger, and at the end of 1974, Ford, believed in "quiet diplomacy."[27] As Nixon told a group of Jewish leaders justifying this approach, "The walls of the Kremlin are very thick. If you are inside, there is a chance that they will listen to you; if you are outside you are not even going to be heard."[28]

While Kissinger, Jackson, and the Soviets negotiated, the Senate held hearings on the amendment. Somewhat surprisingly, the Senate Foreign Relations Committee never held hearings. That responsibility fell to the Senate Finance Committee which was also considering the administration-backed Trade Reform Act. Normally, Senator Russell Long the powerful chairman of the Finance

Committee, would have been expected to have wielded a great deal of influence, but on this issue, Jackson, Ribicoff, and Javits held the power.[29] In his testimony before the Finance Committee, Kissinger called the Trade Reform Act "one of the most important pieces of legislation that has come before the Congress in years." Kissinger also noted that "the domestic practices of the Soviet Union are not necessarily related to detente which we primarily relate to the conduct of foreign policy."[30]

In contrast to the Nixon-Ford-Kissinger foreign policy linkage strategy, Jackson explicitly linked MFN to changes in Soviet domestic policy. Following Kissinger's appearance before the Senate Finance Committee, he met with Jackson, Ribicoff, and Javits in an attempt to work out an acceptable solution to the MFN-emigration issue. Prior to and during these tripartite negotiations, a number of other individuals and organizations were attempting to influence the outcome of the debate over the Jackson-Vanik Amendment.

Interest Groups within the United States

There were many interest groups within the United States that actively lobbied both in favor and against the passage of the Jackson-Vanik Amendment. The most influential nongovernmental opposition to the amendment came from the business community. The National Association of Manufacturers (NAM) lobbied tirelessly against Jackson-Vanik. In February 1973 and again a year later, NAM lobbyists assisted Soviet officials who were visiting congressmen seeking support for expanded U.S.-Soviet trade. When Brezhnev visited Washington in June 1973, NAM hosted a series of meetings between Brezhnev and prominent American businessmen. During the hearings in the Senate Finance Committee on the Trade Reform Act, business groups testifying against Jackson-Vanik included NAM, the U.S. Chamber of Commerce, the National Foreign Trade Council, and the East-West Trade Council.[31]

Supporting passage of the amendment was a coalition of labor, academic-scientific, and Jewish groups. The AFL-CIO and its venerable president, George Meany, supported the Jackson Amendment and opposed the Trade Reform Act, which Meany felt would, if passed, result in the export of U.S. technology and the loss of jobs for Americans. Nixon had threatened to veto the trade bill if it was passed with the Jackson-Vanik Amendment. If the Trade Reform Act could not be defeated outright, which did not appear likely at that time, then Meany hoped for the passage of the Jackson-Vanik Amendment and a Nixon veto of the entire bill. Commenting on the 1972 Soviet-American Trade Agreement, George Meany testified: "There is no economic benefit for the United States in this deal. All the economic benefits flow to the Soviet Union. The most we can hope for are political benefits—but these are very, very doubtful."[32]

The AFL-CIO was joined in its support of the Jackson-Vanik Amendment by a number of American academic organizations following the stepped up repression of prominent Soviet dissidents in the summer of 1973. These groups included the Federation of American Scientists, the National Academy of Sciences, and the American Psychiatric Association. Dr. Jeremy Stone, the director of the Federation of American Scientists whose membership in 1974 included over half of the United States' Nobel Prize winners, pointed out why many U.S. scientists felt an affinity for Soviet Jewish scientists:

> Many of the American scientists are Jews as am I. Indeed, most of the Jewish scientists emigrated from Russia to America three generations ago. These scientists feel an especially close identification with Soviet Jewish scientists of which there are many. And the desire of some Soviet Jewish scientists to go to Israel and Soviet refusals to permit it, will keep these protests alive.[33]

Scientists were not alone in their concern about Soviet Jews; indeed, since the early 1960s various Jewish leaders and groups had tried to convince the U.S. government to pressure the Soviet government to halt its repression of Soviet Jews. In September 1963, Senators Javits and Ribicoff and Supreme Court Justice Arthur Goldberg met with President Kennedy to discuss the plight of Soviet Jews. In the fall of 1963, a group of concerned individuals founded the Cleveland Committee on Soviet Anti-Semitism, the forerunner of the Union of Councils for Soviet Jews. A group of the major Jewish organizations in the United States sponsored the establishment of the American Jewish Conference on Soviet Jewry (AJCSJ) in 1964.[34] Although leaders of the AJCSJ met with U.S. government officials in the executive branch, "it remained legislatively dormant from 1964 to 1971."[35]

Some members of the American Jewish community were dissatisfied with the AJCSJ's approach of lobbying through conventional political channels. Consequently, several other "antiestablishment" organizations were founded, the most militant of which was the Jewish Defense League. In December 1970, Soviet authorities in Leningrad arrested and tried eleven dissidents (nine of whom were Jewish). All eleven were convicted and several were given death sentences, which, after international protest, the Soviet Supreme Court commuted to a sentence of fifteen years of hard labor. The Leningrad affair activated a number of Jewish groups that had not previously taken an active interest in the plight of Soviet Jews. One of the newly activated groups was the American Israel Public Affairs Committee (AIPAC) which was the Jewish community's registered lobby group in Washington. Prior to the Leningrad case, AIPAC had been almost exclusively concerned with American-Israeli issues; however, following the Leningrad "trials," AIPAC became more involved in the Soviet Jewry cause.

Although there was some division among the various Jewish organizations, these groups, nevertheless, were able to play important roles in the fight to gain passage of the Jackson-Vanik Amendment. Several examples illustrate the kind of influence that these organizations were able to exercise. In mid-January 1973, two weeks after Vanik's aide, Mark Talisman, began enlisting cosponsors for the Jackson-Vanik Amendment, Isaiah Kenen of AIPAC sent letters to 1,000 Jewish leaders throughout the United States.[36] Kenen, who worked closely with Jackson's staff, described the process of generating pressure: "We will send out a notice to the leadership of the American Jewish Community letting them know what developments are occurring, [and] they in turn will do what they can."[37]

In some cases, influential members of the Jewish community were able to do a great deal. For instance, when Congressman Vanik introduced the amendment into the House of Representatives, Wilbur Mills was not a cosponsor. However, Kenen asked two prominent Jewish families with interests in Arkansas to "do what they could," and on February 7, 1973, Mills announced his cosponsorship.[38] Two and a half months later, after reading over two Soviet communications indicating that the exit tax would be suspended and that emigration levels would be maintained at 35,000 per year, Mills withdrew his cosponsorship. Richard Perle then contacted a mutual friend of Jackson and Mills, a retired Jewish businessman from New York named David Hermann. Mills met with Hermann who told him Soviet Jews were facing a new holocaust.[39] On May 2, Mills once again added his name as a cosponsor. Hermann's visit was certainly not the only factor that contributed to Mills' change of heart, but it undoubtedly helped.

Nixon attempted to coopt Jewish support for his campaign against the Jackson-Vanik Amendment. On April 19, 1973, nine days after Nixon sent the Trade Reform Act to Congress, he met with a number of leaders of prominent Jewish organizations including Charlotte Jacobson, vice-chairman of the National Council on Soviet Jewry, Max Fisher, a wealthy Jewish philanthropist and one of the founders of the 1972 committee to re-elect Nixon, and Jacob Stein, the chairman of the Conference of Presidents of Major American Jewish Organizations.[40] Following the meeting, these three leaders issued a statement expressing support for Nixon. A number of other leading Jewish leaders criticized the statement. Later in June, when Fisher and Stein attended a White House dinner for the visiting Brezhnev, Jewish students picketed Stein's home and several Jewish organizations strongly criticized Stein and Fisher.

There were, then, both Jewish supporters and opponents of the Jackson-Vanik Amendment, but the overwhelming majority of Jewish leaders and organizations supported passage of the legislation. Perhaps part of the explanation for this orientation was the support of the amendment by Jewish dissidents themselves.

Transnational and Transgovernmental Actors

Keohane and Nye have defined transnational actors as nongovernmental actors whose decisions and actions are not wholly controlled by one state's decision makers.[41] Transgovernmental actors are "sub-units of governments on those occasions when they act relatively autonomously from higher authority in international politics."[42] During the fight over the Jackson-Vanik Amendment, both of these new actors were involved.

Soviet Jews, in the early 1970s, forged transnational contacts with American Jewish organizations. For instance, in April 1973, following the circulation of the statement by Max Fisher, Charlotte Jacobson, and Jacob Stein praising Nixon for his efforts on behalf of Soviet Jewry, more than 100 Soviet Jewish activists sent an appeal to U.S. Jewish leaders.[43] Later in 1973—in September, following the stepped-up repression of the summer—Andrei Sakharov, a highly respected physicist and one of the most prominent Soviet dissidents, wrote a letter in which he called for Congress to support the Jackson-Vanik Amendment. According to Sakharov, "Adoption of the amendment . . . cannot be a threat to Soviet-American relations. All the more, it would not imperil international detente. . . . As if the techniques of 'quiet diplomacy' could help anyone, beyond a few individuals in Moscow. . . ."[44] Because of this letter, historian Arthur Schlesinger, Jr., writer I.F. Stone. and *New York Times* columnist Anthony Lewis registered their support for the amendment. Referring to Sakharov, Schlesinger wrote, "Always trust the man on the firing line."[45]

Transnational contacts were not limited to those supporting the amendment. American businessmen joined their Soviet counterparts in establishing the U.S.-Soviet Trade and Economic Council and the U.S. Chamber of Commerce. In addition, the two governments established the Joint Commission on Scientific and Technical Cooperation. At meetings of these organizations, American and Soviet industrialists had the opportunity to interact and to discover common interests. These contacts proved to be useful to U.S. businessmen when they went to Moscow and to Soviet officials who visited Washington seeking congressional support for the 1972 Trade Agreement.

THE OUTCOME

In a series of discussions with Soviet Foreign Minister Gromyko in Geneva in April, in Cyprus in May, and in Moscow in July, U.S. officials sought to clarify Soviet emigration policies. In the late summer of 1974, the tripartite negotiations among Kissinger, Jackson, and the Soviets came to a head. Relations between Kissinger and Jackson and their respective staff members were hostile and, in early October, both Kissinger and Jackson refused further meetings. Stanley Lowell, the chairman of the National Conference on Soviet Jewry, asked 25 leaders of the most prominent Jewish organizations to appeal to Kissinger and to Ford, who had assumed the presidency in August. The appeal worked, and Jackson and Kissinger met. Then, on the basis of the Gromyko discussions, Kissinger wrote a letter to Senator Jackson describing Soviet emigration policies as conveyed by Soviet leaders to the U.S. government.[46] In essence, the understanding stipulated that there would be no interference with applications for emigration, harassment of applicants; nor obstacles to emigration except for reasons of national security; and that the emigration tax which the Soviets suspended in 1973 would remain suspended. Kissinger noted that the Soviet leaders had made assurances, and not commitments, to the U.S. government and that these guidelines would be followed in the future. He also noted that "if any number was used in regard to Soviet emigration, this would be wholly our responsibility; that is, the Soviet Government could not be held accountable for or bound by any such figures."[47] Finally, Kissinger wrote that Soviet leaders had indicated that the United States could informally raise the question of whether these understandings were being carried out if there were questions concerning the implementation of the understandings.

Senator Jackson sent a letter to Secretary Kissinger in which he presented the conditions concerning Jewish emigration which he considered as essential before the United States granted the Soviet Union MFN status. Jackson stipulated that no unreasonable impediments should be placed in the way of persons wishing to emigrate. In those cases of people who had access to "genuinely sensitive classified information," they should become eligible for emigration within three years of the date on which they last had access to such information. Jackson also stipulated that "we understand that the actual number of emigrants would rise promptly from the 1973 level and would continue to rise to correspond to the number of applicants, and may therefore exceed 60,000 per annum"[48] This number was to be a "benchmark as the minimum standard of initial compliance."[49]

The Kissinger and Jackson letters were released to the public by Senator Jackson on the same day that they were exchanged, October 18, 1974, which was two years to the day after the Trade Agreement had originally been signed. The letters contained several obvious discrepancies, and Kissinger, in testimony before the Senate Finance Committee, noted that Jackson's more explicit and rigorous criteria for judging Soviet performance on the issue of emigration would be considered by the President at the time that he would be required to make a determination on whether to extend MFN and credit to the Soviet Union.[50]

Following the exchange of correspondence, members of the administration and Congress worked out a set of principles that empowered the President to waive the provisions of the original Jackson-Vanik Amendment and to grant MFN and credits to the Soviet Union for an initial period of eighteen months. This initial approval was subject to review and the granting of additional approval for one year periods. As part of a three week, worldwide trip, Kissinger stopped in Moscow October 23 to 27 for discussions with Soviet leaders. Brezhnev reportedly reacted very strongly to the publicity that had been given to Moscow's assurances on Jewish emigration.[51] Despite Brezhnev's strong reaction, it appeared that compromise had been reached with the exchange of letters between Kissinger and Jackson.

On December 20, 1974, Congress passed the Trade Reform Act by a 72–4 vote, and the House by a 323–36 vote. As amended, the bill granted the President power to eliminate tariffs of 5 percent or less on goods imported by the United States and to reduce by 60 percent tariffs above 5 percent. The President was also granted the power to eliminate tariffs on goods imported from developing countries. The bill also provided the President with the authority to grant MFN and credit to the Soviet Union.

Concurrent with its consideration of the Trade Reform Act, Congress also voted on an amendment by Senator Adlai Stevenson which placed a limit on Exim Bank credit to the Soviet Union of $300 million for a four-year period. This amendment contained a $40 million sub-limit on the amount of loans or credit guarantees that could be used for exploration of energy in the Soviet Union. To some observers, it appeared that the Stevenson Amendment was designed to inhibit the expansion of Soviet-American trade;[52] however, it should be noted that this ceiling could be raised with congressional approval. It is, therefore, equally plausible that the primary intent of Senator Stevenson was to assert the power of Congress vis-a-vis the President over questions of trade financing.[53]

The Soviet Union reacted strongly to the passage of the Stevenson Amendment and to congressional assertions that the Soviets had agreed to increase Jewish emigration in exchange for MFN. On December 18, 1974, the Soviet news agency Tass released an article that reported that "leading circles" in the Soviet Union "categorically reject as inadmissible any attempts, from whomever they come, to interfere in affairs which are entirely within the internal competence of the Soviet state and do not concern anybody else."[54] On the same day, the text of a letter from Gromyko to Kissinger dated October 26 and previously undisclosed by Kissinger was released. In the letter, Gromyko stated that the Soviets "resolutely reject" any interpretation of Soviet assurances concerning emigration that mention specific numbers.[55] United States congressmen discounted the Tass report and Gromyko letter as face-saving measures; however, Soviet commentators writing after the passage of the trade bill consistently mentioned the unacceptability to the Soviet Union of the understandings contained in the Kissinger-Jackson exchange of letters.[56] Throughout the last part of December, the Soviet press attacked Senator Jackson and "his cold war views." One author favorably quoted a number of U.S. businessmen who supported the expansion of Soviet-American trade and opposed the Jackson-Vanik Amendment.[57]

On January 10, 1975, the Soviet Union informed the United States that it would not enter the provisions of the 1974 Trade Agreement into force. The Soviet Union objected to the limitation placed on Exim credits and the linking of MFN to emigration as violations of the trade agreement and the principle of noninterference in the domestic affairs of other states. Interestingly, the Soviets nullified, rather than cancelled, the Trade Agreement which meant that, if the Soviets decided at some future date to sign the agreement, they could do so.

In other words, the Trade Agreement was still on the books, even though it was never implemented. In response to the Soviet decision, Kissinger announced that the United States would not take the steps to expand Soviet-American trade called for in the agreement.

CONCLUSIONS

The Jackson-Vanik Amendment simultaneously concerned a number of diverse issues and, as the amendment became politicized, it activated many different groups and individuals. In this concluding section, three questions are addressed: (1) how were the major issues resolved; (2) which actors were the most important in determining the outcome of the debate over the amendment; and (3) what are the lessons to be learned from this case for American foreign policy-making?

Senator Jackson publicly argued that the principal motivation for his amendment was humanitarian: "When people such as those who want to leave the Soviet Union ask for help, the least we can do is provide the tiniest bit of freedom for them."[58] No doubt, many legislators voted for the Jackson-Vanik Amendment because they felt that a vote in favor of the amendment was a vote in favor of human rights. The very substantial support for the amendment from the Jewish community was motivated by a desire to increase Jewish emigration from the Soviet Union. Despite the intention of those who supported the amendment, its passage actually reduced Soviet Jewish emigration as the following figures indicate:[59]

1967 - 1,400	1973 - 30,600
1968 - 380	1974 - 17,000
1969 - 2,900	1975 - 18,500
1970 - 1,040	1976 - 14,500
1971 - 12,900	1977 - 17,000
1972 - 31,200 (SALT I and Trade	1978 - 29,000
Agreement were signed in 1972.)	1979 (January-October) - 43,000 (SALT
	II Treaty concluded.)

The dramatic decline in Soviet Jewish emigration during the years 1974 through 1977 was undoubtedly attributable in part, if not wholly, to passage of the Jackson-Vanik Amendment. The increases of 1978 and 1979 are interesting, and there are a number of hypotheses to explain these increases. Most plausibly, the Soviets wanted to demonstrate "good behavior" while the debate on SALT II was being waged in the United States.

Prior to the passage of the Jackson-Vanik Amendment, the Soviets indicated to Kissinger that they would allow a minimum of 35,000 Jews per year to emigrate. Had this occurred, at least 175,000 Jews would have left the Soviet Union in the 1975–79 period. Instead, only 139,000 Jews were allowed to leave during that five year period. With the demise of SALT II and detente, it is likely that the number of Jews allowed to emigrate will once again decrease. Clearly, the Jackson-Vanik Amendment did not achieve the objective of increasing Soviet Jewish emigration.

When the Soviet Union announced that it would not implement the 1972 Trade Agreement, Kissinger remarked, "Detente has had a setback." Indeed, the Trade Agreement and the expansion of Soviet-American trade had been an integral part of the Nixon-Kissinger approach to the Soviet Union, and its defeat marked a serious reversal in the executive branch's design and implementation of foreign policy. Senator Jackson took advantage of Congress' capability to block the initiative of an administration without proposing a substitute policy of his own. The result created a policy vacuum, and such a situation was hardly desirable.

The Jackson-Vanik case illustrates the potentially close relationship between domestic politics and foreign policy. During the two and a half years that the amendment was debated, Senator Jackson was running for the presidency. He was able to use the issue of Soviet Jewish emigration to increase his support from prominent Jewish individuals and organizations, to strengthen his position with the AFL-CIO (at least until the fall of 1974), to campaign as a staunch supporter of human rights, and to attack the Nixon-Kissinger *realpolitik* policies. Jackson was supported by other legislators because this was a politicized issue about which influential constituents were concerned.

This case demonstrates the importance of a number of different political actors. Jewish organizations were able to exert a great deal of influence. Individual Jewish dissidents in the Soviet Union were able to exert transnational influence through direct contacts with American Jewish leaders and Senator Jackson's office. In addition to these actors, the staffs of Jackson, Javits, Ribicoff, and Vanik played a central role in getting the amendment passed. In recent years, congressional staffs have increased dramatically; during the past decade, House and Senate staff has grown from 10,700 to 18,400, an increase of 70 percent.[60] This development, as this case illustrates, could very likely have an important impact on future American foreign policymaking.

To be sure, the executive branch made some serious errors in dealing with Congress in this case. The administration's foreign policymaking process was excessively centralized in the hands of the White House and particularly Henry Kissinger.[61] In addition, the Nixon administration did not bring Congress into the process of negotiating and implementing the Trade Agreement. For example, there were no congressional representatives on the U.S.-Soviet Joint Commercial Commission. Despite these shortcomings of the executive branch, one should remember that it is the only U.S. governmental actor that can design a coherent American foreign policy. As this case demonstrates, Congress can block the implementation of this design, but it can neither construct nor implement a design of its own.

Events since 1975 have demonstrated that the United States would have been in a far better position in the 1980s to influence Soviet foreign policy without the Jackson-Vanik Amendment than with it. When President Carter sought to penalize the Soviets for their invasion of Afghanistan, there were relatively few ways he could do so. Had Soviet-American trade grown to a level of $5 to $8 billion by 1980, the United States would clearly have been in a better position to influence the U.S.S.R. and to achieve its own foreign policy goals.

NOTES

1. See, for example, Gabriel A. Almond, *The American People and Foreign Policy* (New York: Harcourt, Brace and Company, 1950); and Robert E. Osgood, *Ideals and Self-Interest in America's Foreign Relations* (Chicago: University of Chicago Press, 1953).

2. These instances are cited in William W. Orbach, *The American Movement to Aid Soviet Jews* (Amherst: University of Massachusetts Press, 1979), pp. 118–19.

3. John Lewis Gaddis, *Russia, the Soviet Union, and the United States: An Interpretive History* (New York: John Wiley, 1978), pp. 41–47.

4. U.S., Congress, Senate, *Congressional Record*, 92nd Congress, 2nd sess., 1972, pt. 25: 33661.

5. *New York Times*, April 6, 1973, p. 14.

6. William Safire, *Before the Fall: An Inside View of the Pre-Watergate White House* (Garden City, N.J.: Doubleday, 1975), p. 573.

7. Paula Stern, *Water's Edge: Domestic Politics and the Making of American Foreign Policy* (Westport, Conn.: Greenwood Press, 1979), p. xiv.

8. For an extended analysis of the Nixon-Kissinger grand design and grand strategy, see Dan Caldwell, *American-Soviet Relations: From 1947 to the Nixon-Kissinger Grand Design.* (Westport, Conn.: Greenwood Press, 1981).

9. "Statement of Henry Kissinger," in U.S. Congress, Senate, Committee on Finance, *Hearing on the Emigration Amendment to the Trade Reform Act of 1974*, 93rd Congress, 2nd sess., December 3, 1974, p. 53. (Hereafter cited as *Emigration Amendment Hearing.*)

10. "Statement of Donald M. Kendall," in U.S. Congress, House, Committee on Foreign Affairs, *Hearings on Detente*, 93rd Congress, 2nd sess., May 22, 1974, pp. 102–03.

11. "Statement of George Meany," in U.S. Congress, Senate, Committee on Foreign Relations, *Hearings on Detente*, 93rd Congress, 2nd sess., October 1, 1974, p. 381. (Hereafter cited as *Senate Detente Hearings.)*

12. For recent considerations of executive-legislative relations, see Thomas M. Franck and Edward Weisband, *Foreign Policy by Congress* (New York: Oxford University Press, 1979); and Cecil V. Crabb, Jr. and Pat M. Holt, *Invitation to Struggle: Congress, the President and Foreign Policy* (Washington, D.C.: Congressional Quarterly Press, 1980). The Jackson-Vanik Amendment is not analyzed in detail in either of these books.

13. *United States v. Curtiss-Wright Export Corporation,* 299 U.S. 304, (1936).
14. *New York Times,* October 5, 1972.
15. See Chapter 3 on SALT II by Stephen Flanagan in this volume.
16. Robert O. Keohane and Joseph S. Nye, Jr. (eds.), *Transnational Relations in World Politics* (Cambridge: Harvard University Press, 1971), p. xi.
17. In his memoirs, Nixon pointed out, "From the outset of my administration . . . I planned to direct foreign policy from the White House." Richard Nixon, *RN: The Memoirs of Richard Nixon* (New York: Grosset and Dunlap, 1978), p. 340.
18. In his 1973 foreign policy report Nixon noted ". . . in the earlier years of this administration I linked the expansion of economic relations with improved political relations." Richard Nixon, *U.S. Foreign Policy for the 1970s; Shaping a Durable Peace, Department of State Bulletin* 68 (June 4, 1973). In his memoirs, Kissinger points out: "My own approach was to defer economic programs until there had been political progress." Henry Kissinger, *White House Years* (Boston: Little, Brown, 1979), p. 1152.
19. "Testimony of Henry A. Kissinger," U.S. Congress, Senate, Commitee on Finance, *Hearings on the Trade Reform Act of 1973,* 93rd Congress, 2nd sess., 1974, p. 468. (Hereafter cited as *Trade Reform Act Hearings.*)
20. Kissinger, *White House Years,* p. 48.
21. Peter G. Peterson, *U.S.-Soviet Commercial Relationships in a New Era* (Washington, D.C.: Government Printing Office, 1972).
22. Ohrbach, *The American Movement to Aid Soviet Jews,* p. 132.
23. William Korey, "The Struggle over Jackson-Mills-Vanik," *American Jewish Yearbook, 1974-75* (New York: American Jewish Committee, 1974), pp. 200-10.
24. "Remarks of Senator Henry Jackson," *Congressional Record,* December 13, 1974.
25. Michael Barone, Grant Ujifusa, and Douglas Mathews, *The Almanac of American Politics* (Boston: Gambit, 1972), pp. 816-18.
26. Quoted in Stern, *Water's Edge,* p. 55.
27. Gerald R. Ford, *A Time To Heal* (New York: Harper and Row, 1979), p. 138.
28. Nixon, *RN,* p. 876.
29. Stern, *Water's Edge,* p. 149.
30. *Emigration Amendment Hearings,* pp. 52, 72.
31. *Trade Reform Act Hearings.*
32. "Statement of George Meany," in *Senate Detente Hearings,* p. 382.
33. "Statement of Jeremy Stone," in *Senate Detente Hearings,* p. 165.
34. For the history of the growth of American Jewish organizations to aid Soviet Jews, see the excellent book by William W. Orbach, *The American Movement to Aid Soviet Jews.*
35. Ibid., p. 117.
36. Stern, *Water's Edge,* p. 56.
37. Quoted in *The Washington Lobby* (Washington, D.C.: Congressional Quarterly, 1974), p. 118.
38. Orbach, *The American Movement to Aid Soviet Jews,* p. 136.

39. Stern, *Water's Edge*, p. 72.
40. Ibid., pp. 73–74.
41. Keohane and Nye, *Transnational Relations in World Politics*.
42. Robert O. Keohane and Joseph S. Nye, "Transgovernmental Relations and International Organizations," *World Politics* 27 (1) (October 1974): 41.
43. Stern, *Water's Edge*, pp. 79–80.
44. U.S. Congress, Senate, *Congressional Record*, 93rd Congress, 1st sess., September 17, 1973.
45. Quoted in Stern, *Water's Edge*, p. 86.
46. "Exchange of letters between Secretary Kissinger and Senator Jackson, October 18, 1974," in *Emigration Amendment Hearing*, pp. 36–39.
47. Kissinger in *Emigration Amendment Hearing*, p. 53.
48. Letter from Henry Jackson to Henry Kissinger, October 18, 1974, *Emigration Amendment Hearing*, p. 38.
49. Ibid.
50. Kissinger statement in *Emigration Amendment Hearing*, p. 54.
51. *New York Times*, October 28, 1974.
52. This is the view taken by Daniel Yergin, "Politics and Soviet-American Trade: The Three Questions," *Foreign Affairs* 55 (April 1977): 532.
53. John P. Hardt and George D. Holliday, "East-West Financing by Eximbank and National Interest Criteria," in *U.S. Financing of East-West Trade: The Political Economy of Government Credits and the National Interest*, edited by Paul Marer (Bloomington, Ind.: International Development Research Center, Indiana University, 1975). In an interview with Caldwell, a senior adviser to Senator Stevenson said that the amendment's purpose was "to limit the power of the White House."
54. Foreign Broadcast Information Service, *Soviet Union-Daily Report* 74 (245) (December 19, 1974): B1. (Hereafter cited as FBIS-SOV).
55. Ibid., p. B2.
56. FBIS-SOV 74 (247) (December 23, 1974): B1–B7.
57. "Strelniklov Dispatch," FBIS-SOV 74 (251) (December 30, 1974): B3–B4.
58. Henry Jackson quoted in *Time*, October 1, 1973, p. 23.
59. The figures for 1967-1971 were compiled by the National Conference on Soviet Jewry and are cited by Stern, *Water's Edge*, p. 217. The figures for 1972-1978 were compiled by the Intergovernmental Committee for European Migration and are cited in the *Los Angeles Times*, November 3, 1979, part I, p. 32.
60. Crabb and Holt, *Invitation to Struggle*, p. 192.
61. I.M. Destler, *Presidents, Bureaucrats and Foreign Policy: The Politics of Organizational Reform* (Princeton, N.J.: Princeton University Press, 1972); and John P. Leacacos, "Kissinger's Apparat," *Foreign Policy* 5 (Winter 1971-72).

Chapter 2
Congressional Participation in U.S.-Middle East Policy, October 1973-1976: Congressional Activism vs. Policy Coherence[1]
John F. Roehm, Jr.

OVERVIEW

On the eve of the Yom Kippur War, U.S. Middle East policy had almost settled into a complacent acceptance of the status quo of "no war, no peace," which had ensued following Israel's decisive defeat of the Arabs in the June 1967 "Six Day War." This sense of complacency was at least partially based on a series of congenial assumptions which underlay U.S. Middle East policy in mid-1973: first, Israel's acknowledged military supremacy would ensure stability; second, Soviet influence in the region had reached its limit and U.S.-Soviet detente would serve to minimize the danger of superpower confrontation in the Middle East; and, third, Arab oil could not be used effectively to pressure the West.[2]

These assumptions and the status quo were shattered on October 6, 1973, when the Arab states launched the fourth major Arab-Israeli war since the founding of Israel in 1948 and swiftly followed hostilities with the imposition of an oil embargo against the West on October 17, 1973. As a result, the Nixon-Kissinger administration was confronted with a new situation in the Middle East. The Arab states had achieved a rare state of unity engendered by the "common struggle" and the apparently effective use of the oil weapon. The United States and its Western allies were facing serious economic strain; and their differing perceptions of how to deal with the problem were shaking the unity of NATO. Perhaps most serious of all, the Yom Kippur War was threatening to dissolve the fragile U.S.-Soviet detente while posing a very real danger of a superpower confrontation in the Middle East.[3]

The situation was further complicated by the state of U.S.-Arab relations existing at the time. The United States had no official diplomatic relations with much of the Arab world, including the two major Arab combatant states in the Yom Kippur War—Egypt and Syria.[4] Most of the Arab world viewed the United States as "totally" supporting Israel in the Arab-Israeli dispute and insensitive to the Arab cause. Some of the more radical Arab states accused the United States of either promising what it could not deliver or, more probably, "tricking" the Arab states with offers it would not effect (for example, the Rogers formula).[5]

In response to this new situation, the Nixon-Kissinger administration sought to formulate a new Middle East policy based on U.S. "interests" in the Middle East which Secretary of State Kissinger defined as: (1) our traditional concern for the security of Israel; (2) transformed relations with the Arab states; (3) avoidance of superpower confrontation; and (4) access to Middle East oil.[6] While there was nothing startlingly new in the Nixon-Kissinger definition of these "interests," there were some distinct differences in emphasis and nuance when compared to past U.S. Middle East policy. First, although concern for the security of Israel continued as a basic objective of U.S. Middle East policy, Kissinger made transformed relations with the Arab states the cornerstone of his new policy and sought to reduce the image of the U.S. in the Arab world as "totally" supporting Israel—a policy classified by some as a "tilt toward the Arabs."[7] Second, while there had been a growing trend toward a lessening of the intensity of U.S.-Soviet competition in the Middle East following the heyday of U.S. interventionist policy in the Middle East during the Eisenhower-Dulles administration, Kissinger gave a much more formal and official recognition to the fact that the Soviet Union was firmly entrenched in the Middle East and U.S. policy must learn to live with that fact. Finally, while the United States had always sought to facilitate its own and the West's access to Middle East oil, the bitter lesson of the Arab oil embargo had now raised this objective to "first rank" importance.

In order to launch his new Middle East policy, Kissinger (who, with Nixon becoming ever deeper embroiled in defending his presidency in the midst of the Watergate scandals, became the chief architect of U.S. Middle East policy following the Yom Kippur War) sought to manipulate the Yom Kippur War to create a favorable negotiating situation in which neither side could claim a total victory and the United States would be seen by both sides as an "honest broker" in Arab-Israeli negotiations. Kissinger largely achieved the desired negotiating situation through a combination of carefully managing U.S. resupply of Israel; negotiations with the Soviets, Arabs, and Israelis; a U.S. military alert; rescuing the Egyptian Third Army; and the fortunes of the battlefield.[8]

Building on this foundation, Kissinger developed a "step-by-step" approach to negotiating a settlement of the Arab-Israeli dispute which placed the United States and Kissinger in the central position in Arab-Israeli negotiations and emphasized tackling the peripheral areas of the dispute where agreement was more likely achievable before attempting to confront the harder, more intractable issues.[9] Perhaps the most significant characteristic of Kissinger's new Middle

East policy was the highly personal, noninstitutionalized brand of diplomacy he practiced, exemplified by his frequent applications of "shuttle diplomacy" to achieve Arab-Israeli agreements.

The most visible achievements of U.S. Middle East policy under the tutelage of Kissinger during the period from the Yom Kippur War to the end of the Ford administration (some 39 months) were: (1) the Yom Kippur War cease-fire; (2) first-phase disengagement agreements between Egypt and Israel (January 1974) and Syria and Israel (May 1974), which were the first Arab-Israeli agreements concluded since the 1949 armistice agreement; (3) the lifting of the Arab oil embargo (March 1974); (4) a dramatic turnaround in U.S.-Egyptian relations, transforming Egypt from a bitter opponent to a quasi-ally; and (5) a second-phase disengagement agreement between Egypt and Israel (Sinai Agreement, September 1975).

Kissinger's new Middle East policy also involved a little over $10 billion in U.S. economic and military assistance provided to key Middle East confrontation states, much of it closely linked to the Arab-Israeli agreements negotiated by Kissinger, and a relatively high commitment of U.S. political prestige, which was placed "on the line" as a "guarantor" of Arab-Israeli agreements.[10]

Finally, Kissinger's Middle East policy resulted in a widening of the rift between the United States and the more radical Arab states which, after the Sinai Agreement, included Syria, and contributed to isolating Egypt from much of the Arab world, which bitterly opposed the Sinai Agreement.[11]

Kissinger's Middle East policy was blatantly executive-fashioned. Congress was virtually excluded from the "before-the-fact" decision making process. Kissinger's approach to Congress was generally to rely on his very considerable prestige and persuasive powers to gain support for initiatives already decided and often already set in motion.[12]

In subsequent sections of this chapter, we will briefly examine some of the more significant examples of executive-congressional interaction on Kissinger's Middle East policy, and, in particular, we will examine some of the consequences of rising congressional activism in Middle East policy, which accelerated during this period, on executive policy coherence.

PRINCIPAL ACTORS

William Quandt has identified the traditional actors in U.S. Middle East policy-making as the White House, including the President and numerous staff members; the State Department, including the Secretary, under secretaries, and numerous bureau chiefs; the Department of Defense, including the Secretary, the Joint Chiefs of Staff, and several subagencies; the Central Intelligence Agency; Congress; organized interest groups; influential individuals with access to the President, the Secretary of State, or Congress; and public opinion.[13]

While there is no doubt U.S. Middle East policy from the Yom Kippur War to the end of the Ford administration involved varying degrees of activity from each of these actors, the principal actors participating in the policymaking process for U.S. Middle East policy vis-a-vis the confrontation states in the Arab-Israeli conflict during this period were Presidents Nixon and Ford, Secretary of State Kissinger, the two foreign affairs committees of Congress, the Israeli lobby, the oil and Arab interest groups, and, in a more passive role, American public opinion.

Among the three principal executive branch actors, Presidents Nixon and Ford occasionally played significant roles, but the dominant executive branch actor in U.S. Middle East policy during this period was clearly Secretary of State Henry Kissinger. At the outbreak of the Yom Kippur War, Kissinger held both the positions of Secretary of State and Special Assistant to the President for National Security Affairs, which placed almost all foreign policymaking apparatus effectively under his control. From October 1973 until Nixon's resignation in late August 1974, President Nixon was so absorbed with the defense of his presidency that Kissinger was given exceptional latitude within the executive branch foreign policy decision making system. Not since John Foster Dulles during the period of Eisenhower's incapacity had a U.S. Secretary of State been perceived by domestic and foreign observers alike as so predominant in the direction of U.S. foreign policy.[14] Even after President Ford took office and resolved the crisis of the presidency, Kissinger, despite eventually giving up his position as National Security Advisor, retained his predominance in the direction of U.S. foreign affairs, as Ford, with only a few exceptions, continued to defer to Kissinger's judgment in foreign policy matters, especially those relating to the Middle East.

With respect to Congress, the Senate Foreign Relations Committee and the House Foreign Affairs Committee (renamed the House International Relations Committee in March 1975) were the principal actors with the Senate Foreign Relations Committee enjoying a slight edge due to Kissinger's preference for this committee and the special relationship which he developed with the committee chairman, Senator J. William Fulbright, one of the Senate's most prestigious voices in foreign affairs.[15]

Among interest groups, the Israeli lobby was clearly a major actor in U.S. Middle East policymaking during this period. The spearhead of the lobby was the American Israel Public Affairs Committee (AIPAC), which is officially registered as a domestic lobby with both houses of Congress. The AIPAC serves as an umbrella lobbying organization with Congress for a large number of diverse American Jewish organizations in matters concerning the state of Israel.[16] AIPAC generally draws on the Conference of Presidents of Major American Jewish Organizations ("Presidents Conference"), which is responsible for coordinating the activities of more than 30 American Jewish groups on virtually all foreign policy issues, for its policy positions. The "Presidents Conference" also presents the "Jewish position" to members of the executive branch just as AIPAC does to members of Congress.[17] The influence of the Israeli lobby in U.S. Middle East policy lies in its ability to activate and mobilize the extensive pro-Israeli sentiment in Congress. Robert Trice has noted that Congress' willingness to support pro-Israeli positions is the product of a number of complex factors, with determinants varying with individual congressmen. These factors include responsiveness to constituents' demands, reliance on campaign funds, a personal sense of identification with Israel, a view of Israel as a bastion of democracy which must be kept strong to prevent Soviet domination of the area, and the fact that support for Israel is likely to place the congressman in the mainstream of articulate opinion in his district or state.[18] An example of how AIPAC seeks to activate support for pro-Israel positions is seen in the following statement by AIPAC's Executive Director, Morris J. Amitay:

> if we get a Senator from an industrial state, a state with any sizeable Jewish population and he doesn't come out [in support of a pro-Israeli measure], we don't let him get away with it. That's when we call for outside help. When the word gets out for help, Senators or Congressmen can find themselves deluged with calls and letters.[19]

The effectiveness of this technique is suggested in the statements of two senators who explained their change of mind from not signing to signing the letter of 76 senators sent to President Ford during the "reassessment of U.S. Middle East policy" in May 1975 urging all out support for Isreal as follows: Senator John Culver [D., Iowa]: "The pressure was too great. I caved." Senator Daniel Inouye [D., Hawaii]: "It's easier to sign one letter than answer five thousand."[20] The Israeli lobby played an active role in such initiatives as the emergency military aid bill for Israel in October 1973; aid for Israel in Middle East aid packages in 1974, 1975, and 1976; arms sales to Arab states in 1975 and 1976; the "reassessment" phase of U.S. Middle East policy, March-August 1975; and the proposal to establish a U.S.-manned early-warning system in the Sinai in September and October 1975.

Arab interest groups, and in particular the oil lobby which often supported their cause, also played a role in U.S. Middle East policy during this period, but their influence never rivaled that of the Israeli lobby. The Arab interest groups were much less organized than their American Jewish counterparts, and they had a problem in establishing their "legitimacy" with the American public and Congress. They generally considered the White House, Department of State, and the Congress as captives of the Israeli lobby and expended little effort on communicating with them.[21] The Arab point of view was frequently presented to Congress by the oil lobby, which was often allied with the Arab groups in attempting to moderate U.S. "total" support for Israel. *Time* magazine reported in June 1975 that American oil companies had donated $9 million over the past eight years to various pro-Arab groups.[22] The oil companies also attempted, through advertisements in newspapers and letters to stockholders, to moderate U.S. support for Israel during the Yom Kippur War.[23] While the influence of the Arab and oil interest groups was far less than that of the Israeli lobby, at least they broke the monopoly of information which pro-Israeli groups had enjoyed in the past.

Finally, the role of public opinion in U.S. Middle East policy during this period was largely passive, although still significant. The public was not consistently concerned with most of the issues involved in the Arab-Israeli conflict. Public opinion surveys in 1974, for example, showed that no foreign policy issue ranked higher than seventeenth in public concern or interest.[24] But the significance lay in the fact that what public opinion was expressed was overwhelmingly favorable to Israel compared to the Arabs. A mid-1976 Gallup poll showed that 65 percent of Americans polled rated Israel "favorably" while only 25 percent held unfavorable views.[25] Robert Trice has noted that, on the basis of publicly recorded behavior from 1966-1974, the dominant policy stance of the articulate public has been one of very strong support for Israel relative to that exhibited for relevant Arab states.[26] Thus, public opinion has added "legitimacy" to the efforts of AIPAC and facilitated a congressman coming out in favor of a pro-Israeli measure.

FACTORS AFFECTING CONGRESSIONAL SUPPORT FOR KISSINGER'S NEW MIDDLE EAST POLICY

In attempting to achieve congressional support for his new Middle East policy, Kissinger faced a number of potential difficulties. First, Congress was solidly in the hands of the party opposite to the President's.[27] While the U.S. political system is not noted for strict party loyalty (and the 94th Congress was certainly no exception),[28] party does provide an automatic incentive for congressional opposition to executive branch initiatives, especially those for which it has had little input. It was, for example, the Senate Democratic Caucus which, in September 1974, launched the first serious attacks against Kissinger's direction of U.S. foreign policy.[29] In addition, a Republican House Foreign Affairs Committee member stated that the bitter congressional-executive branch confrontation over missiles for Jordan in July and August 1974 would not have occurred if the President had been a Democrat.[30] Thus, in the absence of a clearly perceived external threat, politics does not necessarily "stop at the water's edge" and Kissinger could expect a certain amount of "built in" opposition to his Middle East initiatives, the more so because Congress was virtually excluded from the policymaking process.

Second, the Congresses faced by Kissinger (the 93rd and 94th) manifested a growing determination to exert their independent voices in foreign affairs. These

Congresses have been termed by Franck and Weisband "revolutionary" because of their successful efforts to increase congressional participation in foreign policy and reduce executive branch discretion.[31] Congressional resurgence in foreign policy was the result of a combination of factors. By the early 1970s, the foreign policy consensus which had sustained presidential foreign policy through a succession of post-World War II crises had broken down partly as a result of a perceptible lessening in the American people and Congress of the perception of the threat to U.S. national security from a monolithic, communist bloc. As the perception of threat lessened, there was less incentive to rely solely on executive discretion in foreign policy. This trend was reinforced by the protracted failure of presidential policy in Vietnam which resulted in a loss of confidence among both Congress and the public in the President's handling of foreign policy.[32] The series of revelations of abuses of presidential power in domestic affairs (the Watergate scandals) completed the erosion of the presumption that in foreign affairs the President knew best and replaced it with an attitude of deep suspicion and distrust of executive branch competence, integrity, and motives.[33]

Third, one of the potentially most serious difficulties Kissinger faced in gaining support for his new Middle East policy was the formidable strength of pro-Israeli sentiment in Congress. Former Senator J. William Fulbright, who was the chairman of the Senate Foreign Relations Committee in the 93rd Congress, stated that "the interests that support Israel have seventy-five to eighty votes in the Senate on nearly any issue in which the interests of Israel are involved."[34] A mid-1975 *Washington Post* poll found that 87 percent of House members affirmed that the United States had a moral obligation to prevent the destruction of Israel.[35] A measure of the strength of pro-Israeli sentiment in Congress was demonstrated by the fact that resolutions introduced in Congress supporting Israel at the outbreak of the Yom Kippur War were cosponsored by two-thirds of the Senate and 279 members of the House.[36] Pat Holt, Chief of Staff of the Senate Foreign Relations Committee in the 93rd Congress, states that pro-Israeli sentiment in Congress was "a constraining factor in the policy-making process within the executive branch."[37]

Finally, the organization and practices of Congress presented difficulties to Kissinger as they had in the past presented difficulties to other executive branch officials. Kissinger frequently complained that he and his aides were being caught up in jurisdictional disputes among several congressional committees seeking to exercise their independent voices in a particular foreign policy area. Kissinger also complained that consultation with Congress on foreign policy was becoming more difficult because the number of congressmen and senators concerned with foreign policy had expanded beyond the traditional foreign affairs committees.[38] In addition, many members of the post-Vietnam and Watergate Congresses refused to accept executive consultation with committee chairmen as adequate consultation with Congress.[39] Kissinger was especially concerned with Congress' frequent inability to maintain the confidentiality of classified information provided it by the executive branch. This concern was the basis of one area of congressional-executive conflict during congressional hearings on the U.S. proposal to establish an early-warning system in the Sinai as part of the Sinai Agreement.

The Kissinger Factor

One of the most unique aspects of congressional-executive interaction on U.S. Middle East policy during this period was the influence on such interaction exercised by Secretary of State Henry Kissinger. At the time of his appointment to this position in September 1973, Kissinger enjoyed tremendous prestige as a result of his being generally credited while National Security Advisor to President Nixon with opening contact with the Peoples Republic of China, negotiating the first Strategic Arms Limitation Agreement (SALT I), and negotiating the Vietnam Peace Treaty, for which he was corecipient of the Nobel Peace Prize in 1973. In 1973 and 1974, Kissinger topped the Gallup Poll's list of most admired men.[40]

The combination of Kissinger's prestige, his acknowledged brilliance, and his excellence as a "briefer" on foreign policy issues, and Congress' concern not to subject U.S. foreign policy to narrow partisan debate during the disintegration of the Nixon presidency facilitated Kissinger's initially overcoming many of the difficulties in gaining approval for his executive-fashioned Middle East policy discussed above. In Kissinger's initial appearances before Congress he was met with almost a sense of diffidence concerning his handling of U.S. foreign affairs.[41] His initial successes in achieving Arab-Israeli agreements (cease-fire and first-phase disengagement agreements) reinforced his prestige with Congress and added to the deferential treatment he was afforded by Congress.

After the resignation of Nixon in August 1974, Congress' attitude toward Kissinger's handling of U.S. foreign policy changed considerably; and such aspects of Kissinger's personality and diplomatic style as his overly personalized, noninstitutionalized approach to diplomacy, his high self-esteem, his autocratic temperament, his penchant for secrecy, and his insistence on holding all decision making power in his own hands resulted in growing congressional criticism. Kissinger, however, retained considerable persuasive power with Congress, especially with the two foreign relations committees, throughout his term in office.[42]

Substantive Issues

Kissinger's new Middle East policy during the period from the Yom Kippur War to the end of the Ford administration involved three issues which generated the most congressional-executive friction: arms sales to Arab confrontation states, the balance in aid to Israel versus aid to the Arab states, and the degree of flexibility to be permitted the executive in fashioning U.S. Middle East policy.

The issue which generated the most friction was probably the issue of arms sales to Arab states. Kissinger had made such sales an integral part of his efforts to transform relations with the Arab states. These efforts were vigorously opposed by the Israeli lobby. In addition, many in Congress believed that providing arms to Arab states was "destabilizing," likely to accelerate the arms race in the Middle East, and a threat to the security of Israel. Some in Congress even viewed arms sales to Arab states as reminiscent of the type of commitment which had led to U.S. involvement in Vietnam.[43]

The question of the proper balance between the amount of total aid to be provided the Arab states versus that to be provided Israel was also a cause of congressional-executive confrontation. Many in Congress, under pressure from the Israeli lobby, sought to commit Congress to "total" support of Israel. Kissinger, on the other hand, strove to develop a more balanced approach, to disassociate the United States from some of Israel's more extreme positions (for example, Israel's insistence on its right to build Jewish settlements in occupied Arab territory), and to portray the United States as an "honest broker" in Arab-Israeli negotiations—a policy seen by some in Congress as too far a "tilt" toward the Arabs.[44]

The third issue, the degree of flexibility to be permitted the executive in Middle East policy, was often a significant part of the confrontations which developed over the first two issues. We have already noted that the breakdown in the foreign policy consensus, Vietnam, and Watergate had predisposed Congress to limit sharply executive flexibility in foreign policy. After 1974, Kissinger's personality and diplomatic style added fuel to these efforts.

There were a number of seemingly important issues involved in Kissinger's new Middle East policy which surprisingly sparked little debate. Congress, for example, did not seriously debate the relative merits of the "step-by-step" approach versus a comprehensive peace plan, although critics outside the government, such as George Ball, frequently raised this issue.[45] Nor did Congress conduct any extensive debate of such issues as the advisability of excluding the Palestinians from negotiations (although the House International Relations Committee did hold relatively inconsequential hearings on the subject in 1975),[46] the implications of isolating Egypt from the radical Arab states for a final peace settlement, and the impact of the Sinai Agreement on future Arab-Israeli negotiations and U.S. flexibility in such negotiations (Kissinger's "secret" protocols which accompanied the Sinai Agreement operated to narrow U.S. flexibility in future negotiations).[47] While a number of reasons could be offered for Congress' relative neglect of these issues, one contributing factor was probably that Israel and the Israeli lobby favored or did not oppose the Kissinger position on these issues and, thus, there was no incentive for Israel's many supporters in Congress to raise the issues.

CONGRESSIONAL ACTIVISM VERSUS KISSINGER'S NEW MIDDLE EAST POLICY

Kissinger had little difficulty in achieving congressional support for his major Middle East initiatives during the period from the Yom Kippur War through 1974. Congress overwhelmingly endorsed the major initiatives of this period—the $2.2 billion emergency aid bill for Israel, the Yom Kippur War cease-fire agreement negotiated by Kissinger, the two first-phase disengagement agreements between Egypt and Israel and Syria and Israel, and the sizable Middle East aid package included in the fiscal year 1975 foreign aid request. All of these initiatives had strong support from the Israeli lobby and none raised, to any significant extent, the contentious issues previously identified.

The one exception was the offer by President Nixon, in June 1974, to sell nuclear reactors and fuel to Egypt and Israel. This offer raised a storm of controversy in Congress, much of it concerning the failure of the executive branch to adequately consult with Congress before announcing the offer. Three separate congressional committees held independent hearings on the subject; and, although Congress did not actually veto the offers, it did place such stipulations on them that the conclusion of final agreements was delayed over two years.[48]

Although Congress was, on the whole, highly supportive of Kissinger's new Middle East policy during this initial period, Congress was concerned with the extent of executive flexibility exercised by Kissinger in foreign policy in general. This concern was translated into a provision in the 1974 Foreign Military Sales Act (the Nelson-Bingham bill) which permitted Congress to veto U.S. government arms sales to foreign governments of $25 million or more.[49] This provision set the stage for future congressional-executive confrontations over arms sales to Arab states.

In examining closely Kissinger's success in gaining congressional support, there is some evidence that Congress exercised a significant "prenatal" influence on the development of some of Kissinger's Middle East initiatives. Pat Holt, Chief of Staff of the Senate Foreign Relations Committee in the 93rd Congress, has stated that a "quid pro quo" for any kind of aid to the Arab states was more aid for Israel.[50] The $2.2 billion emergency military aid bill for Israel may well be a case in point. The Pentagon had considered $850 million adequate to cover the cost of resupplying Israeli arms expended during the Yom Kippur War and administration witnesses were unable to tell Congress exactly how $1 billion of the total $2.2 billion would be used by Israel.[51] There is a strong implication that the higher level of aid for Israel was requested by the administration in order to moderate opposition from pro-Israeli congressmen to initiatives favorable to the Arabs.

There is also some indication that Kissinger's selection of the "step-by-step" approach to negotiations was partially motivated by his concern that attempts to move Israel too far, too fast, as would be likely in a comprehensive peace plan, would cause the Israeli lobby to activate its "legions" of supporters in Congress and thereby threaten Kissinger's efforts to transform relations with the Arabs. In reviewing the accomplishments of the "step-by-step" process, Kissinger stated: "Its easy to say what we've done is not enough. . . . They were the attainable—given our domestic situation."[52] A Kissinger aide remarked that pro-Israeli sentiment in Congress was "the greatest constraint" in U.S. Middle East policy and "the constraint became the determinant."[53]

During 1975 and 1976, Kissinger encountered considerably more difficulty in gaining congressional support for his Middle East initiatives than he did during the earlier period. While Congress continued to support Kissinger's negotiating efforts and approved relatively large amounts of aid to Middle East states to support the negotiations, it proved far less supportive of specific initiatives, such as large arms sales to Arab states and U.S. commitments to Middle East states, made without the prior knowledge and consent of Congress (for example, the "secret" protocols accompanying the Sinai Agreement). Congress proved during this period much more determined to make its voice heard in the formulation of foreign policy.

The issue of arms sales to Arab confrontation states was at the center of three of the more intense congressional-executive confrontations during this period. The first of these confrontations occurred in July and August 1975 over the administration's proposal to sell Jordan fourteen batteries of "Hawk" ground-to-air missiles and eight batteries of "Vulcan" antiaircraft guns at an estimated cost of $325 million. The Israeli lobby mounted an intense campaign to defeat the missile portion of this package. AIPAC prepared a memorandum emphasizing the offensive capabilities of the weapons proposed for sale to Jordan and the danger such "offensive weapons" posed to Israel, and sent it to every congressman and to 397 city and regional Jewish organizations. In addition, AIPAC organized a telephone blitz of Congress from both AIPAC officials and the "grass roots" constituencies to drum up support for a House resolution blocking the proposed missile sale to Jordan, which achieved nearly 100 co-sponsors.[54]

Congressional action on the proposed sale of missiles to Jordan was spearheaded by the House International Relations Committee, which held its hearings on the subject prior to those scheduled by the Senate Foreign Relations Committee. As a result of the pressure of the Israeli lobby, the significant number of co-signers for the House resolution of disapproval of the sale, and the feeling of many members of the committee that the magnitude of the proposed missile sale to Jordan could upset the military balance in the Middle East and encourage Jordan to become an active participant against Israel in future hostilities (Jordan had used the excuse of a lack of air defense for not participating actively with the Arab Front in the Yom Kippur War), the House International Relations Committee initially voted to veto the proposed sale. This action and growing opposition among members of the Senate Foreign Relations Committee caused the administration to withdraw its proposal before it reached the House or Senate floors.[55]

Intense negotiations conducted by Kissinger and his aides with Congress and by Kissinger with Jordan's King Hussein resulted in a compromise acceptable to Congress and finally acquiesced in by Hussein which permitted the sale of the original number of weapons but sharply restricted their mobility, thus greatly reducing their capability to be employed to support offensive operations.[56]

Congress' actions on the administration's proposal incensed King Hussein, whose moderate stance in the Arab-Israeli conflict was considered by Kissinger as highly beneficial to his negotiating efforts. The administration sought, through its missile sale proposal, to demonstrate U.S. confidence in Jordan and support for the king's moderate policies. Instead, Congress' actions resulted in King Hussein stating that he was "shocked and humiliated by the way he was treated by the U.S. Congress and by the administration." When Kissinger visited Jordan shortly after the Congressional action, he received a "frosty reception" from the king.[57]

In March and April 1976, the issue of arms sales to Arab confrontation states surfaced again when the administration submitted its proposal to sell six C-130 military transport aircraft to Egypt. The administration's proposal initiated another Israeli lobby effort to block the proposed sale. Israel's Prime Minister Rabin expressed strong opposition to the sale.[58] It also inspired Democratic presidential hopeful Senator Jackson, who at the time was campaigning in Florida and anxious to strengthen his hold on the Jewish vote, to publicly attack the administration's Middle East policy:

> The Kissinger policy of launching a military supply relationship [with Egypt] is cynical and indeed dangerous. It can only increase the chance of war in the Middle East and the severity of a new conflict there.59

Israeli lobby and congressional opposition to the sale of military transport aircraft to Egypt focused not on the danger of upsetting the military balance, which all agreed was minimal, but on establishing a precedent of a military supply relationship with Egypt, Israel's chief protagonist, which might expand in the future.

Congress was particularly sensitive to the Israeli lobby's pressure since 1976 was an election year and the lobby had the capability to activate the Jewish population in a congressman's constituency. But Congress was also sympathetic to the administration's argument that President Sadat should be rewarded for his new moderation in the Arab-Israeli conflict and for his part in improved U.S.-Egyptian relations.[60] The congressional battle this time was fought principally by the Senate Foreign Relations Committee. The strength of the opposition in that committee finally forced a reluctant Kissinger to negotiate another compromise with both Congress and President Sadat. As a result of the compromise, which was accepted by the House International Relations Committee as well as the Senate Foreign Relations Committee, Congress agreed to the sale of transport aircraft to Egypt but required the administration to officially declare it would request no more arms sales to Egypt during the remainder of 1976.[61]

In August 1976, a third major confrontation over arms sales to Arab nations erupted when the administration submitted a proposal to sell 1,000 "Sidewinder" air-to-air missiles and 1,500 "Maverick" air-to-surface missiles to Saudi Arabia. As in the Jordan missile sale and the sale of C-130 military transport aircraft to Egypt, the Israeli lobby was active in trying to drum up support to block the proposal. AIPAC's Executive Director appeared before the Senate Foreign Relations Committee to testify against the proposal, and an AIPAC representative patrolled the halls outside the committee room during consideration of the proposal to encourage opposition to the administration's proposal.[62] Opposition to the administration's proposal among members of the Senate Foreign Relations Committee centered on three points: (1) concern that the missiles for Saudi Arabia might be used against Israel; (2) the administration's lack of a coherent arms policy; and (3) the failure of the administration to take into account Congress' concern over excessive arms sales.[63]

The strength of the opposition once again forced Kissinger to modify the administration's initial arms sales proposal. Kissinger worked out an agreement with Senators Humphrey and Javits, two of the committee's staunchest supporters of Israel, whereby the number of "Sidewinder" missiles would be reduced from 1,000 to 850 and the number of "Maverick" missiles from 1,500 to 650. The compromise, however, failed to hold up in the entire committee, principally because Senator Case, the ranking Republican member on the committee, refused to go along with an agreement to which he had not been a party. As a result, the committee initially voted to block the sale. Kissinger, however, succeeded in reversing the decision by stressing, during a personal appearance before the committee, that refusing to approve the modified sale of missiles to Saudi Arabia could cause Saudi Arabia to be less supportive of holding down OPEC oil prices. With the reversal of the Senate Foreign Relations Committee's vote, the House International Relations Committee decided to table a similar resolution of disapproval and the modified sale was allowed to proceed.[64]

The intensity of the congressional-executive confrontations over arms sales to Arab states, especially the missile sales to Jordan and Saudi Arabia, was exacerbated by Congress' deep dissatisfaction with Kissinger's failure to consult with Congress "before the fact" on arms sales. During the House International Relations Committee's hearings in 1975 on arms sales to Persian Gulf nations, including Saudi Arabia, Representative Lee Hamilton [D., Indiana] stated that what bothered him most was not the sale of a particular weapon system but that there had been no prior consultation with the committee.[65]

The issue of the proper balance in the amount of support provided to Israel versus that provided the Arabs underlay congressional debate on a number of Kissinger Middle East initiatives (for example, Congressional review of Kissinger's Middle East aid packages included in the annual foreign aid requests). This issue was also at the center of the congressional-executive confrontation which occurred over the administration's announcement of a "total reassessment" of U.S. Middle East policy following the breakdown in late March 1975 of Kissinger's efforts to negotiate a second-phase disengagement agreement between Israel and Egypt. Although Kissinger publicly proclaimed that reassessment was not directed against Israel,[66] there were numerous indications that Kissinger might be using reassessment as a tool to pressure Israel to adopt a more flexible stance in negotiations with Egypt—for example, President Ford sent a letter to Israeli Prime Minister Rabin warning him that, if negotiations should break down, a "reassessment" of U.S. Middle East policy would follow; Kissinger, in supposedly private conversations (widely publicized), reputedly criticized Israeli intransigence in the negotiations; and the administration initiated a slow-down in already agreed to arms deliveries to Israel while, at the same time, proposing a missile sale to Jordan.[67]

Reacting to these indications, and under intense pressure from the Israeli lobby, 76 senators signed a letter sent to President Ford (drafted in part by AIPAC) on May 21, 1975, which called on the President to be "responsive" to Israel's urgent military and economic needs and to make clear that:

> the United States acting in its own national interests stands firmly with Israel in the search for peace in future negotiations, and that this premise is the basis of the current reassessment of U.S. policy in the Middle East.[68]

Senator Humphrey, who played a prominent role in the senatorial letter, argued that, while the letter may have been ill-timed, the expression of the senators' views was "absolutely necessary."[69] It has also been suggested that the letter provided Israel the necessary confidence in U.S. support to proceed with the negotiations.

Assuming these effects may be true, the letter also had some very negative effects on the coherence of Kissinger's Middle East policy. It was published just prior to President Ford's meeting with Egypt's President Sadat in Salzburg, Austria, at a time when the two nations were engaged in delicate negotiations aimed at resuming the Israeli-Egyptian second-phase disengagement talks. The Egyptian People's Assembly bitterly denounced the letter as demonstrating "a flagrant bias in favor of Israel" and characterized the signers as "hostile to peace."[70]

The *New York Times* carried a story from Jerusalem which quoted a senior Israeli official as stating:

> Buoyed by recent demonstrations of Congressional support, Israel has decided to ignore repeated U.S. requests that it produce new negotiating proposals before the American-Egyptian meeting in Salzburg. . . .[71]

One White House official claimed that the senators' letter cost the United States an extra $500 million in aid tied to the Sinai Agreement.[72] George Ball has argued that the pro-Israeli strength demonstrated by the letter weakened Kissinger's hand in trying to move Israel toward additional concessions and may have increased the amount of "subsidy" the United States had to pay Israel in order to achieve the Sinai Agreement.[73]

Regardless of what else it may have accomplished, the senatorial letter distorted Kissinger's attempt to portray the United States as an "honest broker" in Arab-Israeli negotiations, and raised the question in Middle East capitals of whether Kissinger could still speak for the United States. There is also no doubt that the letter virtually "pulled the teeth" of any serious "reassessment" of U.S. Middle East policy and reduced the credibility in the eyes of the Israelis of any attempts by Kissinger to use the possibility of withholding economic, military, or political aid from Israel as a means of "persuading" Israel to make concessions in Arab-Israeli negotiations.

The issue of executive flexibility and executive consultation with Congress "before the fact" in Middle East policy was at the heart of the executive-congressional confrontation that developed during the congressional hearings in September and October 1975 on Kissinger's proposal to establish a U.S. manned early-warning system in the Sinai as an integral part of the Sinai Agreement which he had negotiated. Although some congressmen were concerned that the proposal elicited shadows of Vietnam, the early-warning system proposal, itself, aroused little serious opposition and was eventually overwhelmingly approved by Congress.[74]

What sparked the confrontation was a series of "secret" assurances Kissinger made to Israel and, to a lesser extent, Egypt as a "secret addendum" to the basic Sinai Agreement. Kissinger argued that these assurances had been necessary to move the parties to final agreement. The most important of the "secret assurances" involved promises to provide Israel increased sophisticated armament on a long-term basis, help with its oil requirements, and support for its position concerning the Palestine Liberation Organization.[75] Kissinger had not planned to make public the full contents of these "secret assurances," which the administration considered executive agreements not requiring congressional approval. The "secret assurances," however, rapidly found their way into the press and the two congressional foreign relations committees demanded full disclosure of all of them before they would consider the early-warning proposal.

During the sometimes bitter debate on the "secret assurances," members of the two foreign relations committees expressed considerable suspicion concerning Kissinger's penchant for secrecy in the Arab-Israeli negotiations and anxiety that Kissinger and the administration were seeking to make new U.S. commitments to the Middle East without the knowledge or consent of Congress.[76] Many members argued that, for the assurances to be valid, they would have to be submitted to the Senate for approval as treaties.[77]

The constitutional argument over whether the assurances were executive agreements or treaties was left unresolved during the hearings, but Congress translated its opposition to both the form and content of the "secret assurances" into specific language inserted into the joint resolution establishing the U.S. manned early-warning system which stated that congressional approval of the early-warning system did not constitute approval of any commitments implied in the "secret assurances," nor did it provide any new authority to the President to introduce U.S. military forces into hostilities in the Middle East that he did not already possess. In addition, Congress gave itself the authority to remove the U.S. civilian technicians who would man the early-warning system in the Sinai if it deemed necessary.[78]

An additional area of executive-congressional controversy developed during the hearings of the early-warning proposal concerning the Senate Foreign Relations Committee's decision to publish in its committee report the complete "secret assurances" following the publication of excerpts in the press. Kissinger argued strongly, but unsuccessfully, that such publication in the committee's report would give official sanction to press reports and exacerbate the difficulties the unofficial press reports were already causing Egypt's President Sadat with the radical Arab states and with some elements in Egypt.[79]

Whatever the merits of Congress' actions during the hearings on the early-warning proposal, Congress and Kissinger were clearly at cross purposes concerning the U.S. approach to the Sinai Agreement and future negotiations. Kissinger sought, through the intential use of ambiguous language and secret executive agreements, to maximize U.S. (and his own) flexibility, in order to move Egypt and Israel, two states with very substantial areas of disagreement, closer to agreement. Congress, on the other hand, sought to reduce the ambiguity surrounding U.S. commitments to the Middle East (in effect, with respect to the Sinai Agreement, to reduce the implied commitments) and to reduce sharply the amount of executive discretion to be permitted in U.S. Middle East policy.

One of the more significant effects of congressional action on the Sinai Agreement was to once again raise serious doubts in the minds of Middle East leaders and governments as to the ability of Secretary of State Kissinger and the administration to speak for the United States in Middle East policy.

CONCLUSIONS

Based on our brief examination of executive-congressional interaction on U.S. Middle East policy vis-a-vis the confrontation states in the Arab-Israeli conflict from the Yom Kippur War to the end of the Ford administration, several significant conclusions can be drawn.

First, congressional activism in this policy area—for example, its actions on missile sales to Arab states, the senatorial letter sent to the President and widely publicized during the administration's announced "reassessment" of U.S. Middle East policy, and its virtual disavowal of the "secret assurances" made by Kissinger in order to achieve the Sinai Agreement—clearly distorted the coherence of Kissinger's Middle East policy, especially his efforts to portray the United States as an "honest broker" in Arab-Israeli negotiations and no longer committed to "total" support of Israel. Further, Franck and Weisband have pointed out that Congress' public, often brutal treatment of foreign nations seeking U.S. aid has often tended to cancel out whatever goodwill the transaction was intended to achieve (the Jordan and Saudi Arabia missile sales are two cases in point).[80] The executive branch certainly has no monopoly on being right; in fact, Congress may have a better understanding of what policy the public will support. But when Congress seeks to make its own moves in foreign policy, the problem this presents to a coherent foreign policy has been succinctly stated by Secretary of State Kissinger:

> It is as if when you are playing chess, a group of kibitzers keeps making moves for you. They may be better chess players, but they cannot possibly get a coherent game developed. Especially, if at the same time you have to explain each of your moves publicly so that your opponent can hear it.[81]

Second, while U.S. Middle East policy is not dictated by the Israeli lobby— Congress approved modified sales to Arab states over the objections of the Israeli lobby—the Israeli lobby in conjunction with the extensive pro-Israel sentiment in Congress (supported by a general public also sympathetic to Israel) has succeeded in slanting U.S. Middle East policy strongly in favor of Israel. During the period of this study, Congress worked smoothly with the executive branch on Middle East policy whenever Kissinger's initiatives were favored by Israel and, thus, supported by the Israeli lobby—for example, emergency military aid for Israel in October 1973, high level of aid for Israel in annual foreign aid requests, and the U.S. manned early-warning system in the Sinai. On the other hand, whenever Kissinger's Middle East initiatives were opposed by Israel and the Israeli lobby, Kissinger encountered extreme difficulty—for example, arms sales to Arab states and his attempt to use "reassessment" to gain further concessions from Israel. In effect, the Israeli lobby, the extensive pro-Israeli sentiment in Congress, and public sentiment generally sympathetic to Israel have combined to make support for Israel an almost automatic response from Congress. This response can be disrupted if the administration can make a strong enough case that supporting the Israeli position seriously endangers the national security or economic well being (as Kissinger succeeded in doing when he argued that vetoing the modified missile sale to Saudi Arabia could cause that country to withdraw its support of moderate oil prices and, thus, threaten the economic well being of the United States). In addition, Congress' strong pro-Israeli stance has essentially denied the United States a critical tool (reduced aid) that might be used on occasion to persuade Israel to adopt diplomatic positions more congenial to U.S. interests. The senatorial letter during the administration's reassessment of U.S. Middle East policy is probably a case in point.

The lack of credibility in administration threats to withdraw aid from Israel, based on past experience, may well have contributed to Israeli Prime Minister Begin's recent hard line in the summer of 1980 following the initial euphoria of the September 1978 Camp David Accords (for example, planting new settlements in occupied Arab territory, officially proclaiming Israeli sovereignty over all of Jerusalem and making the unified city the official capital of Israel, and taking a very narrow interpretation of Palestinian autonomy), despite efforts by the Carter administration to moderate the Israeli government's hard line.[82]

Finally, our examination of executive-congressional interaction in Middle East policy reemphasizes the dilemma faced by executive policymakers in pursuing an effective and coherent foreign policy. A foreign policy developed with the participation of Congress, in which a consensus is "hashed out" between the executive and Congress through debate, is likely to gain greater legitimacy and improve the chances that future costs of the policy will be supported by Congress and the public. But subjecting a policy to congressional debate before it is to be implemented, with the public exposure such a debate entails, may well cancel out the benefits the policy was designed to achieve. Had Kissinger, for example, fully consulted Congress "before the fact" on some of his Middle East initiatives—for example, the incentives he was prepared to offer Israel and Egypt, if necessary, to move them to agreement—it is likely, considering the strength of pro-Israeli sentiment in Congress, that individual items of Kissinger's policy might well have been rejected piecemeal before he could present the final agreement with a balanced package of pro-Israeli and pro-Arab incentives. At the very least, his flexibility in achieving agreements would have been significantly narrowed. Kissinger's strategy of keeping Congress essentially "in the dark" on the conduct of the negotiations, however, frequently backfired. Lack of consultation became as much an incentive for Congressional activism as the substance of the policy itself.

Marvin Feuerwerger states that congressional restraint and executive willingness to share power offers the greatest hope for avoiding diplomatic disasters.[83] Our study does not offer a very optimistic expectation that such a desirable executive-congressional "modus operandi" can be easily achieved. A first step would seem to be the need to reconstitute a state of trust between Congress and the White House which Vietnam and Watergate helped destroy. Certainly, it is not desirable to return to the days of unbridled executive discretion; but a measure of executive discretion would seem essential if the United States is to pursue an effective and coherent foreign policy.

NOTES

1. This chapter is drawn in part from: John F. Roehm, Jr., "Congressional Participation in Middle East Policy" (Ph.D. diss., University of Pittsburgh, 1980).
2. William B. Quandt, *Decade of Decision: American Policy Toward the Arab-Israeli Conflict, 1967–1976* (Berkeley: University of California Press, 1977), p. 200.
3. Roehm, "Congressional Participation in Middle East Policy," pp. 55–58.
4. *Department of State Bulletin* 75 (August 16, 1976): 236.
5. Steven Spiegel, "The Fate of the Patron: American Trials in the Arab-Israeli Dispute," *Public Policy*, 16 (1973); 179; Nahum Goldmann, "The Psychology of Middle East Peace," *Foreign Affairs*, 54 (October 1975): 115.
6. U.S., Congress, Senate, Committee on Foreign Relations, *Foreign Assistance Authorization: Hearing on S.3394*, 93rd Cong., 2d sess., 1974, p. 13.
7. Theodore Draper, "The United States and Israel: Tilt in the Middle East?" *Commentary*, 59 (April 1975): 29–45; Roehm, "Congressional Participation in Middle East Policy," pp. 100–23.
8. Walter Laqueur, *Confrontation: The Middle East and World Politics* (New York: Quadrangle/New York Times Book Co., 1974), p. 172; *Department of State Bulletin* 70 (January 21, 1974): 48: Roehm, "Congressional Participation in Middle East Policy," pp. 62–77.
9. U.S., Congress, House of Representatives, Committee on International Relations, *Middle East Agreements and the Early Warning System in Sinai; Hearings*, 94th Cong., 1st sess., 1975, p. 4.
10. Roehm, "Congressional Participation in Middle East Policy," pp. 123–31.
11. Ibid., pp. 97–98.
12. Ibid., pp. 219–30.
13. William B. Quandt, *Domestic Influences On U.S. Foreign Policy In The Middle East: The View From Washington,* The Rand Corporation (P-4309), April 1970, pp. 2–6.
14. Bruce Mazlish, *Kissinger: The European Mind in American Policy* (New York: Basic Books, 1976), p. 228; George Ball, *Diplomacy for a Crowded World* (Boston: Little, Brown, 1976), p. 143.
15. Stanley Karnov, "The Kissinger-Fulbright Courtship," *The New Republic*, 169 (December 29, 1973): 16; *Washington Post*, December 20, 1973, pp. G1-2.
16. *The Middle East: U.S. Policy, Israel, Oil and the Arabs*, 2d ed. (Washington, D.C.: Congressional Quarterly, October 1975), p. 61.
17. Robert H. Trice, *Interest Groups and the Foreign Policy Process: U.S. Policy in the Middle East*, Sage Professional Paper in International Studies, vol. 4, no. 02-047 (Beverly Hills: Sage Publications, 1976), pp. 37–40.
18. Ibid., p. 57.
19. *Washington Post*, November 23, 1974, p. A10.
20. Russell Warren Howe and Sarah Hays Trott, *The Power Peddlers: How Lobbyists Mold American Foreign Policy* (Garden City, N.Y.: Doubleday, 1977), pp. 272–73.
21. Trice, *Interest Groups and the Foreign Policy Process*, p. 59.

22. "Pushing the Arab Cause in America," *Time* 105 (June 23, 1975): 17, 20.
23. Howe and Trott, *The Power Peddlers*, p. 354; "Pushing the Arab Cause in America," p. 20; *Washington Post*, January 9, 1975, p. A8.
24. Robert S. Ingersoll, "The Executive and Congress in Foreign Policy," *Vital Speeches* 42 (March 1, 1976): p. 317.
25. Marvin C. Feuerwerger, *Congress and Israel: Foreign Aid Decision-Making in the House of Representatives, 1969-1976* (Westport, Conn.: Greenwood Press, 1979), pp. 86-87.
26. Trice, *Interest Groups and the Foreign Policy Process*, p. 30.
27. The 93rd Congress comprised 243 Democrats and 190 Republicans in the House and 58 Democrats and 42 Republicans in the Senate; the 94th Congress comprised 286 Democrats and 145 Republicans in the House and 62 Democrats and 38 Republicans in the Senate (*Congressional Quarterly Almanac*, 1974 & 1976).
28. Congressional Quarterly, *A Guide to Current Government* (February 1975), p. 2.
29. *New York Times*, September 22, 1974, p. 3.
30. Feuerwerger, *Congress and Israel*, p. 152.
31. Thomas A. Franck and Edward Weisband, *Foreign Policy By Congress* (New York: Oxford University Press, 1979), pp. 143, 158.
32. Roehm, "Congressional Participation in Middle East Policy," pp. 175-84; John C. Stennis and J. William Fulbright, *The Role of Congress in Foreign Policy* (Washington, D.C.: American Enterprise Institute for Public Policy Research, 1971), p. 64.
33. *Department of State Bulletin* 73 (November 17, 1975); 691; Bayless Manning. *The Conduct of United States Foreign Policy in the Nation's Third Century* (New York: The Foreign Policy Association, June 1976), p. 17.
34. U.S., Congress, Senate, Committee on Foreign Relations, *Emergency Military Assistance for Israel and Cambodia, Hearings*, 93rd Cong., 1st sess., 1973, p. 162.
35. William Greider and Barry Sussman, "U.S. Called Threat to Peace," *Washington Post*, July 1, 1975, pp. 1ff.
36. *Congressional Record, 93rd Congress, 1st Session*, vol. 119-Part 27, Oct. 18-Nov. 5, 1973, Washington, D.C.: U.S. Government Printing Office, 1973, pp. 34614-17, 34730, 34771, 34873, 35035, 35311, 35590; *Congressional Record, 93rd Congress, 1st Session*, vol. 119-Part 28, Nov. 6-15, 1973, Washington, D.C.: U.S. Government Printing Office, 1973, pp. 36038, 36273, 36410, 36891, 37192; *Congressional Record, 93rd Congress, 1st Session*, vol. 119-Part 29, Nov. 16-29, 1973, Washington, D.C.: U.S. Government Printing Office, 1973, p. 38740; *Congressional Record, 93rd Congress, 1st Session*, vol. 119-Part 30, Nov. 30-Dec. 6, 1973, Washington, D.C.: U.S. Government Printing Office, 1973, p. 39420.
37. Pat M. Holt, Chief of Staff of the Senate Foreign Relations Committee, 93rd Congress. Views were expressed in a letter to Roehm, dated February 24, 1978.
38. *Department of State Bulletins* 72 (February 17, 1975), 204; 74 (February 9, 1976): 149-50; 75 (July 26, 1976): 142.

39. U.S., Congress, House of Representatives, Committee on International Relations, *Congress and Foreign Policy*, Print, 94th Cong., 2d sess., (January 2, 1977), p. 20.
40. *New York Times*, December 30, 1974, p. 16.
41. Roehm, "Congressional Participation in Middle East Policy," pp. 201–03, 231–32.
42. Ibid., pp. 204–05.
43. U.S., Congress, Senate, Committee on Foreign Relations, *U.S. Missile Sale to Jordan, Hearings*, 94th Cong., 1st sess., 1975, pp. 3–4; U.S., Congress, Senate, Committee on Foreign Relations, *Sale of Missiles to Saudi Arabia, Report*, 94th Cong., 2nd sess., 1976, pp. 6–7; U.S. Congress, Senate, Committee on Foreign Relations, *Foreign Assistance Authorization, Arms Sales Issue, Hearings*, 94th Cong., 1st sess., 1976, pp. 109, 125, 240.
44. U.S., Congress, House of Representatives, Committee on Foreign Affairs, *Fiscal Year 1975 Foreign Assistance Request, Hearings*, 93rd Cong., 2nd sess., 1974, pp. 112–19, 143, 207; Roehm, "Congressional Participation in Middle East Policy," p. 454.
45. Eugene V. Rostow, "Where Kissinger Went Wrong: A Basis for Peace," *The New Republic* 172 (April 5, 1975): 14; Ball, *Diplomacy for a Crowded World.*
46. U.S., Congress, House of Representatives, Committee on International Relations, *The Palestinian Issue in Middle East Peace Efforts, Hearings*, 94th Cong., 1st sess., 1975.
47. Edward R. F. Sheehan, *The Arabs, Israelis, and Kissinger* (New York: Reader's Digest Press, 1976), pp. 245–57.
48. Roehm, "Congressional Participation in Middle East Policy," pp. 313–17, *Congressional Record, 93rd Congress, 2nd Session*, vol. 120, Part 16, June 24–July 1, 1974, Washington, D.C.: U.S. Government Printing Office, 1974, p. 21767.
49. *Congressional Quarterly Almanac*, 93rd Cong., 2nd sess., 1974, 30 (1975): 542, 546.
50. Holt, Letter to Roehm dated February 24, 1978.
51. Sheehan, *The Arabs, Israelis, and Kissinger*, pp. 69–70; U.S., Congress, Senate, "Report No. 93-620: Foreign Assistance and Related Programs Appropriations Bill, 1974, Dec. 13, 1973," *Senate Reports, 93rd Congress, 1st Session*, vol. 9 (Miscellaneous Reports on Public Bills), Washington, D.C.: U.S. Government Printing Office, 1973, pp. 121–23.
52. Sheehan, *The Arabs, Israelis, and Kissinger*, p. 201.
53. Ibid., p. 202.
54. Howe and Trott, *The Power Peddlers*, p. 295.
55. "Congress and Arms Sales," *The Progressive* 30 (October 1975): 8.
56. U.S., Congress, House of Representatives, Committee on International Relations, *Survey of Activities of 94th Congress, 1st Session*, Print, 94th Cong., 2nd sess., 1976, p. 35.
57. Sheehan, *The Arabs, Israelis, and Kissinger*, p. 197; *Congressional Quarterly Almanac*, 94th Cong., 1st sess., 31 (1976): 347.
58. *New York Times*, March 8, 1976, p. 9.
59. Ibid., p. 30.

60. Howe and Trott, *The Power Peddlers*, p. 298.

61. *New York Times*, March 26, 1976, p. 2; April 3, 1976, p. 2.

62. U.S., Congress, Senate, Committee on Foreign Relations, *U.S. Arms Sales Policy: Second Session Hearings on Proposed Sales of Arms to Iran and Saudi Arabia, Hearings*, 94th Cong., 2nd sess., 1977, pp. 68–72; *New York Times*, September 25, 1976, pp. 1–2.

63. Senate, *Sale of Missiles to Saudi Arabia*, pp. 7–8.

64. *New York Times*, September 29, 1976, pp. 1, 3; *Congressional Quarterly Almanac*, 94th Cong., 2nd sess., 1976, 32 (1977): 526.

65. U.S., Congress, House of Representatives, Committee on International Relations, *The Persian Gulf, 1975: The Continuing Debate on Arms Sales, Hearings*, 94th Cong., 1st sess., 1976, p. 18.

66. *Department of State Bulletin* 72 (April 14, 1975): 464.

67. Sheehan, *The Arabs, Israelis, and Kissinger*, pp. 159, 165; *New York Times*, March 25, 1975, p. 10; March 26, 1975, p. 1; Ball, *Diplomacy for a Crowded World*, p. 142.

68. Sheehan, *The Arabs, Israelis, and Kissinger*, p. 175; Howe and Trott, *The Power Peddlers*, pp. 272–73; *New York Times*, May 22, 1975, pp. 1, 11; Roehm, "Congressional Participation in Middle East Policy," pp. 190–91.

69. U.S., Congress, House of Representatives, Committee on International Relations, *Congress and Foreign Policy, Hearings*, 94th Cong., 2nd sess., 1976, p. 190.

70. *New York Times*, May 30, 1975, p. 5; Foreign Broadcast Information Service, "Middle East and Africa," *Daily Reports*, May 27, 1975, pp. D3–15.

71. Howe and Trott, *The Power Peddlers*, p. 546.

72. Feuerwerger, *Congress and Israel*, pp. 170–71.

73. George Ball, "How to Save Israel in Spite of Herself," *Foreign Affairs* 55 (April 1977): 471.

74. U.S., Congress, Senate, *Early Warning System in Sinai, Report*, 94th Cong., 1st sess., 1975, p. 345; House of Representatives, *Survey of Activities, 94th Congress, 1st session, Print*, pp. 22–24; *New York Times*, September 4, 1975, p. 8.

75. Sheehan, *The Arabs, Israelis, and Kissinger*, pp. 253–57.

76. *Congressional Quarterly Almanac*, 94th Congress, 1st session, 1975, 31 (1976): 293.

77. U.S. Congress, House of Representatives, *Congress and Foreign Policy-1975, Print*, 94th Congress, 2nd session, 1976, p. 50.

78. *Congressional Quarterly Almanac*, 94th Congress, 1st sess., 1975, 31 (1976): 348; House of Representatives, *Survey of Activities, 94th Congress, 1st session*, p. 23.

79. U.S., Congress, Senate, Committee on Foreign Relations, *Memorandum of Agreements Between the Governments of Israel and the United States, Early Warning System in Sinai, Hearings*, 94th Cong., 1st sess., 1975, p. 237.

80. Franck and Weisband, *Foreign Policy by Congress*, p. 103.

81. *Department of State Bulletin* 73 (November 17, 1975): 691.

82. *Christian Science Monitor* (Western Edit.), July 15, 1980, p. 3; July 31, 1980, p. 2.

83. Feuerwerger, *Congress and Israel*, p. 186.

Chapter 3

The Domestic Politics of SALT II: Implications for the Foreign Policy Process*

Stephen J. Flanagan

OVERVIEW

On the evening of June 18, 1979, only hours after he and Soviet President Brezhnev had signed the relevant documents in Vienna, President Carter proceded to Capitol Hill to request the Senate's advice and consent to the Treaty on the Limitation of Strategic Offensive Arms, more commonly known as SALT II. This event marked the initiation of the final stages of an intense debate on American foreign and defense policies which raged during the nearly seven years that the treaty was under negotiation. Because the SALT II negotiations involved central aspects of U.S. national security, had pervasive international implications and were conducted in the context of mounting skepticism about Soviet intentions, their evolution was destined to involve a major domestic political battle. However, the chaotic manner in which this struggle was waged caused many observers at home and abroad to question, in yet another instance, whether Washington is capable of executing coherently its major foreign policy initiatives.

Indeed, the history of SALT II illustrates many of the problems with executive-congressional relations in the shaping of American national security policies.

*A good deal of the author's material is drawn from confidential interviews and personal observations during the final stages of the SALT II debate. Elaboration of issues discussed in this chapter can be found in Stephen J. Flanagan, "Congress and the Evolution of Strategic Arms Limitation Policy: A Study of the Legislature's Role in National Security Affairs, 1955–1979", Ph.D. Dissertation, Fletcher School of Law and Diplomacy, 1979. The author is grateful to Dr. Coit D. Blacker of Stanford University for helpful comments on an earlier draft of this chapter.

Congress provided several positive stimuli to the initiation and the sustenance of the SALT I negotiations and then lapsed into a period of benign neglect. As disagreements about the achievements of SALT I and U.S. goals in SALT II emerged, a political guerilla war erupted between critics and supporters of the process which complicated the negotiations and the American decision-making process. Presidents Ford and Carter had to struggle to build support for SALT initiatives with several factions of the divided SALT bureaucracy. Policymakers on both sides of the issue found strong allies among the increasingly assertive and suspicious Congress of the post-Vietnam, post-Watergate era. Various congressional forces undertook fragmented actions in support of like-minded elements in the executive branch and to ensure that there was no retreat on issues of particular concern. To be sure, the executive branch made its share of tactical blunders. But at times, particularly during the Carter stewardship, the White House's dealings with Congress on SALT II assumed almost as much importance as, and often interacted with, the negotiations with Moscow. The SALT II experience points to the need for a new *modus operandi* in the development of American foreign policy which will retain congressional collaboration without imprudently encumbering executive diplomacy and decision making.

THE SUBSTANCE OF THE SALT PROCESS

SALT was initiated in 1968 as an effort to control aspects of the Soviet-American strategic competition, thereby lessening tensions and facilitating amelioration of political relations between the two states. As it evolved, SALT became the centerpiece of the Nixon, Ford, and Carter administrations' policies toward Moscow. A symbiotic relationship emerged between SALT and detente. SALT became both the touchstone and the leading edge of this policy. As such, developments in SALT had a trickle-down effect on other aspects of the Soviet-American relationship. In the absence of progress in SALT, other elements of the detente process stagnated. Obversely, deterioration of other facets of Soviet-American interaction repeatedly hampered progress in SALT.

But SALT has remained much more than a vehicle for improving political relations. During more than a decade of negotiations, SALT has involved efforts to reconcile selected aspects of strategic forces which the two powers believe are essential to their security. SALT had a complex interrelationship with the evolution of the strategic balance and with U.S., and possibly Soviet, strategic planning during the 1970s. SALT was undertaken initially to avoid a costly and dangerous arms race in defensive strategic weapons based on early anti-ballistic missile (ABM) systems — which neither state really wanted but feared the other was about to initiate. The other principal U.S. goal in SALT was to constrain the growth and improvement of Soviet offensive strategic forces. Both these developments threatened to undermine two pillars of deterrence in the nuclear era: the vulnerability of the two superpowers' populations to nuclear annihilation, and the inability of one party to launch a disarming first-strike against the other's retaliatory forces.[1]

While the SALT I ABM Treaty has been effective in preserving this first pillar of deterrence by sharply limiting ABM systems, unconstrained qualitative improvements in both parties' offensive forces during the SALT period left the latter pillar in jeopardy. Of particular concern has been the fact that in the early 1980s the Soviet ICBM force is expected to attain a theoretical capability for preemptive destruction of the entire U.S. land-based ICBM force. As negotiations dragged on, domestic political pressures on both sides forced reconciliation of strategic needs by means of a highest common denominator approach. Agreements became negotiable because they set fairly high numerical force ceilings and allowed for most qualitative improvements. SALT appeared to codify, with some significant adjustments, the strategic plans of the two parties. While this limited achievement contributed to stability by enabling more rational strategic planning, the SALT process yielded, at best, modest control of strategic armaments.

The value of any proposed limitation was judged first with regard to its impact on the strategic balance and U.S. force planning. Domestic reaction often varied because of differing views on the state of the balance and on what force improvements were desirable. SALT considerations interacted with U.S. strategic planning in several ways. Various strategic initiatives have been vaunted for their contribution not only to U.S. military capabilities but also to U.S. bargaining strength at SALT. In another vein, some supporters of arms control in Congress believe that new weapons systems of all kinds have been developed with little consideration for arms limitation objectives. Several legislators of this latter persuasion demanded, with mixed success, that authoritative arms control impact statements for all nuclear weapons systems be presented to Congress along with the Defense budget so that they could be evaluated in line with U.S. arms control objectives.[2] While strong proponents of arms control contend that their concerns have never been integral factors in U.S. strategic planning, critics of the SALT process charge that arms limitation considerations have repeatedly distorted defense policy and stymied force modernization efforts.

SALT emerged on the scene during a period when the postwar foreign policy consensus had begun to collapse. Perennial adversary Moscow became a sometime negotiating partner, and Americans were never comfortable with nor in agreement on how to conduct this new relationship. Similarly, there was only limited consensus about what U.S. objectives in SALT II should be. While some held that SALT should be pursued independently of other aspects of Soviet-American relations, others argued that SALT should shape strategic stability and moderate Soviet foreign and domestic policies. Without feasible and widely agreed goals, Presidents Ford and Carter were continually subjected to criticisms from right and left. Any revisions of opening positions became subject to charges of capitulation to Soviet demands or, at best, bad bargaining.

SALT has not been conducted in an international vacuum nor without impact on other key aspects of American foreign policy. SALT addresses aspects of the security interests of U.S. allies by imposing constraints on threatening Soviet weapons and on U.S. forces which are designed to provide them with a nuclear umbrella. As such, the basic thrust of U.S. policy in SALT has been coordinated or at least acquiesced to by members of the NATO Nuclear Planning Group and Japan, although the allies often complained that this consultative process was inadequate. Furthermore, as SALT II began to deal with the so-called "gray area" forces — those nuclear weapons with both theater and strategic capabilities — the need to protect allied interests in SALT became more acute.

SALT has had a significant impact on the progress of other components of East-West detente, particularly on the principal negotiating forums. A chill in SALT caused the Mutual Force Reduction (MFR) talks to "catch a cold"; and, conversely, it came to be expected that success at SALT would allow for progress in these efforts to reduce the level of conventional forces in central Europe. A similar, though less direct, effect has been felt on the Conference on Security and Cooperation in Europe (CSCE), which includes the European neutral and nonaligned states. However, each of the allied states has more (France and West Germany) and less (Britain and Canada) distinctive relationships to pursue with the USSR. Thus, when the SALT process became very uncertain in 1980, several of the NATO allies began to consider whether they shouldn't pursue their interests in detente more independently of Washington.

Moreover, it is not just alliance relationships which have interacted with SALT. Because SALT addresses issues of interest to China and Eastern Europe, Washington has conducted its relations with these states at various times in ways designed to express displeasure with complications or bolster progress at SALT. SALT has also had an impact on the proliferation of nuclear weapons. Washington's efforts to convince nuclear threshold states from exercising their weapons option became much more difficult as superpower arms control efforts foundered.

THE PRINCIPAL ACTORS AND THE TOOLS OF THEIR TRADE

SALT has involved several sets of negotiations beyond those at the international conference table. Political differences between the two states have generally been hammered out at the highest levels of authority, while the delegations have been assigned the task of either reducing technical differences to a set of political questions or translating a political decision into provisions that accomplished precisely what was agreed.[3]

On another level, but often interacting with these bilateral negotiations, are the debates within the policymaking structures of the two parties. Insights into Soviet decision making for SALT are few, but it is almost certainly less complicated than its American counterpart.[4] Within the United States, there are really two constituencies with which the President and his staff must struggle to build a policy consensus: the various bureaucracies involved with SALT, over which he has considerable leverage; and the key members of Congress and their aides, with whom he has only indirect influence. To separate these two components of the U.S. domestic debate is a difficult task because like-minded elements in the two branches reinforce each other's positions. Thus, proponents of a negotiating proposal in the bureaucracy often seek out the assistance of their allies on Capitol Hill. In turn, the legislators need these officials for information and as representatives at the councils of state.

The Salt Policymaking Machinery

Obviously, so complex an undertaking as SALT requires input from a number of executive branch agencies coupled with a firm centralized direction, if not control, by the White House. While this control was realized under Henry Kissinger's closed diplomacy during the early SALT period, it became nearly impossible as the Ford administration became divided over its goals in SALT.[5] In this latter context, Congress gained a better understanding of the issues. Congress was afforded greater information on policy disagreements as a consequence of its new assertiveness and cooperation from disgruntled officials in the executive branch. This management problem was even more pronounced for the Carter administration, which had multiple power centers and had pledged to, and initially did, conduct a very open diplomacy.

The bureaucratic organization for SALT policymaking is reflected in the composition of the SALT negotiating team. The Chief SALT Negotiator, or head of the delegation, was generally either the Director of the Arms Control and Disarmament Agency (ACDA) or a senior Ambassador. Each of the organizations which played a role in SALT policymaking had a representative on the delegation: the Department of State, the Office of the Secretary of Defense (OSD — the civilian component of the Pentagon), and the Joint Chiefs of Staff (JCS). Policy disagreements sometimes reflected divergent bureaucratic interests, but often were based on ideological or tactical disputes among the various actors. For example, the JCS, as representatives of the uniformed military, have both an obligation and an inclination to take the most skeptical view of the negotiations; and generally advances the worst-case assessments of Soviet intentions, capabilities, and possibilities for cheating. The JCS are

allied with hardliners in Congress, particularly on the Armed Services Committees, and elsewhere in the bureaucracy and the White House. Similarly,
during the Carter administration, ACDA, consistent with its charter and the
disposition of its senior officials, was the most forceful advocate of the SALT
process, and worked closely with supporters in various quarters.

At the second level in all these agencies are senior civil servants compris-
ing a permanent SALT bureaucracy whose assets are an historical memory
and often access to media figures and congressional supporters. By leaking
information on policy struggles, senior bureaucrats have been able to have
a much greater impact on policy covertly than they ever could overtly, generally by subverting objectionable initiatives. However, the most skilled leakers
are to be found in high levels of the administration and some quarters of
Congress.

The role of the intelligence community in SALT planning is one of providing information and monitoring assessments rather than recommending
policy options. Nonetheless, there have been times when the intelligence community's assessments of a Soviet weapon system's capability or of the moni-
torability of a proposed limitation shaped policy discussions.

The Congress

It is simply a shorthand technique to speak of Congress, for there is obviously
no such unitary actor in the policy process. The legislature is divided by
chamber, committee, party, region, and ideology — to name but a few barriers.
Because of its traditional predominance in foreign policy and unique role in
treaty making, the Senate has generally been the locus of SALT-related activity
on Capitol Hill. The SALT I framework of treaty and executive agreement
did bring the House into the endorsement process. Although the Carter administration considered using the executive agreement vehicle as Senate opposition
grew, it was presumed that the SALT II accords would be submitted as a treaty,
leaving little formal role for the House. Nonetheless, several members of the
House were influential in the development of the SALT II debate, and committees in the lower chamber reviewed the agreement's implications for
American foreign and defense policies.

In the history of nuclear arms control, and even during SALT I, Congress
had been a significant actor in this process only when an accord was actually
presented for endorsement. The Senate's constitutional power of consent
to ratification of treaties and both houses' statutory authority to pass on any
agreements that limit U.S. armed forces are the ultimate sources of congressional clout. Another source of congressional influence on SALT decisions
stems from its power to authorize and appropriate funds for strategic weapons
programs. Congress has supported programs judged critical to U.S. bargaining

strength, and questioned the consistency of some systems with U.S. arms control objectives.

There are several less-obvious aspects of congressional involvement with SALT policy which were linked to these two powers. Anticipation of congressional predilections affects policy planning, and on occasion, particularly during the Carter administration, influential legislators actually entered the President's inner circle to gain more direct input to this process. Congress has also become involved in a variety of ways with the negotiating process. Congressional predispositions have been used as a bargaining lever in efforts to extract concessions from the Kremlin. On several occasions, American officials suggested that certain provisions in an emerging agreement were unacceptable because they would never obtain congressional endorsement. Similarly, the Soviets learned that courting and making occasional leaks to key members of Congress and the press enable them to influence the tone of SALT policy debate in the United States – although these efforts often backfire.

Finally, the congressional response to developments in SALT has a powerful impact on allied reactions. Many officials and opinion leaders in the NATO countries looked to key congressional figures as guides in assessing SALT provisions. Indeed, for some legislators the allies became another attentive constituency whose interests they endeavored to protect.

During the SALT II debate, the Senate was divided into three camps, largely along ideological grounds. Approximately 40 members could be classified as arms controllers due to their general support of the SALT process and conviction that some reasonable accord was preferable to an unconstrained arms race. There was another bloc of about 20 moderate senators who, because of limited interest or experience in this field, were swing votes. The balance was comprised of about 20 irreconcilables in dealings with the Soviet Union and roughly 15 members who were very skeptical of arms control but could be satisfied with a tough accord. Thus, this "hardline" faction included both those who believed that any SALT agreement was likely to be bad, and those who were genuinely convinced that the United States was involved in a most dangerous game wherein only limited compromise was prudent.

President Nixon easily won the votes of arms controllers and extracted the loyalty of hardliners and swing votes in the Republican Party for SALT I. While President Ford enjoyed a similar political line-up, he had to contend with doubts about the SALT process. But President Carter's only certain supporters on SALT were the arms controllers. Conservative and several moderate Democrats, disillusioned with the Carter administration's foreign policy, revived the Coalition for a Democratic Majority, which advocated a more vigilant policy toward Moscow and larger defense expenditures than President Carter was willing to pursue. It was this wing of the Democratic Party along with the majority of Republicans who were most skeptical of SALT II.

After SALT I, hardliners in the Congress were initially more effective and had firm leadership, while the Ford and Carter Administrations were slow in developing strong allies. Henry Jackson, long recognized as the Senate's foremost authority on strategic affairs, assumed an even more imposing stature than he previously enjoyed. During the Ford administration, Jackson kept a wary eye on Henry Kissinger's efforts to conclude an agreement based on the Vladivostok formula. As chairman of the Energy Committee and the Armed Services Subcommittee on Arms Control, the Senator from Washington seemed likely to control the fate of two of the centerpieces of the Carter administration's legislative programs — SALT and the energy bills. In the early months of the Carter administration, Jackson offered his counsel and support to the new President on several issues. However, as differences emerged, the Senator parted company with the administration on SALT and other matters.

An equally influential skeptic of SALT was Senator Sam Nunn. Nunn had emerged as the Senate's leading expert on European military affairs and a defender of NATO's interests in SALT. Once Jackson's vote was lost, winning Nunn's support was crucial to the Carter SALT strategy in the Senate. Senator John Glenn, who possessed a background in flight testing, was well prepared to seize the verification issue. Glenn dominated public discussions of U.S. intelligence capabilities to monitor Soviet compliance with the various Treaty provisions.

Another key figure in the SALT II debate was Minority Leader Howard Baker. Baker, a moderate, appeared disposed to support a tough, verifiable SALT II accord, and demonstrated a willingness to work with the Carter administration during the Panama Canal Treaty debate — a move which injured his standing among conservative Republicans. However, as the SALT II agreement neared completion, Baker made it clear he was not satisfied. Perceived as one of Carter's leading challengers for the White House in 1980, it appeared that the Senator from Tennessee saw SALT as an opportunity to make amends for his Panama stand and to visibly demonstrate his distance from President Carter on an issue that was certain to attract extensive media coverage. However, the most unabashed GOP criticism of SALT has emanated from the "new right" members of Congress and their support groups, who find little if any value in the SALT process as it has been conducted. Senators such as Jake Garn, Jesse Helms, and Malcolm Wallop took forceful stands unalterably opposed to the SALT II treaty.

During the Ford administration, a bipartisan group of Senate arms controllers, including Senators Kennedy, Mondale, Humphrey, Cranston, Javits, and Mathias, attempted to provide support to Kissinger's efforts to conclude an accord. However, neither their lobbying nor policy resolutions found broadbased support on Capitol Hill during 1975 and 1976. The advocacy role played by Senators John Sherman Cooper and J. William Fulbright during the SALT I period was never really replicated during the SALT II negotiations

— a consequence of reforms that reduced the power of the Senate leadership, as well as other factors. The passing of Hubert Humphrey in 1978 resulted in the loss of one of the Carter Administration's most valued and experienced allies on Capitol Hill.

The Foreign Relations Committee failed to seize the initiative on SALT II under the helm of John Sparkman, and no other committee member stepped into the breach. Senator Frank Church had mixed success in his efforts to reverse the decline of the panel's influence over SALT when he assumed the chair in January 1978. Church had to cope with a committee that was more divided on ideological and party lines. A new bloc of conservative Republicans forced a break with the committee's bipartisan tradition by demanding the creation of a separate minority staff. Nonetheless, committee member Joseph Biden did develop into one of the Senate's most effective advocates of SALT. Other forceful voices in support of SALT emerged from different corners of the Senate, including Armed Services Committee members Gary Hart, John Culver, and Thomas McIntyre. Majority Whip Alan Cranston formed a study and strategy planning group for pro-SALT Senators and their staffs, which met regularly with administration and other experts to discuss the emerging treaty.

Just the recitation of this roster suggests another novel dimension of the politics of SALT II. During the first five years of SALT's history, only a handful of legislators monitored the development of the negotiations. After 1975, as allegations of Moscow's violation of SALT I accords surfaced and as concern with Soviet military might grew among the public, more and more members of Congress felt compelled to speak out on SALT, and the support of greatly expanded expert staffs has enabled them to do so with greater authority. The prestige of the Oval Office suffered a sharp decline as a consequence of the conduct of the Vietnam War and the Watergate crisis, and this made Congress less deferential to executive authority.[6] In addition, the Carter administration's close consultations with Congress, not to mention numerous leaks from the executive branch, facilitated this burgeoning attention.

The Carter administration undertook several efforts to fulfill its commitment to make the Congress a fuller participant in the SALT planning. At the outset, it attempted to bring hardliners into the process by consulting them on the development of SALT negotiating positions. As Senator Jackson noted, the new "give and take" allowed Congress more influence over the SALT policy planning, and Minority Leader Baker praised the President for making genuine steps towards a bipartisan foreign policy through such consultations.[7] Administration officials noted the fundmental liability of such a strategy, commenting that, while they were willing to apprise senators of developments in SALT and solicit their views on policy, they did not intend to allow the information shared to be used to disrupt the administistation's diplomacy. Preventing this from happening proved extremely difficult.[8]

The Soviets did not let these internal SALT negotiations go unnoticed. In a bitter editorial, *Pravda* lamented that Senator Jackson and other "enemies of detente" had "become unseen participants at the conference table."[9] Judging from the repeated denunciations of the hardliners' role in SALT that appeared in the Soviet press, and the number of Soviet diplomats scurrying around Capitol Hill, it was evident that the Kremlin was as anxious to monitor U.S. domestic bargaining as Congress was to learn of developments in Geneva.

The Carter administration also established a mechanism to provide Congress with further insights into the SALT process by actual participation in the negotiations. In June 1977, Vice President Mondale announced the appointment of a diverse group of 14 representatives and 30 senators as advisors to the SALT delegation. Nearly all senators on the Advisory Group visited with the negotiators in Geneva, where they participated in both formal and informal discussions with the Soviet delegation and reviewed the draft text of the SALT II agreement. Hardliners' initial fears that membership in this group might be coopting proved ironic when several advisors expressed publicly their displeasure with U.S. negotiating positions after concluding stints in Geneva.

This extensive congressional involvement with the SALT II process during the Carter administration was a marked departure from the earlier SALT period and is unprecedented in the modern history of treaty negotiations. Legislators have long defended the right of Congress under Article II of the Constitution to provide its *advice* on, as well as consent to, treaties. However, the scope of the recent counsel has been extraordinary.

Other Voices in the SALT II Debate

The SALT I package was greeted with broad-based support from a variety of public interest groups and academic experts, with only extreme right-wing groups and a few proponents of ABM waging a very modest campaign against approval of the accords. However, during the years that SALT II was under negotiation the mood of the country shifted considerably. Doubts about the value of military spending gave way to alarm with Soviet military expansion and involvement in the Third World. This disillusionment with detente inspired a harder look at SALT II.

Several anti-SALT groups with good access to the media emerged on the scene after 1975. The most effective among them was a group of prominent conservative business, academic, and former governmental figures known as the Committee on the Present Danger. The committee's spokesman on strategic issues, former SALT negotiator Paul Nitze, produced a number of anti-SALT papers, and he and other members of the committee conducted briefings on Capitol Hill and elsewhere around the country. The committee's position carried considerable weight with conservative and moderate members of Congress.

The academic community was also divided on SALT II and many prominent strategic and political experts expressed their displeasure with the SALT process. Many "new right" groups that had worked together against the Panama Canal Treaties viewed this earlier campaign as a warm-up exercise for the more important SALT II debate. These well-financed groups caused difficulties for supporters of the SALT and Panama pacts, whom they "targeted" for defeat during the 1978 and 1980 Congressional elections. These groups were also effective in sniping at selected aspects —some of which were neither under consideration nor included in the final text — of the emerging SALT II Agreements.

Private groups who were active in support of the SALT process were not as well organized as their adversaries, and they did not take up a very active struggle until the SALT II Treaty was signed. The most effective public policy effort on behalf of the SALT process was undertaken by the Carter administration, which had a multitude of officials on the road debating critics of the process for nearly 18 months before the SALT II Treaty was completed.

Public opinion polls throughout the negotiations revealed strong support (in excess of 70%) for SALT II in the abstract, although few Americans knew much about the specific issues involved. A similar percentage of those polled repeatedly expressed considerable suspicion of Soviet intentions in SALT as well as the belief that Moscow would endeavor to cheat on most limitations. This disposition reinforced the centrality of satisfaction with U.S. capabilities to monitor Soviet compliance for many members of the Senate. Public opinion was almost equally divided on the issue of whether the negotiations could be pursued independently of other Soviet activities, such as human rights violations or involvement in Africa, until the invasion of Afghanistan, when most Americans felt that linkage should be invoked. Some of the anti-SALT groups commissioned opinion polls of their own which they contended revealed much weaker support for SALT than the major national polls would suggest. However, most of the questions in these polls were weighted with leading questions that couched provisions of the SALT II Treaty in terms inimical to the United States.[10]

CONGRESS AND THE EVOLUTION OF SALT I

An improved political climate in the late 1960s facilitated Soviet-American dialogue, but the driving force leading to the initiation of SALT was the desire of both Moscow and Washington to avoid an arms race in ABM technology. The Soviets had constructed a small ABM installation near Leningrad in 1962 and had begun deploying a more extensive system around Moscow in 1965. Pressure mounted in Congress for procurement of one of the ABM systems under development at U.S. test ranges. However, President Johnson attempted to forestall initiation of deployment, and use this congressional pressure for bargaining leverage in approaching the Kremlin about an agreement to limit ABMs. Johnson's ploy proved initially unsuccessful during his discussions with Soviet Premier Kosygin at the 1967 Glassboro Conference, and a limited American ABM program was begun.

As a consequence of a number of political developments, Moscow finally agreed in May 1968 to commence negotiations on limiting strategic arms.[11] Many hardliners in Congress were convinced that it was the administration's decision several months earlier to proceed with deployment of an ABM program, whose initial construction had been given final congressional approval only three days before Moscow announced its change of heart, that provided the impetus for the Soviets to go to the negotiating table. This thesis that vigorous strategic programs could serve as bargaining chips in negotiations became an enduring theme in military procurement debates during the SALT period. While President Johnson intended to advance a significant arms limitation proposal at a September 1968 summit, the Soviet invasion of Czechoslovakia in August resulted in U.S. cancellation of the conference. It was left to the Nixon administration to initiate what had become known in Washington as the Strategic Arms Limitation Talks – SALT.

By the time the Nixon administration began the initial, exploratory round of SALT in October 1969, Congress had become skeptical of any ABM program as a consequence of expert criticism of the technology and strong public opposition to "bombs in the backyard." A coalition of liberal and moderate senators staged an unprecedented series of legislative challenges to this major strategic program between 1968 and 1971, which energized the Nixon administration's quest of severe limitations on ABM deployments in SALT.

Another, less-prominent, but equally controversial debate at this time concerned the question of whether the United States should seek limitations on multiple independently-targetable, re-entry vehicles (MIRVs). MIRVs multiply the lethality of each ICBM or SLBM on which they were fitted by enabling a missile to disperse several nuclear warheads on a number of different, widely-spaced targets. Once testing was initiated, MIRV limitations were encumbered by the severe problems in determining if deployed missiles of a type tested with MIRVs are actually so equipped.[12] One of the most positive congressional efforts to influence SALT I policy sought to prod the executive branch into seeking limitations on this destabilizing technology which was about to reach the flight-test stage of its development. Just prior to the first substantive round of the SALT I talks in April 1970, the Senate overwhelmingly endorsed a resolution sponsored by Senator Edward Brooke which urged U.S. negotiators to propose a mutual MIRV test moratorium during the negotiations and to pursue a comprehensive accord limiting both offensive and defensive strategic weapons.[13]

The vigorous legislative challenges to ABMs and MIRVs led may observers to expect Congress to play an important role in strategic arms control matters. But, after spurring the negotiations, Congress became a largely uninformed observer by acquiescing to Henry Kissinger's secretive diplomacy. This information gap, coupled with a preoccupation with the Vietnam War and a continuing attitude of deference toward the President in the conduct of foreign affairs, rendered Congressional influence over the SALT I process tangential.

The SALT I package signed by President Nixon and General Secretary Brezhnev at the May 1972 Moscow summit was comprised of a long-term treaty constraining ABMs and a five-year executive agreement imposing numerical ceilings on offensive forces.

The ABM Treaty limits the parties to two ABM radar sites, each armed with 100 interceptor missiles, and precludes the development of a base for a nationwide defense. The parties also consented to certain qualitative constraints on ABM technologies, limitations on radar construction, and bans on certain test practices which could form the basis for a rapid breakout capability. The Treaty also stipulates that the parties discuss limitations on ABM systems based on other physical principles – i.e., lasers or beam weapons – that may emerge in the future and bring into question the viability of the accord.

The five-year Interim Agreement was essentially a freeze on the numbers of ICBM and SLBM launchers operational or under construction in 1972. Modernization of missiles was allowed, as was some substitution of new SLBM launchers for dismantled ICBM and older SLBM launchers – an effort to move strategic forces to the more secure ocean environment. There were no qualitative limitations on missiles other than indirect limits on their size, and the MIRV capabilities and bomber forces of both parties were unconstrained. SALT I left the United States with 1,700 launchers, of which 54 were for so-called "heavy" ICBMs, and the USSR was limited to 2,400 launchers, including 308 "heavies." The Interim Agreement was cast as a breathing spell which would facilitate realization of more rigorous limitations in SALT II.

The severe constraints on ABM systems dismayed congressional hardliners who had labored dutifully for the administration's ABM plan. The President assured critics that the accord's launcher ceilings forestalled U.S. ICBM vulnerability and that the threat would be attenuated by MIRV or throw-weight limits in SALT II. The 40 percent higher Soviet launcher ceilings were more than offset by American advantages in unconstrained bombers and MIRVs—including a seven-to-one lead in SLBM warheads—as well as the general qualitative superiority of U.S. strategic forces. While this disparity was tolerable to hardliners at a time of clear U.S. strategic superiority, there was considerable concern about the dangers of these asymmetries as the Soviets attained qualitative force enhancements and reached their SALT I ceilings.[14]

While the ABM Treaty received a relatively easy 88-2 endorsement for ratification, the debate over the Interim Agreement was more complicated.

Many lawmakers believed that any future SALT agreement should have equal numerical ceilings and rough equality in other indexes of power. It was argued that the perception of inequality in the Interim Agreement eroded international respect for American might. Thus, Senator Henry Jackson found considerable support for an amendment to legislation endorsing the Interim Agreement which would have advised the administration to emulate the equality of the ABM Treaty in any SALT II pact and to provide the United States with an escape hatch should the Soviets develop Minuteman-threatening MIRV capabilities during the Interim Agreement period. The administration wanted to avoid an acrimonious debate on the Interim Agreement, and Jackson recognized that his measure was unlikely to pass without the White House's endorsement. As a result, the two worked together to make the Jackson Amendment mutually acceptable. The Senate's 56–35 endorsement of the Jackson Amendment advising the Administration that in future SALT agreements the United States should not be limited to "levels of intercontinental forces" inferior to those allowed the Soviet Union was initially perceived as an endorsement of equal ceilings on delivery vehicles which the Nixon administration had proposed in 1971 and which the JCS and others in the SALT bureaucracy were pushing for in SALT II. However, the open-ended meaning of equal levels was skillfully used by SALT critics to incorporate a number of stipulations – throw-weight and others. In addition, the use of the term "intercontinental forces" in the Jackson Amendment put the administration on notice that U.S. nuclear capabilities based in Europe which could strike the USSR – the so-called forward-based systems – should be excluded from the SALT II agenda as they had been in SALT I.

THE SALT II NEGOTIATIONS

The SALT II negotiations began in November 1972. The talks continued for nearly seven years, under the direction of three Administrations, during a period of domestic political upheaval and increasing international tension. The parties had to grapple with the complex qualitative issues which were deferred in SALT I as well as some new technologies which had emerged on the scene. The White House also had to deal with allegations of Soviet violations of SALT I, Soviet efforts to take advantage of SALT I loopholes – some of which had been oversold to Congress – and a general disillusionment with detente compared with the halcyon days of the Nixon-Kissinger "era of negotiations."

The Nixon administration attempted unsuccessfully in 1973 and early 1974 to obtain Moscow's agreement to limitations on the payload that its missile forces could deliver, thereby constraining the number of MIRVs that the Soviets could place on their much larger missiles. Little progress was possible during these months because of disagreements within the U.S. policymaking community over goals and strategies, Soviet inflexibility on a few key issues, and political uncertainty in the United States as the Watergate scandal unfolded. By early 1974, the principal SALT policymakers, Kissinger and Defense Secretary Schlesinger, reached agreement, after some intense haggling, on how to proceed in SALT II. On the issue of the MIRV/throw-weight problem, the new scheme was based on two separate formulas which would together produce "essential equality." One component would maintain the ICBM launcher freeze and impose equal limitations on the aggregate number of strategic delivery vehicles – ICBMs, SLBMs and heavy bombers – with a freedom to mix the composition of the force. Control of MIRV was to be achieved by constraining the overall throw-weight of the two powers' land-based missile forces.

The pace of high level diplomatic contacts quickened as President Ford moved quickly after his inauguration to breathe life into SALT. After a six-month suspension of front-channel dealings, the negotiating teams sat down in Geneva in September 1974. This activity paved the way for a summit conference at Vladivostok in November 1974, where Ford and Brezhnev agreed in an *aide memoire* to a formula for the completion of a ten-year SALT II treaty. The treaty would impose a ceiling of 2,400 on stragegic delivery vehicles, no more than 1,320 of which could be MIRVed missiles or bombers armed with long-range missiles. The treaty was to last until 1985, with reductions in these ceilings to be negotiated in talks starting in 1980. Kissinger noted that the accord was possible only because the Soviets had finally agreed to exclude U.S. forward-bases systems, and predicted that remaining details could be ironed out in time for a mid-1975 Washington summit.

After Vladivostok, the negotiations foundered, and bureaucratic infighting and domestic squabbling escalated—symptoms of both technical and political impediments. The issue of how SALT II would address the cruise missile, which had emerged as an important facet of U.S. strategic modernization plans, and the Soviet Backfire bomber, whose intercontinental capabilities were subject to dispute in the intelligence community, emerged as the most enduring complications at the negotiating table. However, the Soviets also resisted key U.S. proposals such as the MIRV launcher-type counting rule. The deterioration of other aspects of the Soviet-American relationship also began to affect the negotiations.

The Vladivostok formula satisfied few domestic critics of SALT who believed that Soviet throw-weight and, hence, MIRV capabilities would not be sufficiently constrained. Arms controllers felt that the ceilings were too high but were willing to go along with the formula as the best of possible options. Congress lapsed into general disinterest with SALT between 1973 and 1975, preoccupied with the Watergate scandal, the Middle East, and the termination of American involvement in Southeast Asia. But, by mid-1975, many legislators were becoming disillusioned with the value of SALT as the Soviets continued their buildup to the agreement's ceilings and stretched its several loopholes to their limit. Charges of Soviet violation of the spirit and the letter of both the SALT I pacts rendered hardliners and moderates skeptical of the value of the SALT process and exacerbated concerns about the verifiability of many limitations. While congressional arms controllers attempted to salvage a Vladivostok-type accord through several policy resolutions, none could find sufficient support to be adopted.

Confronted with the challenge to his renomination from Ronald Reagan, and a skeptical Senator Jackson, it appears that President Ford decided – many observers believe erroneously – that conclusion of a SALT II accord before the summer of 1976 would have been an act of political suicide. Congressional hardliners feared that when Schlesinger was removed from the Administration, so, too, was the counterweight to Kissinger's lust for an accord. Moreover, Ronald Reagan's first campaign address on foreign policy decried prospective limits on cruise missiles and charged that Ford was rushing into a SALT II agreement for political gain. The cruise missile and Backfire problems, coupled with these domestic political considerations and developments in external events, stymied progress in the negotiations until the end of the Ford/ Kissinger tenure.

President Carter took office committed to reductions of the Vladivostok ceilings. The administration's initial, highly-publicized SALT proposal of March 1977 called for such reductions along with sharp constraints on large ICBMs, force modernization, and missile flight testing. Moscow found this "deep-cuts" proposal unacceptable. The administration's fall-back proposal of Vladivostok, with deferral of the cruise missile and Backfire issues, was also rejected at the time. Negotiations continued for the next two years in an effort to reconstruct the Vladivostok formula to incorporate some reductions and some elements of the Carter "deep-cuts" proposal. The administration undertook quiet diplomatic initiatives which yielded a formula for SALT II that was agreed to by Secretary of State Vance and Foreign Minister Gromyko in May 1977. A major breakthrough came four months later, when many of the specifics of this scheme were established. A three-tiered accord would be pursued: a treaty lasting until 1985 which codified the Vladivostok guidelines with some reductions; a three-year protocol addressing controversial issues; and a statement of principles, incorporating some elements of the "deep-cuts" proposal, which would serve as a guidepost for future negotiations.

The 21 months between the September 1977 breakthrough and the Vienna summit in May 1979 were consumed by negotiations on the nature of limitations to be imposed on cruise missiles, mobile missiles, the Backfire bomber, and several definitional problems (particularly those related to monitoring compliance). A premature debate on SALT II was avoided in late 1977 as the Interim Agreement reached its expiration date. Both Moscow and Washington wanted the SALT I limitations to remain in effect while negotiations on the follow-on accord continued, but many members of Congress were insisting that any such action would require the prior approval of both houses of Congress. The administration finessed the issue by allowing the Interim Agreement to lapse, while both parties issued "parallel declarations of intent" to continue to abide by the SALT I limitations on offensive forces. The Senate disliked this circumvention but passed a resolution authorizing the President's stated intent.

After September 1977, the administration was forced to battle openly with congressional hardliners all the way to the Vienna summit. As the details of the September framework became known, hardliners set out to stop the protocol (which they feared would threaten the modernization of U.S. strategic forces) and to modify the treaty. Supporters of the accords attempted to convince their colleagues that while the limitations were not ideal, the threat to the United States and the countervailing spending on strategic forces that would be required in their absence would be much worse.

By the fall of 1978, SALT II was judged by many observers in and out of government to be at a critical turning point. The slow negotiations allowed critics of the emerging accord to snipe at it without full rebuttal. The White House was also fearful that Brezhnev's health was failing and that the Soviet President's incapacitation could force a delay of SALT until the Kremlin succession struggle was resolved. The final stages of the negotiations were very complicated because all of the small, and several of the major issues that remained had to be resolved together, and neither side wanted to make the last concession. Most of these issues were worked out in a series of Vance-Dobrynin meetings, the last of which took place on May 7, 1979.[15]

President Carter's send-off to the Vienna summit foreshadowed the bitterness of the ratification debate. Senator Jackson likened the trip to Neville Chamberlain's mission to Munich in 1939 when the British Prime Minister tried to appease Hitler. Speaker of the House O'Neill denounced Jackson's preemptive attack, and cautioned that no nation should mistake the domestic American debate over SALT II for a lack of resolve in the negotiations. However, this incident highlights the fact that American diplomacy is increasingly hampered by domestic discord.

MAJOR AREAS OF CONGRESSIONAL INTEREST

Congressional interaction with SALT negotiations and policymaking was extensive and diverse, but an elaboration of several major categories of activity which had particular prominence or impact is illustrative of the nature of executive-congressional relations during this period. Several legislators oversaw the negotiation and policymaking process. While verification was the acid test for any agreement on Capitol Hill, all members agreed that this consideration was secondary to the merits of the provisions — particularly their impact on the strategic balance — and Congress debated these issues thoroughly. A particularly contentious issue in the congressional debate was the question of linkage.

Oversight of the Negotiations and the Policymaking Process

One of the indirect congressional levers over foreign policy evolves from the Senate's power to confirm certain presidential nominations and influence appointments to posts not subject to such review. In the SALT case, the Senate exercised this capability with vigor.

During the SALT I ratification debate, several senators seized on allegations that, while the White House had made major policy decisions, the delegation had exerted excessive influence on several key limitations. Indeed, some hardline senators accused ACDA and the delegation of "selling out," and sharply criticized the views of several members of the negotiating team. When this criticism of the SALT apparatus surfaced, the White House found it particularly useful to replace key officials in ACDA and the delegation with individuals more acceptable to hardliners on the Hill. The ACDA director was relieved of his job as Chief SALT Negotiator because hardliners argued that the ACDA director's role as principal advocate for arms control conflicted with the mandate of the Negotiator to cut the best possible deal for the United States. The responsibilities of Chief Negotiator were assigned to a career diplomat who was expected to represent faithfully the dictates of policymakers in the White House. All but one of the principals on the delegation, Paul Nitze, were replaced. ACDA was effectively denied a SALT policymaking role for several years. Nearly all of the agency's senior experts were either replaced or relocated elsewhere in government and its already meager budget was reduced by one-third. The effect of all of this was to remove a wealth of experience from the SALT II process and to disrupt the progress of the negotiations.

After this flap, both congressional hardliners and arms controllers monitored the policymaking and negotiating processes with considerable skepticism. While one side feared subjugation of arms control considerations, the other worried that U.S. military options were being sacrificed in the overeager search for agreement.

It was not surprising when the Carter administration took over the SALT negotiations in 1977 that its organization for SALT policymaking came under close scrutiny from congressional hardliners. While hardliners were not enthused by many of these appointments, the decisions to reunite the responsibilities of Chief SALT Negotiator and Director of ACDA and name an outspoken liberal to these posts set off a major row. In fact, the nomination of former

Deputy Secretary of Defense Paul Warnke to these two jobs proved a catalyst for the administration's first major debate on national security policy. Warnke's past opposition to several strategic weapons systems and his advocacy of "parallel restraint" as a possible alternative to and complement of negotiated arms limitation caused shivers among hardliners who feared he would not be a tough bargainer with Moscow. The debate over Paul Warnke's nomination waxed from a discussion of the man's capabilities and credibility to a far-reaching controversy over America's role in the world.

Hardliners strove to deny Warnke a plurality on his confirmation vote, hoping thereby to render the nominee ineffective and to present the administration with a *de facto* mandate for a tough negotiating strategy. The 58-40 confirming Warnke as SALT negotiator fell short of the margin of support that the administration desired. The President was successful in bringing along several "swing" senators who were inclined to vote with the hardline faction on national security issues. However, he lost all but 10 of the chamber's 38 Republicans.[16] Though the President downplayed the impact of the "exact vote" totals on the conduct of the negotiations, there was considerable evidence to the contrary. Senate leaders noted that the Warnke vote was a signal to the White House and the Kremlin of the chamber's determination to exercise independent judgement in assessing the final SALT II accord.

Until the very end, the domestic negotiations over SALT II were repeatedly ruffled by rumors that State and ACDA were attempting to force "retreat" on one issue or another while Defense and the NSC were holding the line. President Carter found himself particularly vulnerable to having prudent compromises so criticized because the tough March 1977 "deep-cuts" proposal set a benchmark by which less restrictive accords would be judged.

Salt Verification: Monitoring the Verifiers

It was widely known on Capitol Hill that monitoring of Soviet compliance with the limited provisions of SALT I could be accomplished with a high degress of success using available technical intelligence collectors, primarily photoreconnaissance satellites. Moreover, the Senate lacked the political interest and a structure for conducting a review of such matters. Thus, verification was not a contentious issue during the SALT I debate. It became clear, however, that the extensive qualitative limitations under consideration for a SALT II treaty would place much greater demands on U.S. intelligence capabilities such that the administration asked for funding to improve the monitoring system during the SALT I debate.

As allegations of Soviet violations of the SALT I accords surfaced and an understanding of the difficulties in assessing certain Soviet strategic weapons characteristics developed, the monitoring issue took on greater importance in the domestic SALT debate. Moreover, these allegations of Soviet violations were accompanied by charges that the White House was suppressing intelligence information concerning such ambiguous Soviet activity and was refraining from raising some of these practices with the Kremlin.[17] These charges caused an erosion of confidence in the arms control process. While the administration made CIA Director Colby and other senior officials available for confidential reviews of these issues, it refused to have Kissinger testify in this charged political atmosphere for fear of leaks and because of a recognition that Senate hardliners had already found the Secretary and the Soviets guilty. The Kissinger stonewalling strategy, while desirable from a diplomatic perspective, had the effect of allowing debilitating wounds to fester.[18]

Already suspicious of his appointment as ACDA Director, hardliners were particularly alarmed when Paul Warnke announced plans in April 1977 to reorganize the agency. In the most significant move, the functions of the separate Verification Bureau, which was charged with assessing U. S. ability to monitor compliance with arms control proposals, were reincorporated into the other functional divisions. The goal of this reshuffling was to make verification an integral part of the work of all the bureaus — as it had been until a 1973 reorganization by the Nixon administration — rather than an appendage. However, several legislators alleged that Warnke was purging the verifiers so as to minimize bureaucratic resistance to concessions at SALT. In response, the House adopted a measure which would have required the ACDA Director to provide extensive information to Congress on the verifiability of arms limitation proposals and on Soviet compliance. A coalition of hardliners and arms controllers in the Senate recognized the disruptive potential of this legislation and adopted a counterpart measure, which prevailed in conference, stipulating more reasonable reporting requirements.[19]

Recognizing that verification would be a critical issue in the SALT II ratification debate, the Foreign Relations Committee asked the Senate Intelligence Committee in 1977 to conduct a study of U.S. capabilities to monitor Soviet compliance with provisions of the emerging accord. The Intelligence Committee undertook an exhaustive two-year study of all intelligence material bearing on this question and, in October 1979, presented the Senate with a lengthy classified report and a series of unclassified summary findings.

The importance of verification waxed and waned in response to a variety of political and technical developments. Due to sanguine judgments by several members of the Intelligence Committee and the focus of attention on the state of the strategic balance, it appeared for a while that verification would be a secondary issue. Then, in March 1979, just three months before the treaty was signed, the United States lost access to intelligence facilities in Iran which monitored Soviet weapons developments. Suddenly, verification was thrust to the top of the political agenda, and Senator Glenn made it clear that he could not support the Treaty until he was satisfied that the capabilities of the Iranian sites were recouped. At about the same time, there were reports of a number of Soviet test practices which could complicate SALT monitoring, including encoding of missile test data.

The Intelligence Committee's unclassified findings, released on the eve of the floor debate, noted that, while the Treaty's quantitative and many qualitative provisions could be monitored with relatively high confidence, there were several provisions where low monitoring confidence was found.[20] Hardliners focused their attention on the low-confidence provisions. However, Treaty proponents emphasized the committee's overall judgement that SALT II enhanced U.S. capabilities to monitor aspects of Soviet strategic forces limited by the Treaty.

Linkage

A fundamental difference between the Carter administration's SALT diplomacy and that pursued under the guidance of Henry Kissinger during the two previous administrations related to views on the negotiations' relationship to other issues on the Soviet-American agenda. SALT was the touchstone of Kissinger's design for detente. Discord in other aspects of the Soviet-American relationship could not leave SALT unscathed. SALT was fundamentally a political issue pursued in an effort to enable military detente to have a spill-over effect on political detente and allow for mutually beneficial cooperation in the economic and scientific realms. Kissinger believed that the United States could manipulate this cooperation, particularly in the trade area, in a way which would induce Moscow's restraint in other areas. The Soviets did not often respond appropriately. The Kremlin did not appear to have its own policy of linkage. Brezhnev did not allow Nixon's opening to Peking and America's intensified bombing of North Vietnam just before the 1972 Moscow summit to impede the conclusion of SALT I.

In contrast, the Carter administration moved quickly to eschew the linkage concept.[21] This view of some of the leading architects of the Carter administration's SALT policy was compatible with the President's declared interest in sharply reducing the size of the superpowers' nuclear arsenals. Marshal Shulman, Vance's senior advisor on Soviet affairs, viewed SALT as a process whereby the U.S. and the USSR can work for mutual interests such as avoidance of nuclear war and the enhancement of crisis stability, that should be pursued independently of the bulk of other issues where the interests of the two states diverge. Shulman believed that within this two-track design SALT could still have a beneficial effect on other aspects of superpower relations. National Security Advisor Brzezinski appeared willing to go along with this scheme, but believed that the Soviets' commitment to these goals needed to be tested in early SALT proposals. When Moscow rejected the March 1977 "deep-cuts" plan and expanded its intervention in the Third World, Brzezinski argued that the Kremlin could not go unpunished for destabilizing actions in other spheres.

A critical factor in the domestic political equation became the dispute between, and within, the Carter administration and a large segment of the Congress over the question of linkage. Many influential legislators firmly embraced this notion as originally enunciated by Henry Kissinger. Indeed, Congress has applied this concept to an extreme that Kissinger did not endorse, by predicating the progress of detente upon favorable developments in Soviet domestic as well as foreign policies. The Jackson-Vanik Amendment to the Trade Act of 1974, which tied extension of most-favored nation status to the Soviet Union to a loosening of its emigration restrictions, is perhaps the most prominent example of Congressional determination to impose this linkage.[22] Similarly, the vigorous objections to conclusion of a SALT II pact while Soviet-supported Cuban intervention in the Angolan Civil War persisted was a major factor in the Ford administration's decision to forego an accord in 1976.

Applications of the linkage concept have not met with success. Secretary Kissinger's effort in early 1976 to trade progress at SALT for Soviet assurance of Cuban troop withdrawals from Angola proved futile. Even though its chief theoretician became disillusioned with its usefulness in the SALT context, linkage retains considerable support on Capitol Hill and in the Reagan Administration.

Despite these disclaimers, the controversy over linkage was never resolved. When Brzezinski declared that the intrusion of Soviet power into the conflicts in the Horn of Africa complicated both the negotiation and ratification of a SALT II accord, he revealed the existence of lingering differences within the Administration. Moscow swiftly decried Brzezinski's comments as a blackmail attempt. Secretary Vance and ACDA Director Warnke hastened to assert that conclusion of a SALT pact remained in the national interest. Nonetheless, all the official spokesmen who reacted to Brzezinski's statement affirmed his assessment of the domestic political impact of the Kremlin's activities. Clarifying the administration's position, President Carter noted that while Washington did not initiate the linkage, continued Soviet military presence in Africa would lessen the confidence of Congress and the American people in Moscow's intentions and make it more difficult to ratify a SALT agreement.

With or without a declaratory policy of linkage, the overall tenor of Soviet-American relations influences the domestic debate on SALT. Congressional perceptions of Soviet credibility and peaceful intentions have always colored and may even determine, the ultimate fate of the SALT II Treaty. Indeed, the successive shocks of the revelation of the presence of a Soviet combat brigade in Cuba, the fall of the Shah, and the taking of American hostages in Teheran had already made the climate for SALT so inhospitable that the Soviet invasion of Afghanistan was but the final blow which turned American attention from the control of arms to U.S. efforts to rebuild its conventional and strategic might. By 1980, many of its American proponents began to argue that linkage is much too indirect a "punishment" for Soviet interventionism and that a military buildup is a much more effective means of expressing displeasure and alarm. Similarly, Moscow began to wonder about the wisdom of pursuing SALT in the face of increased American defense spending, several efforts to play "the China card" as a means of intimidation, and the expansion of nuclear forces in Europe.

Protection of Allied Interests

During SALT I and the early stages of SALT II, several members of Congress endeavored to reinforce the American negotiating position that U.S. nuclear forces deployed in Europe capable of striking targets in the USSR (FBS) were not to be addressed. The Soviets had repeatedly pressed for limitations on FBS but finally relented just prior to the Vladivostok breakthrough. As SALT II progressed, members of Congress became concerned that the treaty might impede European access to American weapons technology and undermine the credibility of the U.S. nuclear deterrent.

European interest in modernization of American FBS and of their own nuclear and conventional weapons grew markedly in the late 1970s in response to significant expansion of the capabilities of Soviet theatre nuclear forces, particularly the SS-20 mobile intermediate-range ballistic missile. Because of its relatively low-cost and extraordinary accuracy (enhancing the effectiveness of each missile), U.S. cruise missile technology became a very attractive option for West European governments which were encountering domestic resistence to increased defense spending for modernizing their forces. And cruise missiles were not the only weapons of interest. The British were considering how best to modernize their aging submarine-launched Polaris missiles, and two systems under consideration were the U.S. cruise and Trident ballistic missiles.

Eager to prevent the introduction of cruise missiles in Western Europe, particularly in West Germany, and to drive a wedge between the NATO allies in the process, Moscow pressed for strictly-defined range limitations of 2,500 km. on air-launched and 600 km. on ground- and sea-launched cruise missiles. The Soviets also advocated a rigid proscription on the transfer of SALT-limited weapons or technology to third countries, similar to provisions in the ABM Treaty. Apprised of this development in the talks, members of Congress took it upon themselves to ensure that NATO interests were not neglected by the executive branch in the quest of a final agreement. Senator Sam Nunn, an effective advocate of NATO interests, was therefore courted and consulted by the White House on these and other issues.

U.S. negotiators hung firm, and in April 1978 realized Soviet acquiesence to very vague language in which the parties pledged not to circumvent the provisions of the agreement. This pledge became Article XII of the SALT II Treaty. While the administration heralded this provision as simply preventing the United States from transfering weapons systems actually banned by the treaty, critics viewed the ambiguity as a liability which could be used by Moscow to threaten abrogation in the event of a variety of technology or weapons transfers to the allies. The State Department made a unilateral declaration to the NATO ministers which was conveyed to the Kremlin prior to the Vienna summit, noting that the transfer of technology and the continuation of existing allied weapons cooperation was not affected by Article XII.

As for the other facets of the cruise missile problem, the Carter administration had to make several trade-offs in order to move the cruise missile bans from the treaty itself to the protocol; and, in the wake of the cancellation of the B-1 bomber, was trying to free the air-launched cruise missile from the restrictive range limitations advocated by the Soviets. When an opportunity to lift range limits from the air-launched cruise was presented, the White House, somewhat reluctantly agreed to accept the *quid pro quo*, strict 600 km. range limits on sea- and land-launched cruise missiles deployed during the protocol. The consolation to this compromise was that the United States could still develop and test such missiles which were not even expected to be ready for deployment until after the protocol expired.

Senator Nunn and the JCS were not completely satisfied by this plan because it did not allow exceptions for non-nuclear cruise missiles, particularly those launched from aircraft. Moreover, skeptics of this arrangement were concerned that the protocol limitations on cruise missiles would be extended if a follow-on pact were not realized by the expiration date. During the ratification debate several senators sought administration assurances that the protocol limitations would not be extended, as had the Interim Agreement, without congressional approval. To ensure that there was no doubt about congressional resolve, the Foreign Relations Committee adopted a reservation which stipulated that neither the treaty nor the protocol could be extended beyond their expiration dates without positive legislative action.[23]

Several senators undertook an effort to assess the administration's assurance that the allies fully supported SALT II and that rejection of the pact would shatter confidence in Washington's leadership and vastly complicate allied involvement with the several pending efforts to enhance NATO defense capabilities. A number of senators contended that the allies were actually worried that SALT would have an adverse impact on the state of the strategic and theatre nuclear balance and that allied endorsements were a consequence of intimidation by Washington and political expediency in the face of strong domestic support for detente. The administration and its Senate supporters brought forth a number of officials and private figures from both sides of the Atlantic, including a number of allied parliamentarians who affirmed that their country's support was genuine, to refute these charges. While no civilian or military European leader emerged from the closet to declare opposition to SALT II, doubts lingered on Capitol Hill.

Strategic Considerations

Throughout the negotiations, the consensus in Congress was that SALT II should have a positive effect on the strategic balance and enhance crisis stability. As the agreement developed, attention was directed to the equity of various limitations and their impact on key American strategic forces. Congress also closely scrutinized the administration's contentions that SALT II enhanced American security by preserving the integrity of U.S. strategic forces and obviating major expenditures on these forces, which would have an adverse effect on other vital military efforts. Several esoteric strategic issues, which cannot be treated fully here, were debated by strategic experts from a variety of perspectives in highly charged political forums.

During the ratification proceedings, both the Senate Foreign Relations and Armed Services Committees reviewed the military implications of the Treaty.[24] And although the issues were familiar to the military panel from its recent reviews of the strategic forces budgets, the Foreign Relations members were somewhat startled by what they learned. The House Armed Services Committee undertook its expected review of the military implications of the Treaty as well, but in a surprising effort at preemption, hardliners on the panel forced through a highly critical report of what was known of the agreement six months before the Vienna summit.[25] Yet, before the Senate committee hearings were very far along, they had the effect of shifting public attention away from specifics of the treaty toward consideration of the appropriate levels of spending for improvement of U.S. strategic and general purpose forces.

As the treaty provisions were finalized, the debate focused on whether they did, in fact, impose modest but significant limitations on Soviet strategic forces which would grant the United States additional time and leeway to redress the impressive Soviet momentum. Treaty proponents pointed to the launcher and fractionation ceilings as prime examples of where the Soviet threat would be constrained. The administration made a convincing case that, while subject to some uncertainties, the Soviets were likely (and in some instances had already demonstrated the capability) to exceed these ceilings. Executive branch figures noted that, without warhead limitations, the planned U.S. mobile ICBM, the MX, (which is to be shuttled among a variety of launch points to conceal its true location from Soviet targeteers) would enter service in 1986, already behind in the race between shelters and warheads that is its rationale. Critics countered with the contention that Soviet ICBMs were already so numerous and accurate that future force enhancements would be expected, both with and without a treaty, in the area of operational effectiveness rather than numerical expansion. But most found the argument that SALT limitations enhanced stability by providing predictability in assessing the evolving threat quite persuasive. Moreover, a consensus emerged on Capitol Hill that, just as SALT I was not responsible for the adverse shift in the U.S. strategic posture, so, too, SALT II alone could not be expected to redress this shift. The legislators recognized that arms control and prudent modernization of strategic forces are collateral means of shaping strategic stability.

The long vexing problem of Minuteman vulnerability, which many had hoped to forestall by throw-weight and fractionation limits in SALT II, was overtaken by technology and the slow pace of negotiations. Several analysts aptly noted the limited near-term military significance of Minuteman vulnerability given the health of the two other elements of the triad; however, all recognized the destabilizing political implications of this situation and the need to correct this deficiency in the most potent indicator of strategic power. Thus, the debate turned to the question of whether the treaty's bans on deliberate concealment measures and construction of new, fixed ICBM launchers would allow the U.S. to construct the multiple launch point MX ICBM system. Not completely assuaged by administration assurances that a multiple-launch point MX could be deployed under SALT II, the Foreign Relations Committee added an understanding to the ratification document which declared U.S. intent to deploy a verifiable MX system of this kind.

Because the limitations in the treaty allowed most other likely modernization efforts to continue unabated, the limitations in the protocol became the target of congressional critics. Extension of the protocol's ban on mobile ICBMs and its stiff limitations on cruise missile range were inimical to the two most important U.S. strategic initiatives. Thus, Congress took great pain to reinforce the administration's declaration that there was no implied commitment to extending the protocol's limitations beyond the document's duration.

Some critics were concerned with the inequity of the agreements which allowed the Soviets 308 heavy ICBMs and the United States none, and excluded the Backfire from the aggregate force ceilings. This criticism of the heavy ICBM asymmetry was dulled somewhat as it became clear that it was a unilateral U.S. force planning decision to develop light, highly-accurate ICBMs and that there were threats to Minuteman other than the SS-18. Nevertheless, SALT critics charged that the heavy missile limitations were inconsistent with the Jackson Amendment, and recommended that the U.S. reserve the right to build an equal number of heavy ICBM launchers even if it never intended to exercise that option. Senator Howard Baker introduced a "killer amendment" (one which would require renegotiation of treaty language) which delineated this argument, and it was narrowly defeated in the Foreign Relations Committee. The Backfire was subject to similar cries of outrage, and one killer amendment sought to have the Soviet aircraft count as 3/4 of a delivery vehicle. However, the Foreign Relations Committee was also satisfied here with shoring up the Carter administration's declarations that the Backfire limitations were viewed as an integral part of the SALT II package and that the United States reserved the right to deploy an aircraft with similar capabilities.

It was ironic that one of the initial criticisms leveled at the treaty by hardliners was that it would have an euphoric effect on Congress and the public, creating a false sense of security which would inhibit realization of the several strategic initiatives that most parties in the debate believed were necessary. In the end, the final stages of the SALT II debate focused attention on the shifts in the strategic balance and was instrumental in forging a broad consensus that something had to be done to reverse the perception that the Soviets were gaining the upper hand. As the Senate committee hearings drew to a close, the debate had really shifted away from consideration of the merits of the treaty to a battle over what increase in defense spending would constitute a sufficient response to the Kremlin's challenge. Hardliners harbored fears that the Carter administration's commitments to increased defense spending and the MX programs were unreliable and only undertaken in order to garner support for SALT. In order to allay these fears, the White House was forced to offer previews of its five-year defense plan to several groups of hardline lawmakers. The SALT debate had been transformed into a preparedness debate.

THE RATIFICATION DEBATE IN COMMITTEE

The major issues in the SALT II Treaty were well known, perhaps too well known, by the time the agreement was taken up in the Senate. Nonetheless, the Foreign Relations Committee began four months of nearly continuous public and closed hearings covering all facets of the treaty — this contrasts with the four weeks the committee took to review the Panama Canal Treaties. The Intelligence Committee undertook a secret review of verification issues. Later, the Armed Services Committee held a series of hearings on the military implications of SALT II. As these sessions droned on, their most striking feature was their staleness. Treaty opponents, who had been so effective in delivering their message in the preceding years, were unable to mount a fresh assault so their efforts lost momentum. However, supporters of the accord were able to muster only lukewarm support which essentially found the political and military implications of rejection far more troubling than the treaty's numerous failings. And, as noted above, by late 1979, the details of the Treaty had ceased to be the focus of the debate.

After defeating a number of "killer" amendments to the treaty by very close margins, the Foreign Relations Committee endorsed the pact with 23 other conditions appended to the resolution of ratification by a hardly propitious 9 to 6 vote.[26] With the prospect of many of the "killer" amendments surfacing again during the floor debate, where they were likely to find greater support, the chances of the treaty emerging unaltered from the Senate seemed remote. Pundits foresaw a repeat of Wilson's fight for the League of Nations, as President Carter indicated that the treaty could not be renegotiated. Moreover, the climate for consideration of SALT II was inauspicious. The brouhaha was just subsiding from the disclosure by Senators Church and Stone of intelligence reports on the previously unnoticed presence of a Soviet combat brigade in Cuba. Linkage was once again being invoked as senators decried the fact that while this brigade watched over Cuba, Cuban soldiers were advancing Soviet interests in Africa. Then, only a week before the treaty was reported out of committee, American diplomats were taken hostage in Teheran. The Iranians' action, yet another in a series of blows to American prestige, seemed likely to hold the fate of the SALT II hostage as well.

As 1979 came to a close, the treaty's prospects rose and fell with the day's events. But, even on the best days, the most optimistic vote counts never reached the critical 67 ayes. When the news was bad, Senate oddsmakers projected barely a simple majority of the Senate would support the pact. On December 21, ten hardliners on the Senate Armed Services Committee took the unprecedented move on issuing a report on the treaty — which was not in their bailiwick—over the objection of Chairman John Stennis and the six other members.[27] This action was but another illustration of the lingering struggle between the Foreign Relations and Armed Services Committees for influence over SALT II. Not surprisingly, the panel's report was highly critical, concluding that the treaty was not in the nation's best interest and counseling alteration. A day later, 19 senators urged President Carter to postpone a vote on the treaty rather than risk outright rejection. These blows, while injurious, were not as devastating as the one delivered by the Kremlin a few days later with its invasion of Afghanistan. Once again, extraneous events had intervened to stymie SALT II. Though he hardly needed to, President Carter asked the Senate to postpone final consideration of the treaty until the Soviets withdrew from Afghanistan. The entire SALT process faced a very uncertain future.

CONGRESS AND SALT: AN ASSESSMENT

The domestic debate over SALT II undoubtedly improved the executive branch's perception of what provisions would be acceptable to attentive members of Congress. During the Carter administration's conduct of an open diplomacy, Congress attained unprecedented access to information that enabled it to influence important decisions. Ironically, this opportunity presented itself at a time when Congress lacked discipline, clear leadership, and even a general foreign policy consensus. Thus, while SALT policymaking may have been more representative of the *vox populi,* or at least the loudest voices, this was realized at the expense of complicating and often confusing American diplomacy. To be certain, the Ford and Carter administrations made several tactical errors in dealing with Congress. Moreover, the underlying source of tension was the fundamental disagreement throughout the government about the achievements and the goals of the SALT process. Nonetheless, presented with the opportunity to offer advice on SALT issues over the past few years, Congress extended this counsel in a highly fragmented manner. Congress failed to provide the White House with a focal point on consultation and clear guidelines in conducting SALT diplomacy. Congressional influence over SALT grew, but primarily in a negative rather than a constructive way. Similarly, the Carter administration seemed unable, for a variety of reasons, to forge an effective collaborative relationship with Congress.

Some observers have reviewed this record and concluded that the evolution of SALT diplomacy under the Carter administration vindicates the wisdom of Henry Kissinger's secretive approach to the negotiations. However, it was this closed diplomacy which exacerbated congressional doubts about SALT II. When the SALT I accords were thrust upon it in May 1972, Congress found itself with a scant understanding of their implications and few options for action. The ambiguities of the Interim Agreement were not fully appreciated by the ill-informed lawmakers. As these shortcomings became apparent, deep reservations surfaced about the value of arms control arrangements with the Soviet Union.

A return to a secretive SALT process would have jeopardized the realization of any accord. Moreover, it is doubtful that any President could undertake such an effort considering the fundamental changes in congressional capabilities and disposition. The statutory legacy of this period will linger long after the Watergate scandal is forgotten. But, even if it were possible to return to this diplomatic style, it would be undersirable. If Congress had been closed out of the SALT process between 1977 and 1979, it would have been forced to offer its advice at the time of ratification. Rejection or amendment, which would necessitate renegotiation, would be the legislature's *only* tools, and their employment would have been far more damaging to American foreign policy than the long public debate on SALT II.

Indeed, several observers have surveyed this scene and decided that the swing of the pendulum toward congressional government has gone too far, and that executive dominance of foreign affairs is once again essential to successful diplomacy. However, such discussions of congressional or presidential ascendancy in foreign policy are counterproductive. The SALT experience, just as Wilson's troubles with the Treaty of Versailles, demonstrates that the legislature and the executive must be strong partners in the formulation of successful foreign policies. American diplomacy has been most dynamic in instances when this was the case.

There are several steps which might be taken to help attain a new partnership. There is a need for a refinement of the consultative process and a renewed sensitivity to the demarcation of authority between the two branches. The President should solicit advice from legislators on general goals to be pursued in negotiations, but Congress must facilitate this process by undertaking some reform of its own operating style. Rather than briefing a number of congressional committees each time there is some development in a negotiation, a central point of contact would simplify and enhance such consultations. Perhaps a joint select committee on national security, comprised of several members from each of the attentive standing committees and the leadership, could serve this function on SALT and other major issues. Such a body could integrate the work of several standing committees and serve as a focal point of executive–Congressional consultation on pressing and sensitive matters.

As much as Congress should reflect public opinion, it also has a duty to shape these perceptions by education. Thus, public hearings on major foreign policy issues remain a crucial aspect of Congress' distinct role in foreign affairs. This need of debate is particularly acute in the case of SALT because it would help shape a consensus about U.S. goals in the negotiations. At the outset of international negotiations, Congress should, as it has in the past, agree on feasible goals and then provide the executive branch with a flexible mandate. Such measures can strengthen bureaucratic resolve on key issues and expand U.S. bargaining leverage with other countries. In such a situation, executive-legislative consultations would more likely be pursued in a spirit of cooperation rather than combativeness.

NOTES

1. For a basic introduction to the nature of deterrence theory and its relationship to the ABM debate see John Barton and Lawrence Weiler (Eds), *International Arms Control: Issues and Agreements* (Stanford, CA.: Stanford University Press, 1976); and Lawrence Martin, *Arms and Strategy* (New York, McKay, 1973). The classic in the field is Bernard Brodie, *Strategy in the Missile Age*, (Princeton, N.J.: Princeton University Press, 1965).
2. For an analysis of the failings of the arms control impact statement process see U.S. Congress, House Committee on International Relations, 95th Cong., 2d sess. Committee Print, *Evaluation of the Fiscal Year 1979 Arms Control Impact Statements*, 1978.
3. There were occasions when the principals took control of the entire process, with often problematical results. See Raymond Garthoff, "Negotiating With the Russians: Some Lessons from SALT," *International Security*, Spring 1977, pp. 3–24.
4. For a discussion of Soviet decisionmaking for SALT see Thomas Wolfe, *The SALT Experience* (Cambridge, MA.: Ballinger, 1979), pp. 49–77.

5. See John P. Leacacos,"Kissinger's Apparat,"*Foreign Policy* 5 (Winter 1971–72), pp. 3–27; for a discussion of the Kissinger Verification Panel system. See also Wolfe, *The SALT Experience*, pp. 23–45; for a comparison of the Carter and Kissinger structures.

6. See the introductory chapter in this volume by John Spanier for a more detailed discussion of the changing mood of Congress during this period.

7. The unprecedented degree of consultation with Congress during the later stages of the negotiations is illustrated by the following statistics. Between February 1977 and the Vienna summit, senior Carter Administration officials addressed SALT issues at nearly 50 Senate hearings. A variety of officials briefed senators on 140 occasions and groups of staffers on more than 100 occasions about developments in the negotiations. These exchanges, coupled with innumerable informal contacts between individuals in the two branches, provided Congress with detailed insights into SALT diplomacy and policymaking.

8. Carter went so far as to ask Jackson to develop a proposal for the first session of the SALT negotiations under his Administration. Jackson advanced a tough package, which some policymakers feared would disrupt the negotiations because it marked a sharp departure from earlier U.S. positions. However, the Jackson memorandum provided greater impetus to a strategy to test Moscow's commitment to deep reductions that had been gaining strength in White House deliberations. The March 1977 "deep-cuts" proposal, which was advanced in a highly public way, set back the negotiations and became a benchmark against which subsequent formulas were judged by Senate hardliners. This episode is elaborated in Stephen J. Flanagan, "Congress, the White House and SALT," *Bulletin of the Atomic Scientists*, November 1978, pp. 36–7; and Strobe Talbot, *Endgame: The Inside Story of SALT* (New York: Harper & Row, 1979), pp. 52–55.

9. Sergi Vishnevsky, "SALT," *Pravda*, June 26, 1977, p. 4 (*Current Digest of the Soviet Press*, July 27, 1977, p. 1). The Kremlin made considerable strides in appreciating the role of and dealing with Congress during the decade of negotiations. However, when backed to the wall, the Kremlin often returned to the counterproductive technique of threatening Congress. See a denunciation of the use of the threat of Senate ratification as a bargaining tactic in "The Task of Limiting Strategic Arms," *Pravda*, February 11, 1978, p. 4 (*Foreign Broadcast Information Service – Soviet Union*, February 13, 1978, pp. A1-9), for example.

10. Lewis Harris, "Most Still Have Hope for SALT," *Chicago Tribune*, June 16, 1977, p. 8; and the CBS-New York Times Poll, *New York Times*, June 30, 1978, p. A9 are representative of these trends in public opinion. In contrast, see the report on a poll commissioned by the Committee on the Present Danger, "Public Attitudes on SALT II," Pamphlet distributed by the Committee, April 1979.

11. For a history of the early SALT negotiations, see John Newhouse, *Cold Dawn: The Story of SALT* (New York: Holt Reinhart, 1973).

12. For a discussion of the technical details and bureaucratic battles involved in the development of MIRVs, see Ted Greenwood, *The Making of MIRV* (Cambridge, Mass.: Ballinger, 1975).

13. While the Nixon Administration did advance two MIRV limitation plans during the early stages of SALT I, it became apparent that these proposals were disingenuous, designed mainly to appease Congressional arms controllers. Technical disagreements about U.S. MIRV monitoring capabilities coupled with strong bureaucratic opposition stifled the moratorium idea. There was little political interest in MIRV constraints as was confirmed when Kissinger and Dobrynin removed the problem from the SALT I agenda. For a comprehensive insider's view of the MIRV debate see Alton Frye, *A Responsible Congress: The Politics of National Security* (New York: McGraw Hill, 1975), chapters 3 and 4. Frye's view of the role of Congress in foreign affairs contrasts with many of the chapters in this volume.

14. For the text of the SALT I accords and an appreciation of the debates, see the Foreign Relations and Armed Services Committee Hearings. U.S. Senate, Committee on Foreign Relations, 92d Cong., 2d sess., Committee on Armed Services, 92d Cong., 2d sess., Hearings, *Military Implications of the ABM Treaty and the Interim Agreement*, June–July 1972. Debate on the floor is in *Congressional Record*, August–September 1972.

15. For an account of the negotiations during the Carter Administration, particularly in the latter stages, see Talbot, *Endgame.*

16. See U.S. Senate, Committee on Foreign Relations, 95th Cong., 1st sess., Hearings, *Warnke Nomination*, February 8-9, 1977; and *Congressional Record*, March 4 and 9, 1977.

17. U.S. House of Representatives, Select Committee on Intelligence, 94th Cong., 1st sess., Hearings, *U.S. Intelligence Agencies and Activities: Risks and Control of Foreign Intelligence*, Part 5, November and December 1975; charges by Admiral Elmo Zumwalt, pp. 1602-1649; Administration response, pp. 1927-62.

18. The Carter Administration finally issued a review of all the allegations of Soviet violations. While the document contended that the Soviet activities of concern were either not violations of the pact or were resolved in bilateral consultations, it did not silence critics. See U.S. Department of State, Special Report, "Compliance With the SALT I Agreements and Verification of the Proposed SALT II Agreement," February 1978, reprinted in *Department of State Bulletin*, April 1978.

19. The evolution of this controversy is traced in the Senate debate. See the *Congressional Record*, June 16, 1977.

20. U.S. Senate, Select Committee on Intelligence, 96th Cong., 1st sess., Committee Print, *Principal Findings on the Capabilities of the U.S. To Monitor the SALT II Treaty*, October 1979.

21. The Kissinger view is expressed in "U.S. Foreign Policy for the 1970s: Building for Peace," A Report by Richard M. Nixon to the Congress, February 25, 1971 in the *Department of State Bulletin*, March 22, 1971, p. 405. The Carter Administration's position was first enunciated in "News

Conference of Secretary Vance," February 3, 1977, *Department of State Bulletin*, February 22, 1977, pp. 148-9.

22. See Chapter 1 on Jackson-Vanik by Dan Caldwell.

23. The nature of congressional concerns in this area is elaborated in the Foreign Relations Committee's Report, *The SALT II Treaty*, November 19, 1979, pp. 228-52.

24. U.S. Senate, Committee on Armed Services, 96th Cong., 1st sess., Hearings, *Military Implications of the SALT II Treaty*, Parts 1-4, July-Oct. 1979.

25. U.S. House of Representatives, Committee on Armed Services, 95th Cong., 2d sess., Report 95-95, *SALT II: An Interim Assessment*, December 23, 1978.

26. Committee on Foreign Relations Report, *SALT II*, pp. 27-78. The report includes the complete text of the SALT II Agreements and a helpful series of commentaries on pp. 319-453.

27. This report, drafted by a few hardline staff members, was not immediately reported out and printed. However some of its contents were leaked to the media. See Richard Burt, "Senate Panel Votes Anti-Treaty Report," *New York Times*, December 21, 1979, p. 10.

Chapter 4

Negotiations and Ratification of the Panama Canal Treaties

William L. Furlong

INTRODUCTION

Despite major efforts in 1967 by both the Johnson administration and the Panamanian government, the first major attempt to replace the 1903 Hay-Bunau-Varilla Treaty ended in failure. Presidents Nixon and Ford also talked of a new treaty, and Ellsworth Bunker began negotiations in 1973, but little was actually done. Finally, under President Carter, serious negotiations with Panama began in early 1977 and Ambassador Bunker continued to act as principal negotiator.

Negotiations were completed in August 1977, and the new treaties were signed in an elaborate ceremony in Washington, D.C. on September 7, 1977. Before the treaties were completed and implemented, four House and four Senate committees had held numerous hearings on the treaties, 42 senators and a number of congressmen had traveled to Panama, 38 days of Senate floor debates had been held, and over 90 reservations, understandings, and conditions, were considered and two amendments had been added to the treaties. In some instances, senators were forced into negotiating directly with the Panamanians over some of these changes. On other occasions, the Senate leadership had to pull votes together where the administration had failed. Even after the treaties were ratified, the House of Representatives came very close to destroying them when it formulated and passed implementation legislation that disagreed with and contradicted specific aspects of the treaties. The House continued its opposition role up to the last moment.

IMPORTANT DATES

1973, September: Ambassador-at-large Ellsworth Bunker confirmed as new chief Panama Canal negotiator

1974, February: Secretary of State Henry Kissinger and Panama's Foreign Minister Juan Antonio sign "statement of principle"

1977, January: Former OAS Ambassador Sol Linowitz appointed co-negotiator with Ellsworth Bunker

1977, August 10: Negotiators announce agreement on the treaties

1977, September 7: Treaties signed in Washington D.C. in elaborate ceremony

1977, October 23: Plebiscite in Panama ratifies treaty by a 2 to 1 margin

1978, January 30: Treaties reported out of Senate Foreign Relations Committee by a vote 14-1

1978, February 8: Debate on treaties begins in Senate

1978, March 16: Senate approves Neutrality Treaty by a vote of 68-32

1978, April 18: Senate approves the Panama Canal Treaty by a vote of 68-32

1979, September 26: Implementation legislation is approved by the House

1979, October 1: Implementation of Canal Treaty begins

HISTORICAL BACKGROUND

Few foreign policy issues in the history of the United States have involved the Congress more than negotiations and relations regarding the Panama Canal. It began in the 1840s and has continued until today. Not unlike today, Secretary of State John Hay in 1900 had a major confrontation with the Senate. He bitterly denounced the treaty approval process in the following terms:

> I long ago made up my mind that no treaty . . . that gave room for a difference of opinion could ever pass the Senate. When I sent in the Canal Convention I felt sure that no one out of a mad house could fail to see that the advantages were on our side. But I underrated the power of ignorance and spite, acting upon cowardice. . . . there will always be 34% of the Senate on the backguard side of every question. . . . A treaty entering the Senate is like a bull going into the arena; no one can say just how or when the blow will fall—but one thing is certain—it will never leave the arena alive.[1]

Despite his attitude, Hay persisted, and a new treaty was later negotiated and ratified.

Congress continued to be the major political battleground for most of the important issues related to the Panama Canal; its location, construction, and the eventual agreements between the United States and Panama. The conditions set down in the 1903 Hay-Bunau-Varilla Treaty were quite severe on Panama but were favorable for the United States. Philipe Bunau-Varilla stated that, although some provisions of the treaty were innovations in international law, they were included in order to guarantee that the U.S. Senate would approve the treaty.[2]

From 1903 to 1955, three major attempts were made to change the 1903 Hay-Bunau-Varilla Treaty. Panama refused to ratify the first in 1926. Panama accepted the other two attempts, while the U.S. Senate took three years to ratify the 1936 treaty and over two years to ratify the 1955 treaty.

Serious negotiations began in 1965 and three new treaties were agreed upon in the Spring of 1967. Nevertheless, the texts of the treaties were never submitted to the Senate for their "advice and consent." The idea of new treaties with Panama at that time met with vehement opposition in Congress.[3]

Senate and House resistance to any changes in the status quo over the canal and the zone continued through 1977. Serious negotiations began in 1973, and in 1974 the Kissinger-Tack agreements on basic principles set the guidelines for the final treaties. The House tried to cut off funds to the Department of State that might be used for negotiations in 1975, 1976, and 1977. Despite these efforts, however, successful negotiations continued from May through August of 1977. Many congressmen and senators, however, continued to show their opposition to the whole concept of change. Committees began to hold hearings, and two cases were taken to federal courts to prevent ultimate treaty passage. Despite this vocal and procedural opposition, progress was made and, finally, on August 10, 1977, the negotiators announced agreement "in principle" on two new treaties. The treaties then went through a formal drafting stage and were ready for signing in September. On September 7, 1977, in a ceremony not to be forgotten in Washington, President Carter and Panamanian Chief of Government Omar Torrijos signed the two new treaties. For the next seven months, the Senate played out its part on the treaties; on March 16, 1978, the Neutrality Treaty was approved and, on April 18, 1978, the Senate gave its approval to the new Canal Treaty.

MAJOR TREATY PROVISIONS

The Canal Treaty

Under the new Panama Canal Treaty, the United States will continue to regulate shipping through the canal and to operate, maintain, and defend the canal until December 31, 1999. Panama will increasingly participate in the operation and defense of the canal over this period. A new Panama Canal Commission established by the treaty and by the implementation legislation, will operate the canal until January 1, 2000. Approximately 60 percent of the Canal Zone was turned over to Panama when the implementation legislation became effective on October 1, 1979, and the zone as a separate territory ceased to exist. Other segments of the zone will be transferred during the 22 year life of the treaty. In the year 2000, all remaining territory and property, including the canal itself, will be turned over to Panama. After a 30 month transition period, beginning about January 1982, Panamanian law will apply to all areas of Panama. Starting in October 1979, Panama is to receive thirty cents per net ton in tolls amounting to $40-60 million per year. In addition, they will receive an annual payment of $10 million from operating revenues, $10 million for the provision of public services (e.g., water, sewer, garbage collection), and an additional $10 million contingency payment to be taken from profits when canal revenues exceed expenditures. These benefits are much smaller than those demanded by Panama, who had requested a one-time payment of about $1 billion and an annual subsidy from tolls of from $150 to $200 million.

The new treaty further provides that the United States and Panama must agree on any new negotiations on a sea-level canal, and that the United States will not negotiate for such a canal with any third country unless Panama agrees. It also grants the United States the right to build a third lane of locks on the existing canal.

The treaty goes on at length on employment practices and guarantees. It states the Americans can still hold secure jobs, but the Panamanians must be trained to replace most of them. Early retirement and other benefits are granted to U.S. employees. This section created a significant technical and specific difficulty and makes up the bulk of the implementation legislation.

The Neutrality Treaty

The Neutrality Treaty, which does not take effect until the year 2000, declares that the canal shall be permanently neutral, secure, and remain open to peaceful transit by vessels of all nations equally in times of peace and war. The United States and Panama agree to maintain and defend this neutrality. After the year 2000, only Panama is to operate the canal and maintain defense forces and defense installations within its national territory. The treaty further states that vessels of war and auxiliary vessels of the United States and Panama shall be entitled to "expeditious" passage.

Despite some weaknesses and unresolved issues in the treaties, the United States could not have received many more concessions and had them accepted and approved by Panama. It is even more obvious that Panama could not have received any more concessions and had them approved by the U.S. Senate.

In contrast to the situation in 1967, both sides were very close to the maximum they could expect without destroying chances for ratification in 1977-79.

THE NEGOTIATORS

Ellsworth Bunker

In September 1973, Ambassador-at-large Ellsworth Bunker was confirmed as the new chief Panama Canal negotiator. This was probably one of the strongest and most effective decisions made in the treaty process by the executive branch. Bunker was a wise choice for at least three major reasons. In the first place, he was respected and trusted by the military and the defense establishment. Secondly, the Panamanians learned to trust him; but, even more important, they learned to negotiate without feeling that, anytime they obtained agreement from the United States it was because they had given too much or that somehow they were being out-negotiated. They were able to gain more confidence in their own ability to actually obtain some real gains without hidden loop-holes. Ambassador Bunker's third strength was with the Senate which had confidence in his ability and in his reputation. He was able to convince some senators that the treaties were not a "give-away," but were in our long-run national interest.

Sol Linowitz

The appointment of Ambassador Sol Linowitz, on the other hand, had a negative impact upon the Senate. Despite his previous experience with Latin America and as U.S. Ambassador to the OAS, his appointment met with strong opposition. He was accused of having a conflict of interest over his bank holdings. He was on the Board of Directors and a member of the Executive Committee of the Marine Midland Banks, Inc. This fact was related to the argument by the opponents of the treaties that they were being negotiated to bail out a number of U.S. banks which had lent money to Panama and were concerned about repayment. Senator Jessie Helms (R-NC), who strongly voiced this concern, stated that Ambassador Linowitz's relationship created an obvious conflict of interest and, thereby, was not in the national interest of the United States.[4]

A number of senators were also upset that Ambassador Linowitz's appointment was as a temporary negotiator, which limited his term to six months, and made it possible for his appointment to avoid Senate approval. When the treaty negotiations ended in a flurry of activity and with what appeared to be undue haste, senators implied that it was because Ambassador Linowitz's six-month tenure was also ending and that the negotiators were more concerned with this fact than with the treaties' cost factors and the national interest. The treaty negotiations were completed exactly six months to the day from when Ambassador Linowitz's appointment was made.[5]

Negotiations Staffs

These two principal negotiators required a lot of support and staff people to be able to carry out their functions. Most important among their staff were four military and civilian personnel from the Department of Defense and three specialists from the Department of State. These staff people prepared position papers on various issues and obstacles during the negotiations. These papers were circulated, discussed, and approved by the respective departments, and then formal stands were taken to present to the Panamanians. Staff people also kept the Senate Foreign Relations Committee and staffers of individual senators informed, as well as keeping their own leadership up to date in their own departments. In this fashion, some important support and input were obtained from these two executive Departments and from some of the Senate leadership.[6]

Crucial support from the Department of Defense was thus forthcoming, as the main personnel were kept abreast of the issues and important agreements and were centrally involved during the negotiations. Without the support of the Department of Defense, the treaties would never have been approved by the Senate. Some staff changes in the negotiation team in early 1977 also seemed to facilitate agreement on the treaties.

The individuals who seemed to be at the focal point of this activity and crucial to these staffs were Mike Kozak, Mark Feldman, and Douglas Bennet of the State Department; Colonel Lawrence W. Jackley of the Department of Defense; and Robert Dockery, a staff member for the Senate Foreign Relations Committee. These gentlemen all became experts on the canal and the treaties, and their roles and inputs were significant during negotiations of the treaties and during ratification approval by the Senate.[7]

Torrijos and the Treaty

Despite all of the negative rhetoric heaped on General Omar Torrijos of Panama, it is difficult to envision the resolution of the treaty question in an atmosphere of calm and rational agreement without his influence. Despite the fact that he assumed power through a coup and was an authoritarian ruler, there is a positive side to his role in the treaty process. In the first place, General Torrijos had sufficient power to be able to negotiate with the United States without being seriously weakened by accusations of selling out to them, which had been a problem with his predecessors. He also had sufficient legitimacy and power at home to keep opposition to the treaties at a minimum and to keep the opposition from major riots and street demonstrations. If incidents such as those of 1964 had occurred during the negotiations, it would have been very difficult to have completed them.

He was also able, as in the example of the 1973 U.N. Security Council vote, to obtain worldwide support for the negotiations. He used this support to his advantage and as a major wedge against the United States. Furthermore, he obtained general support from most of the Latin American nations, and especially from his neighbors. Costa Rica and Venezuela gave Panama significant and continual support throughout the whole negotiation and ratification process.

He met personally with nearly half of the senators and discussed the treaties with them and their staffs, although this type of politicking was extremely difficult for him. He showed complete restraint while the Congress took eight months from the signing of the treaties to the ratification and then took over a whole year to pass implementation legislation. Without his leadership, the treaties would probably never have become a reality.

SUBSTANTIVE ISSUES

In any discussion of the major issues of the Panama Canal treaties, one must keep in mind that the President had to fight a multifront battle on most of these major points. The first battleground was within his own executive branch. The major opponent was the Pentagon. Once the Department of Defense, the Department of State and the President were in agreement, then the Panamanians had to agree. Then the real domestic battles in the United States had to be fought with Congress, more with the House than the Senate; with the Republican Party, and especially the Right Wing; and with the American public at large. This particular case study differs from many of the others in this regard. The President and the executive branch, specifically the Department of State, stood almost alone on the major issues of the treaties. It must also be kept in mind that most of the substantive issues pertain to the Canal Treaty and not to the Neutrality Treaty which establishes relationships only after the year 2000.

The Sovereignty Issue

The principal issue in the negotiations between the United States and Panama and between the executive and Congress centered on the question of transferring complete sovereignty and the property in the Canal Zone to Panama and of relinquishing control of the canal to Panama. The argument over the sovereignty clause of the Hay-Bunau-Varilla treaty had gone on since 1903.

The major actors in the creation of that treaty (Secretary of State John Hay, Philippe Bunau-Varilla, President Theodore Roosevelt, and Vice President Howard Taft) had all stated at one time or another that real or titular sovereignty had been retained by Panama and that the United States was only given to power to act as "if it were sovereign" within the Canal Zone.[8] (Bunau-Varilla, 1940:159; LaFeber, 1979:34-46).

Presidents Eisenhower, Johnson, Nixon, and Ford also agreed with these precedents. Nevertheless, during this whole period, Congress consistently rejected the idea that the United States did not own this strip of land. The pattern of behavior in the Congress and particularly in the House of Representatives from 1965 to 1979 indicated very strong sentiment against any action that might alter our acting as sovereign in the Canal Zone, or jeopardize our control of the 51 mile long, 10 mile wide strip of land and our maintaining direct control of the canal itself.

In 1977 and 1978, the House attacked this issue on procedural grounds. The opponents argued that the President and the Senate could not transfer U.S. property without the House also approving. They were joined by the Senate Judiciary Committee's Subcommittee on the Separation of Powers led by its chairman James B. Allen. A number of other senators also agreed with this reasoning.[9] Treaty opponents believed that they could prevent treaty ratification and kill the treaties, if the House had to give its approval as well as the Senate.

A number of congressmen and senators took this question to the federal courts in an attempt to force the President to take the treaties to the House also. Senators Helms, McClure, and Thurmond, Congressmen Flood, McDonald, and Snyder, and a U.S. citizen living in the Canal Zone, William R. Drummond, submitted the suit.[10] Two days before the final vote on the Panama Canal Treaty, the Federal Appeals Court in Washington, D.C. voted in a 2-1 decision to allow U.S. property to be transferred by treaty alone without House action.[11] Four state Attorneys-General (from Idaho, Indiana, Iowa, and Louisiana) and other opponents to the treaties filed another suit in an attempt to prevent the transfer of U.S. property. This suit also failed at the appeals level and was rejected by the Supreme Court.[12]

In the new treaties, the questions of sovereignty, property, and control of the canal were resolved and were supported by President Carter and the Departments of Defense and State. The final agreement created a three stage transfer. On October 1, 1979, approximately 60 percent of the Canal Zone was turned over to Panama. Portions of the remaining Canal Zone land will be transferred over the next twenty years. The final transfer of land and of the canal will occur on December 31, 1999, according to Article 13 of the treaty: "The republic of Panama shall assume total responsibility for the management, operation, and maintenance of the Panama Canal, which shall be turned over in operating condition and free of liens and debts, except as the two parties may otherwise agree."

Economic Issues

Four economic disagreements made up the second major substantive issue. Two of these four economic questions resolved by the Canal Treaty were directly related to the property and canal operation agreements above. The question of property to be turned over to Panama during the life of the treaty is complicated because various methods were used to calculate U.S. investment, replacement costs, and benefits, and whether or not the canal has paid for itself.

The second economic disagreement was over the implementation costs of the treaty. This became a principal issue when the House of Representatives considered the implementation legislation in 1979. The House retaliated because they were left out of the treaty approval process and attacked the treaties and attempted to revise or kill them through their actions on the implementation legislation.

The Panama Canal Treaties attempted to resolve old financial grievances between the United States and Panama by promising Panama a share of toll payments and other direct compensation. Some of the best and most prolonged debates on the floor of the Senate revolved around this third economic issue. Proponents and opponents of the treaties alike criticized some of the direct payments to Panama.

The fourth economic question involved military and economic assistance promised to Panama by President Carter, but not actually included in the treaties. This type of aid was rejected by both houses of Congress. In early 1979, before the implementation legislation was even acted upon, both the Senate and the House deleted the technical and military aid to Panama from appropriation bills that were passed by them.

Defense Issues

Defense of the canal from external and internal enemies was the third major issue of the treaties. The treaty opponents in the Senate strongly indicated that the United States was retreating from its world leadership position, and that the loss of the canal would greatly jeopardize U.S. national security and world image. They downplayed the internal threat within Panama. Opponents also raised the fear of a communist threat with such statements as Senator Orrin Hatch (R-Utah) quoting from Adm. Thomas Moorer, "Do not be surprised if the treaty is ratified in its present form to see a Soviet and/or Cuban presence quickly established in Panama."[13]

The administration used one of its strongest proponents to rebut the opponents and win over a number of senators on the defense issue. Secretary of Defense Harold Brown turned out to be one of the most influential witnesses in the hearing process in the Senate. He placed our defense needs into four categories. The first was free and unimpeded use of the canal by both merchant ships and the U.S. Navy. He stated that the new treaties sufficiently guaranteed this.

The second security requirement, he said, was to have an efficiently operated canal. He was convinced that the provision of the U.S. operation until the year 2000, thus allowing time for training the Panamanians to take over the canal, definitely satisfied this requirement.

Defense of the canal from hostile external threats was his third security requirement. He stated:

> Our armed forces now control and they will continue to control with overwhelming forces, the sea approaches to the canal . . . . It (the treaty) states unequivocally that during the life of the treaty, the U.S. armed forces shall enjoy the right and the primary responsibility to defend the canal itself. It further provides that during that period the United States may station, train, and support units of our armed forces in Panama, and that the United States will decide unilaterally whether and how to modify the force levels we maintain there. All key military bases and training areas which we now operate in the Canal Zone will remain under U.S. control.[14]

He went on to state that we would continue to defend the canal after the Neutrality Treaty went into effect after 2000 and that we could "defend the canal against any external threat. . . ."[15]

The fourth defense requirement was the protection of the canal from internal threats, terrorism, and guerrilla action. He stated: ". . . the treaty contemplates a combined defense agreement between the United States and Panama as a result of which Panama's armed forces will be able to protect the canal against threats from within Panama more effectively than they can at present."[16] This will add real security to the canal, he went on to say. He also implied that the passage of the treaties would significantly reduce internal threats to the canal and its operation and personnel. Despite this optimistic view, some retired military officers (e.g., former Chairman of the Joints Chiefs Thomas H. Moorer; Gen. Maxwell Taylor; and Admiral Elmo R. Zumwalt Jr.) maintained that the treaty would give the Cubans and the Russians a political and a military advantage over the status quo.[16]

Other Issues

United States–Latin American relations was another important issue. Secretary of State Cyrus Vance spoke for the administration when he stated that ratification of the treaties would be the " . . . single most positive action to be undertaken in recent years in our relations with Latin America."[18] Many treaty opponents argued that this would not be the case at all, and that many Latin Americans feared the impact of the new treaties. Donald M. Dozer, Latin

American expert, stated that the treaties would have an adverse effect on United States--Latin American relations.[19]

Another issue that provoked strong arguments in both the Senate and the House centered on the commercial importance of the canal. The administration and some of the proponents argued that the canal was declining in commercial and defense value because a number of modern ships today cannot use it. Related to this issue is the plan for a sea-level canal. The opponents fought this question on the grounds that the Canal Treaty would reduce U.S. options and tie us too closely to Panama and the politics of Panama until the year 2000. The proponents argued that the treaty prevents Panama from allowing others to build such a canal and gives us the first option to build one. Without the treaties, this option for the United States would be completely lost.[22]

An important issue that was not related to the provisions of the treaties but was related to their ratification, concerned the presidency itself. The news media and a number of senators expressed concern that, if the treaties were rejected, the diplomatic bargaining power and foreign policy credibility of the President of the United States would be seriously jeopardized. This aspect of the treaties was important enough that some senators modified their opposition to the treaties. It was also viewed so strongly by the administration that the President, himself, spent many hours personally lobbying with uncommitted senators. He also sent many of his most prominent officials to do the same. Among them were Vice President Walter Mondale, Secretary of State Cyrus Vance, Secretary of Defense Harold Brown, National Security Advisor Zbigniew Brzezinski, White House Adviser Hamilton Jordan, and many others.

In summary, the above strongly indicates that the treaties were in the U.S. national interest. The riots of 1964 could have been repeated with greater intensity if the treaties failed. Threats of damage, transit interruptions, sabotage, and civilian unrest could no longer be ignored. The President, the Department of State, the Department of Defense, and many knowledgeable senators and Latin American experts agreed on the value of the treaties. Nevertheless, many government officials and about 58 percent of the adult American public were against their approval.

RATIFICATION APPROVAL PROCESS

Contrary to popular belief, the U.S. Senate does not ratify treaties. It gives its advice and consent to them. If it does not give its consent, then treaties cannot be ratified. After Senate consent is obtained, the President is responsible for formal ratification. The Senate's role in this process is spelled out in Article II section 2 of the Constitution. A treaty only becomes binding on the United States after the advice and consent is given, the President ratifies, the other party(ies) also ratify, and there is an exchange or deposit of the ratifications.

Upon receipt of a treaty from the President, the Senate may approve the treaty without qualification or it may reject the treaty outright. Rejection, however, is generally done through inaction, rather than by a direct vote to reject. The Senate may also support a treaty but, at the same time, restrict that support in a general or specific way.

Congressional Input

Because of the highly emotional nature of the Panama Canal Treaties, the President attempted to obtain from Congress some inputs on the treaties. Before 1977, however, little of a positive nature was received. Most of the input emanated from the House of Representatives and was of a very negative nature. In 1975, 1976, and 1977, the House either passed or presented amendments to State Department appropriations requesting that no money be spent to support treaty negotiations with Panama that might alter U.S. control of the Canal Zone or sole operation of the canal. This either required the President to ignore Congress or to break off negotiations, as these two issues were central to any new settlement with Panama. Four Presidents, from 1965 to 1977, chose to ignore such inputs and to go on with negotiations.

In the spring of 1977, when it became evident that new treaties could be finalized before the end of the year, the Carter administration began briefings with congressional leadership and critical congressional committee staff members. State Department personnel and Department of Defense staff were also involved in these briefings. In most cases, however, the briefings were one-way communications informing Congress of the developments in the negotiations and not requesting advice instructions on how to approach specific issues in the negotiations.

Hearings and Congressional Negotiations

Before the hearing process was completed, numerous committees and sub-committees had participated. In the House, the Panama Canal Subcommittee of the Merchant Marine and Fisheries Committee held hearings in July and November 1977. The full committee held its hearings in August. The House International Relations Committee held hearings in September and October, while the House Armed Services Committee held theirs in late October. In the Senate, the Foreign Relations Committee held the most extensive hearings of all, from September 26 to October 19 and in January 1978. The Senate Subcommittee on the Separation of Powers of the Judiciary Committee held sporadic hearings in July, September, October, and November

1977. The Senate Armed Services Committee held the last series of hearings from January 24 to February 1, 1978.[21]

On August 18, 1977, three opposition senators traveled to Panama to question people there. This began the most significant aspect of the treaty procedure outside the floor action in the Senate. Before the treaties were approved, 42 senators and numerous staff as well as a number of congressmen traveled to Panama to talk to people, to see the canal in operation, and to investigate various aspects of the treaties.

In a very real sense, this activity constituted a second negotiation phase for the treaties. Many of the senators met with Panama's leader, Omar Torrijos, to discuss specific aspects of the treaties, various amendments, and reservations to the treaties that could be proposed without killing them. This constituted an innovative element in treaty negotiation process.[22]

A good example of this is found in Senator Howard Baker's special report to the Senate in January 1978.

> During intensive discussions with General Torrijos at Farallon, the delegation advised General Torrijos that the treaties as submitted to the Senate had no chance of obtaining the Senate's consent to ratification. He was further advised that there might be enough flexibility in the Senate to secure consent to ratification were guarantees of United States rights more clearly spelled out in the treaties by way of amendment. In particular, reference was made to the need to incorporate the language of the Statement of Understanding previously issued by General Torrijos and President Carter into the text of the treaties with regard to the United States' right to defend the Canal after the year 2000 and to secure priority passage in time of emergency. Torrijos indicated that he was open-minded with regard to modifications of the treaty. . . .[23]

This statement clearly indicates the real nature of the type of negotiations that took place between General Torrijos and a number of senators who visited Panama between August 1977 and April 1978.

Prior to completing their report and making their recommendations, the Senate Foreign Relations Committee held 15 days of hearings and heard 92 witnesses, including 17 members of Congress. Ten of the fifteen committee members traveled to Panama and discussed the treaties with General Torrijos and other American and Panamanian leaders.

Another unique procedural feature of the approval process was incorporated in the Senate Committee of Foreign Relations Report on the treaties. Usually in such a report any recommendations of the committee are included in the resolutions of ratification. But in order to allow the committee to make its views known and, at the same time, allow all the members of the Senate maximum participation in shaping the treaties and their consent to them, the committee merely included its recommendations in the full report.

The committee does not view the procedure as a precedent-setting departure from established procedure. Quite the contrary—the committee views the procedures as *unique,* but one which is necessitated because the situation posed by the consideration of the Panama Canal treaties is in *many ways unique.*[24]

The committee report procedure was followed by an unprecedented 38 days of continuous debate. This was the second longest treaty debate in the history of the Senate except for the debate on the Treaty of Versailles after World War I. In addition, the Senate debate was broadcast live to radio stations in both the United States and Panama.

The procedure used in the floor debate was also unusual. For over 50 years, debate had taken place on the ratification resolution on a treaty as a whole. Senator James Allen (D-Ala), however, reinstituted the "Committee of the Whole Senate" procedure in order that each article of the treaties could be debated and amended on a one by one basis. The procedure more commonly followed requires unanimous consent of the Senate before it can be used in the deliberation phase, and yet it has been the sole process used for treaty ratification since 1922. On these treaties, however, Senator Allen refused to consent to this customary procedure and forced the Senate to consider the treaties one at a time and article by article.[25]

Over 50 amendments and amendments to amendments were considered and voted upon by the Senate on both treaties. Of these, only the two so-called leadership amendments, which incorporated the Carter-Torrijos Statement of Understanding into the Neutrality Treaty, were adopted. In addition to the amendments, about 30 conditions, reservations and understandings were proposed and voted on, and 21 were finally adopted.

In total the Senate considered and voted on nearly 90 such changes and alterations in the treaty.[26] Through these amendments, conditions, understandings, reservations, and amendments to amendments, the Senate did alter the treaties and took a much more active role in the "advice and consent" stage of the treaties than it had done since they rejected the Treaty of Versailles in 1919-1920. Participation to this extent in the treaty approval process is unparalled in the history of treaty-making in the United States.

The Neutrality Treaty was the first of the treaties to be approved. The final vote occurred on March 16; then, on April 18, 1978, the vote on the Resolution of Ratification of the Canal Treaty was taken and resulted in exactly the same (68-32) approval that had been tallied on the March 16 vote. But this did not end congressional action with regard to the treaties. The implementation legislation still had to be introduced and passed by both houses of Congress. The uphill battle for the treaties was to last through most of 1978 as well as 1979.

MAJOR ACTION ON THE TREATIES

The major issue of the defense of the canal worried a number of senators. From the date of implementation until the year 2000 there would be few problems; but, after the termination of the Canal Treaty, the Neutrality Treaty would take effect. The general feeling was that the United States should have the written right to intervene to protect or open the canal if necessary beyond the year 2000 and that, to make such defense easier, the United States should continue to have at least one military base within Panama. These issues resulted in hours of debate and the introduction of a number of amendments, conditions, and reservations to the treaties.

Neutrality Treaty

First Leadership Amendment. One of the two amendments passed and attached to the Neutrality Treaty concerns the issue of defense. The so-called leadership amendment, co-sponsored by Senators Byrd and Baker and 75 other senators, was a verbatim portion of the Statement of Understanding agreed upon by President Carter and General Torrijos on October 14, 1977. This amendment provided that each country could defend the canal against any threat to it or its neutrality in accordance with their own constitutional processes. This amendment was adopted on March 9, 1978, by a vote of 84 to 5.

DeConcini Reservations. In contrast to the leadership amendment which had the support of the administration and the approval of Panama, the introduction and passage of the DeConcini reservation came very close to killing both treaties, causing great alarm in both countries, resulting in a substantial loss of treaty support in Panama and very difficult problems for the Carter administration. (Although this addition to the treaty is popularly referred to as a reservation, it was technically entitled a "condition" which carries more force; nevertheless, we use the more commonly used term of "reservation" in this chapter.) The DeConcini reservation provided that, if the canal were closed for any reasons, either the United States or Panama could take the steps necessary, including the use of military force, to reopen it or put it back in operation.[27]

According to authoritative sources, it was never Senator DeConcini's (D-Ariz) intent to kill the treaties. Like many other senators, he believed that the treaties needed some changes in order to make them more acceptable to the United States Senate and the public at large. Also, like many other senators, he was under great pressure from his constituency (which, incidentally, was still not satisfied even after his recommendation was approved but started a recall move against him in Arizona after the final votes on the treaties were taken).

Apparently, working pretty much on their own, Senator DeConcini and his staff drafted a number of amendments, resolutions, and conditions to be added to the treaties. The one mentioned above became one of the more popular ones and was consequently seriously considered. Once real consideration on the treaties began, the staff along with the senator presented the wording to specific individuals in the administration and in the State Department. The State Department seemed more concerned with the status of the change—whether it would be introduced as an amendment or as a reservation, an understanding or a condition—than with the specific wording. The wording was worked out and approved by both the Department of State and White House staff before going to the floor of the Senate.[28] Senator DeConcini stated that he even cleared it with President Carter.[29] On the floor, the reservation met with phenomenal support and was finally adopted by a vote of 75 to 23 on March 16, 1978, the last day of the debate on the Neutrality Treaty. Support for the Neutrality Treaty was thereby enhanced and it was approved on the same day. This reservation was strengthened by the Hayakawa "understanding" that was also adopted on March 16. It stated that either party could take *unilateral* action to defend the canal and maintain its neutrality.[30]

It was only after the adoption of these two additions to the treaties that it became apparent to the State Department that the Panamanians could not live with these reservations, worded as they were. The Panamanians found the DeConcini wording to be "offensive" and "imperialistic." Some of the strongest treaty supporters in the Panamanian business community began to alter their support and raise questions concerning the ratification process. The leftists in Panama found the reservation to be a central issue and painted walls all over Panama calling for the rejection of the treaties and especially the DeConcini "amendment."

Before the passage of this reservation, it was expected that the main issues in the Senate debate concerning the Canal Treaty would be defense, military bases, and implementation costs. But because of the DeConcini change, much of the effort between March 16 and April 18 centered on the attempts by the administration and the Senate leadership to find a compromise position that would be acceptable to Panama, the U.S. Senate, and the State Department. In a very real sense, the DeConcini reservation became the main issue, and some of the other considerations slipped into the background and were never treated in the depth that their importance indicated.

In the last few days before the final vote was taken, on the Panama Canal Treaty, DeConcini, along with the leadership of the Senate and the Foreign Relations Committee, met with White House people and Departments of Defense and State staffs and negotiated directly with representatives from Panama to attempt to resolve the problems created by the DeConcini reservation. This action placed these senators in the direct diplomatic role of actually negotiating this aspect of the settlement with Panama. These negotiations resulted in a compromise resolution.

Despite these discussions between the branches of government and the Panamanians, the Senate leadership had to convince the State Department and the White House to refrain from trying to sell this compromise to the Senate or to Senator DeConcini. The Senate leadership, on its own, believed that it could better convince fellow senators to support the compromise.

Resolution number 36 (Byrd, Baker, DeConcini, et al.), which was this carefully worded compromise, was adopted just before the final vote on the Canal Treaty on April 18, 1978. It softened the DeConcini reservation and assured Panama that any U.S. effort to reopen the canal or put it back into operation would not become an excuse for intervention into the internal affairs of Panama or to interfere with their "political independence" or "sovereign integrity." This language made the DeConcini reservation more acceptable to Panama. It also helped to ensure the passage of the treaty by the Senate. The Canal Treaty then passed the Senate on April 18, by the same vote that the Neutrality Treaty had passed by March 16.

Defense Reservations. The other aspect of the defense issue that disturbed so many senators was that the United States had made no arrangement to keep military bases within Panama after the year 2000. It appeared to many that, if the United States were going to continue to play a role in the defense of the canal, at least one military base should have been assured us in the treaties.

Senator Sam Nunn (D-Ga) was joined by Senator Herman T. Talmadge (D-Ga) is providing the compromise reservation (Condition #8) on this issue. It was approved on March 14, 1978, just two days before the vote on the Neutrality Treaty. This reservation provided that nothing in the treaty "would" preclude Panama and the United States from making agreements or arrangements for the stationing of U.S. military forces or the maintenance of U.S. defense sites in Panama after December 31, 1999.[31] Because of Senator Nunn's membership on the Armed Services Committee, his support of the treaty had a significant influence on other senators and added credibility to the proponents' argument that passage of the treaties would not be detrimental to U.S. defense and national security. According to Senator Nunn's office, this reservation was critical for his support and the support of at least three other uncommitted senators.[32]

It was opportunities such as this to alter the treaties and suggest changes which saved them, as this process allowed everyone to respond to the treaties, to improve them, to make them more acceptable and clear, and to obtain some political mileage for themselves. The end result also made the treaties more palatable to the American people and made Senate approval possible.

Although Senator Nunn's reservation was passed, some Senators believed that it did not go far enough. Senator Edward Zorinsky (D-Neb), for example, expressed the desire to have included in the Neutrality Treaty a provision guaranteeing a continued U.S. presence in Panama. Although he was a supporter and co-sponsor of the Nunn reservation and had been lobbied by the White House almost to excess, he did not accept the treaties in their final form and voted against both of them.[33]

Second Leadership Amendment. The only other amendment to the treaties to be passed was another leadership amendment on the Neutrality Treaty. It also came from the "Statement of Understanding" and dealt with emergency and expeditious passage of U.S. and Panamanian warships and auxiliary vessels. It gave them the right to go to the head of the line during an emergency. This amendment, like the other one, was co-sponsored by Senators Byrd and Baker and over 75 other senators. This amendment also had President Carter's support and General Torrijos' approval. It was adopted on March 10, 1978, by a vote of 85 to 3. This amendment was further strengthened by the Chafee, et al. understanding (number 13) which allowed each respective nation to unilaterally determine the need for emergency passage.[34] The only other major "understanding" attached to the Neutrality Treaty dealt with toll charges after the year 2000, and stated that these charges would have to be "just, reasonable, equitable, and consistent with international law."

Canal Treaty

There were no amendments attached to the Canal Treaty; nevertheless, a number of reservations, conditions, and understandings were added to it. The modification of the DeConcini reservation to the Neutrality Treaty, already mentioned, was one of the most important. An economic reservation was added which stated that nothing in the treaty or any other accompanying document would obligate the United States to any level of economic or military assistance to Panama.[35] This same understanding had been added to the Neutrality Treaty also and was a result of President Carter's and the Department of State's additional agreements, outside of the treaties, to provide both economic and military assistance to Panama in the amount of $345 million.[36] This understanding was added to the treaty to force the administration to bring such requests for aid through the regular channels of Congress. The first such request was brought to Congress in early 1979. Both houses responded and voted to cut all economic and military assistance to Panama out of the foreign aid and military aid budgets.

One very important procedural change in the treaties was submitted by Senator Brooke of Massachusetts. Ir affected the dates for implementation of the treaties, stating that the ratification of the Canal Treaty was not to be effective before March 31, 1979 and no later than October 1, 1979. This change allowed time for Congress to introduce, to study, and to pass the implementation legislation for the treaty. This length of time proved to be very necessary as the implementation legislation was not approved until September 26, 1979.

MAJOR ACTORS

Treaty Proponents

A number of individual senators, both proponents and opponents of the treaties, played very significant roles in the approval of the treaties and in the many attempts to block that approval. Some were Senate leaders, but many were not.

Although Senator John Sparkman (D-Ala) was chairman of the Senate Foreign Relations Committee, freshman Senator Paul S. Sarbanes (D-Md) played a critical role as floor leader of debate on the treaties. He was praised by Senate Majority Leader Robert Byrd (D-W. Va) for his "dedication to the working of debating, defending, and improving the treaties." According to Byrd, he did an extremely good job.[37] His dedication and thoughtfulness were illustrated by the fact that he was one of the few senators on the Foreign Relations Committee to attend most of their hearings on the treaties. He questioned the witnesses thoroughly, but never revealed his own position until the committee began marking up the treaties in January 1978. Once he announced his support for the treaties, he—along with Senator Frank Church (D-Ida.)—was given the task of managing the floor action on the treaties.[38]

Whereas Senator Sarbanes was the "quiet" floor manager, Senator Church played a very vocal role in the presentations and debates of the treaties. Senator Robert Byrd played one of the most important roles of all. He was called upon for many different tasks. He led the Democrats, he convinced many of them to back the treaty, and he obtained support from a number of key Republicans. He influenced the White House and even urged the President to give his first fireside chat on the treaties. Senator Byrd also headed off a number of situations which, if they had been allowed to develop, would have killed the treaties.

Minority Leader Howard H. Baker (R-Tenn) also played a critical role. Senator Baker's support and ability to convince other Republicans to support the treaties was decisive with respect to eventual passage. Without this support, the treaties would have been rejected.

Senators Byrd and Baker sponsored the so-called leadership amendments to the Neutrality Treaty which incorporated the Carter-Torrijos "Statement of Understanding" into the treaty. Senator Baker negotiated directly with

President Torrijos in Panama on this condition. He told President Torrijos that without these amendments, the treaties would not be approved by the Senate.[39] President Torrijos thereupon agreed to having the amendments attached to the treaties. Senator Baker helped greatly to get these amendments included in the treaties. He also played an important role on the DeConcini reservation along with Senator Byrd as mentioned above.

Treaty Opponents

There were as many reasons for opposition to the treaties as there were opponents to them, but two main groups seem to emerge in this study. In the first group were those who rejected some specific aspects of one of the treaties or the other. For example, Senator Zorinsky was in this group. Senators Cannon, Abourezk, and Hayakawa almost joined Senator Zorinsky but were won over to the supporter's side at the last minute.

The other group of opposition senators, led by Senator James Allen (D-Ala), were against the whole concept of altering the status quo in the Canal Zone or of ever relinquishing the control and/or the defense of the canal itself. They used a number of sophisticated strategies and offered countless amendments and reservations to the treaties in order to block their final passage. Although some of these so-called "killer" amendments met with significant support, none were accepted and most were rejected by more than 34 senators, the number needed to block the treaties in the final two-thirds vote.

Senator Allen led a brilliant parliamentary battle. He was the one who insisted that the treaties be debated by using the old procedure which allowed each article of each treaty to be debated and amended on the floor. Senator Allen also introduced several reservations and amendments to the treaties themselves, as well as changes in other senator's amendments and reservations.

Senator Paul Laxalt (R-Nev) also strongly opposed the treaties. He stated that he could find no reason to support ratification, but found many reasons for opposing it.[40] He also organized and participated in the so-called "truth squad" which traveled around the country and mobilized public opposition to the treaties. Senators Robert Griffin Orrin Hatch (R-Utah), Jessie Helms (R-N.C.), and Robert Dole (R-Kan) were the principal senators to join with Senators Allen and Laxalt in their campaign against the treaties. Although each seemed to have his pet area of opposition, each was against giving up the operation of the canal and control of the Canal Zone under any circumstances.

Political Costs

The destruction of political careers is another interesting aspect of the treaty-approval process. A number of senators were hurt by their votes for the Panama

Canal Treaties. It is difficult to say whether this single issue was the decisive one in their failure to be reelected, but it was definitely one of the main issues in the defeat of William D. Hathaway (D-Maine), Paul Hatfield (D-Mont), Dick Clark (D-Iowa), Floyd K. Haskell (D-Colo), Thomas McIntyre (D-N.H.), and Edward Brooke (R-Mass). Some senators, e.g., Charles Percy (R-Ill), were also hurt politically by their vote for the treaties but they were, nevertheless, re-elected.

Thomas McIntyre was probably the senator hurt most by this single issue. A number of people on the Hill pointed to him as the one who the opponents "got" because of his support for the treaties. In his concession statement on election night he acknowledged the impact of this single issue:

> Some will say that my votes on issues like the Panama Canal Treaties cost me this election. And they may be right. But when I voted for the treaties I said I did so because I believed they were in the best interests of our country. I still believe that, and I am confident that time will prove me right.[41]

Opposition to the treaties was vehement and most senators who voted for them lost electoral support. A proponent of the treaties gained little politically by supporting them. But, on the other hand, his support earned him a hard core of permanent opponents whose hostility would continue for years. James W. Symington summed up this situation quite eloquently when he wrote: "Opponents [of the treaties] can win standing ovations, supporters at best 'adequate reflection.' . . . It is easier to bring a crowd to its feet than to its senses."[42]

Treaty Lobbyists

The New Right was well organized and extremely well financed. Eight organizations were the most active, including the American Conservative Union, the Conservative Caucus, the Committee for the Survival of a Free Congress, Citizens for the Republic, the American Security Council, Young Republicans, the National Conservative Political Action Committee, and the Council for National Defense. The American Conservative Union alone sent out nearly 2 million mailings and spent over $600,000, while the Conservative Caucus sent another 2 million pieces of mail and raised over $800,000 to defeat the treaties.[43]

Senator McIntyre quotes from Howard Phillips, National Director of the Conservative Caucus, to show how revenge and fear tactics would be used against anyone who dared vote against them. "We organize discontent. . . . We must prove our ability to get revenge on people who go against us. . . . We'll be after them, if they vote the wrong way. We're not going to stop after the vote's past."[44]

Lobbying on the proponents' side was also intense, although they were much less active than the conservative groups and had much smaller budgets. A group of prominent treaty supporters organized the Committee of Americans for the Canal Treaties, Inc. The committee included such people as former President Ford, Mrs. L. B. Johnson, and George Meany. New Directions, a liberal-leaning foreign policy group, organized the Committee for the Ratification of the Panama Canal Treaties. This group focused its activities at the state and local levels. Although they had a budget of only $19,000, New Directions paid mailing costs of close to $200,000.[45] The White House and the State Department also sent out their own staff people to attempt to build grass-roots support for the treaties. Officials participated in over 700 forums on the issues, but most of their activities centered around the Washington D.C. area and on television shows.

Despite these efforts, the polls continued to indicate that the majority of adult Americans opposed ratification of the treaties. They also showed that the American people were very unaware of facts concerning the canal and the treaties. Those who understood some of the specifics of the treaties indicated more support than opposition.[46] Communications to senators and congressmen, mostly in the form of letters were well over 50 percent in strong opposition to the treaties.

CANAL TREATY IMPLEMENTATION LEGISLATION[47]

The House keyed in on the above mentioned negative sentiments and continued to fight the treaties even after the Senate approved of them by a two-thirds vote and they were ratified and exchanged by the United States and Panama. When the Canal Treaty implementation legislation was introduced into the House in January 1979, the House took this opportunity to get the revenge it sought. In March of that year, the House voted to cut off most military aid to Panama. Just one week later (on April 5), the House voted to prohibit nearly all economic aid to Panama.

The administration bill for the treaty implementation (HR1716) was assigned to four House Committees: Foreign Affairs, Merchant Marine and Fisheries, Judiciary, and Post Office and Civil Service. Beyond this complication, two additional House bills were also introduced. The most important of these was the so-called Murphy Bill (HR111) authored by John M. Murphy (D-NY), Chairman of the Merchant Marine and Fisheries Committee. The administration bill was attacked, amended, and strongly criticized in the various committees. Although it was finally reported out of these four committees, it suffered a final blow when, on April 26, 1979, the House Rules Committee rejected the administration's bill in favor the Murphy Bill. The Rules Committee did, however, also reject the third proposed bill (HR 3656) sponsored by Congressman George Hansen (R-Ida).[48] The administration suffered a further setback when floor debate on the Murphy Bill, which the White House strongly disliked but had to back, had to be postponed from mid-May to June due to lack of House support even for this bill. In over five hours of debate on May 21, both treaty opponents and supporters attacked the administration and accused President Carter and his aides of misleading them and even lying to Congress on the impact of the treaties and especially on the costs of implementation.[49]

The Murphy Bill was finally adopted by the House on June 21, 1979. Nevertheless, the administration and many senators believed that the bill violated the treaties. Leading Panamanians were convinced of the fact. President Aristides Royo of Panama reacted to the Murphy Bill by sending a very lengthy letter to President Carter. The letter accused the United States and the Murphy Bill of being offensive and in direct conflict with the treaties. He cited nearly 30 articles of the bill that he saw as lacking conformity to the treaty or that were in direct contradiction to it. He went on to detail his criticism article by article and to state that if this bill were adopted, it would raise important legal questions and create havoc with the implementation of the treaties, as Panama would be forced to reject it.[50]

The U.S. Senate, in its consideration of the implementation legislation, did not include the offensive articles found in the House version and worked on a bill that was much closer to the administration position (S-1024). Unlike the House, the Senate leadership referred this bill to only one committee, Armed Services. Hearings were held on June 26 and 27; and, on July 17, the committee reported on a compromise bill that combined provisions of both (HR111) and (S-1024). The bill was then approved by a committee vote of 9 to 8. The Senate continued to expedite the legislation by passing this compromise bill on the floor on July 26, 1979 by a vote of 64 to 30.

The quick passage of the implementation legislation in the Senate was due to two major factors. First, the Senate had dealt with the treaties in 1978 and few wanted a repeat performance. To most of them, the treaties were now the law of the land and should be implemented. Senator Stennis' role in the process is a good example of this. He fought against and voted against the treaties in 1978, but he led the fight in the conference committee for rational compromise between the House and Senate versions for implementation in the summer of 1979.

The second factor contributing to rapid Senate action was the active and thorough role played by two freshman senators, Carl Levin (D-Mich) and J. J. Exon (D-Neb.). These two men did their homework well and worked out the compromise Senate version of the legislation. The implementing costs were their principal concern. They tried to reduce costs without causing major conflicts with any of the provisions of the treaty. Their bill was actually less costly to the U.S. taxpayer than the Murphy Bill that passed the House. Their preparation, knowledge, and ability played a significant role in the Senate's rapid consideration and passage of the Senate version and its subsequent approval of the House and Senate conference report.[51]

The House however, continued to react negatively to the whole issue. On July 30 by a vote of 308-98, the House advised their conferees, by a non-binding mandate, not to compromise the main aspects of their version of the legislation.[52] This brought a strong response from Senator Stennis (D-Miss), Chairman of the Senate Armed Services Committee, and conference committee chairman. He told the House members that if they were not there to negotiate, he would cancel the conference committee. He stated that he would not be pressured by the House advisory vote and that both sides must be willing to negotiate and compromise or there was no reason to hold the conference. He further stated that the Senate members were not going to be stampeded by the House and they would not let the House destroy what had taken so long to put together.[53] The House conferees thereupon agreed to these ground rules. With the ground rules set, the Congress recessed for the month of August. By mid-September the conference committee completed its task and the committee report was submitted to the two houses for their action.

The Senate immediately approved the report. The House got back into its refractory mood when it rejected the conference report on September 20, by a vote of 203 to 192. The House continued to extract revenge on the Senate and on the administration by continued intransigence against implementation. The representatives also continued to orchestrate their actions for the people back home. Finally, with only four days left before the treaties took effect, the House voted on a modified conference report and opened the way for a presidential signature and actual implementation of the 1977 treaty. On September 26, 1979, by a vote of 232 to 188, the House finally approved the legislation. These House actions increased the already strained relationship between the House and the Senate. Their relationship was strained during much of 1978 and, according to some Senate staffers, was more acute than the difficult relationship between the Senate and the administration.[54]

The Panama Canal treaties were not the only issues to separate the House and the Senate in 1979. The strain between the two houses of Congress surfaced again only two days after the treaty implementation bill was passed in the House. This time it was over disagreement on the fiscal 1980 budget.

IMPACT UPON THE ADMINISTRATION

If these treaties are not ratified, then the United States will have lost its place as the moral leader of the community of nations. Our President will have lost credibility as a national and international leader.[55]

These ideas, expressed above by Senator Long, were of the greatest concern to the Carter administration. Many other senators, numerous news writers, and commentators also expressed this same notion. If the President lost the treaty vote, he would lose credibility and acceptance as an international negotiator and leader. To prevent this, the White House and the State Department fiercely lobbied the Senate. The President himself personally contacted, met with, and tried to pursuade individual senators to support the treaties.

This effort was necessitated by the fact that so many senators remained uncommitted during the "advice and consent" process. In late November 1977, UPI published a poll that indicated that there were 37 uncommitted senators and another 16 that were only leaning toward approval or disapproval. As late as March 2, there were at least 13 and as many as 20 uncommitted senators.[56]

During March and April, President Carter ". . . threw virtually every high official of his administration and the nation's defense and foreign policy establishment into the fray. . . ."[57] Yet, just two days before the Neutrality Treaty came to a vote, only 62 senators were sure they would vote for it.[58] By this stage, charges and accusations of vote buying began to circulate throughout the Senate. Senator Robert Packwood (R-Ore) was quoted as saying that he was "disgusted" with the deals President Carter was making to get votes. He accused the President of playing "let's make a deal."[59]

Stories began to appear regarding specific deals made with individual senators in order to assure their support for the treaties. It was said that Senator Talmadge obtained a change in administration opposition to a $2.3 billion emergency farm bill. In order to obtain Senator DeConcini's vote, the White House supposedly reversed itself and supported a plan for the government to purchase $250 million worth of copper. Senator Jennings Randolf of West Virginia stated that the President had done all he could for him, and Senator Walter Huddleston (D-Ky) mentioned that the White House had been "very friendly." Another senator responded that "I expect he'd promise me anything I asked."[60]

Supposedly, other senators were also approached. According to Senator Gary Hart of Colorado, some of the senators who voted for the treaties believed that . . . "they have a chip to cash in the future." Others stated that the President gave out many IOU's in order to gain victory on the vote.[61] In addition, Time Magazine also indicated that special deals were also made with Senators Sam Nunn, Russell Long and Howard Cannon.[62]

Despite these rumors and accusations, Senate staffs interviewed for this study consistently denied that these types of deals had really made any difference. Most of them were of the strong opinion that vote buying had been at a minimum and that the reports of such were media–created and not an accurate reflection of what had occurred in the Senate.[63]

The victory on the final votes was hard-won and came with a number of costs as well as benefits. Many senators believed that the administration handled the whole thing very poorly. Others maintained that the President had learned much from the experience. The victory gave the administration a boost in morale, but it did not give it any long-term momentum or produce much positive spillover on other key problems and issues.[64] In many ways, the cost was very high with regard to the House of Representatives. The bitterness and feelings of revenge were evident when the implementation legislation worked its way through the process in 1979. This high level of criticism, negativism, and malice probably had as much or more negative spillover as did the victory on the positive side. One Democratic leader in Congress expressed the situation aptly by stating that, "The main thing about the Panama vote is that it is damage limitation. It protected the President from a disastrous defeat."[65]

If the Senate had voted against the treaties, it would have been a disastrous defeat indeed. Bitter recrimination between the White House and Congress would have followed. There would have been violent anti-American demonstrations in Latin America and, no doubt, there would have been an outpouring of nationalism in Panama resulting in violence, property destruction, deaths, and perhaps direct assaults on the canal itself.

The administration had a contingency plan ready for such a possibility. The President planned to meet with Senate leaders to consider the military and defense consequences. An air and sea-lift of military reinforcements to the zone was planned. All Latin American diplomatic missions would be placed on alert, and, finally, the President was to appeal over radio and television to the nation and to Panama to maintain peace and order.[66]

Despite the fact that the vote on the canal treaties did not give the President a vote of confidence nor help him to resolve many of his other problems or conflicts with the Congress, it did prevent a national and international crisis; and, due to this fact, it can definitely be defined as a major victory.

CONCLUSIONS

A number of rather unique circumstances are revealed by this study. Unlike most foreign policy (where Congress plays only a peripheral role), on decisions related to the Panama Canal, Congress has always had a significant and continual impact; and all negotiations with Panama have had to keep this consideration in the forefront.[67] Secondly, the American people were strongly against any change in the status quo of the canal and the Canal Zone, and they continued their adamant antagonism to the treaties throughout the whole process. Despite attempts made by the President to go directly to the people to obtain support for the treaties, public opinion remained firmly against them and one of the heaviest mailings to Congress continued unabated.

Although Senate leadership from both parties favored treaty passage, a large number of senators remained uncommitted right up to the final days when the votes were taken. This situation forced President Carter and his staff to make countless personal contacts with these senators, promises had to be made, and rumors circulated that a number of deals were made to assure sufficient votes for treaty passage. This was not merely the result of a resurgent Congress, as even more assertive Presidents have had to make concessions on the Panama Canal. For example, the fear of failure on the floor of the Senate forced President Lyndon B. Johnson to completely withhold his three negotiated treaties from the Senate in 1967.

The fragmentation and weakness of party leadership was also evident. Although the bipartisan support by the Senate leadership played a crucial role in the submission and passage of the "leadership" amendments and in extricating the Senate from the corner that the DeConcini reservation had painted them into, they had real problems delivering the final votes for passage. They, like the executive, had to make promises and had to use their influence at every turn. This required heavy outlays of time, personal commitment, and consistent watchfulness.

Negative political costs were also high. Some senators lost considerable electoral approval due to their support of the treaties. The hours of debate and compromise; the problems created by Senate changes in the treaties; and the open attacks on Panama, the Panamanian people, and President Torrijos created negative results. Increased good will in Panama and throughout Latin America that could have resulted from treaty passage was lost during much of the process. Increased antagonism between the House and Senate also occurred over the way the treaties were handled.

If the treaties would have been rejected, the result could have been disastrous to American national interests. There would have been an increase in threats of violence to the canal, and there was a real possibility of transit interruption, property damage, and loss of life. On the other hand, a treaty less favorable to Panama and more popular in the United States would never have been approved by the Panamanians. Both sides were very close to maximizing their own position and minimizing the concessions with which they could politically survive.

The President's position in national and international leadership was also weakened by the whole process. His appeal to the public at large failed, he could not marshal Senate votes, and the Senate leadership had to save him from disaster. Failures continued as the House refused to pass the implementation legislation. Killer amendments on the treaties and alterations on implementation legislation threatened to destroy the final product time and time again. To obtain the two-thirds vote in the Senate was extremely difficult; to also obtain a majority vote in the House almost proved impossible.

Perhaps, in our troubled times, the treaty approval process may be too difficult. With strong public opinion based on ignorance, a proliferation of strong and active interest groups, weak leadership in Congress, and a weakened executive; the whole treaty process may be so onerous that controversial treaties in the future will seldom be able to be ratified.

NOTES

1. Thomas A. Bailey, *A Diplomatic History of the American People,* 7th Ed. (New York: Appleton-Century-Crofts, 1964), pp. 487–88.
2. Philippe Bunau-Varilla, *From Panama to Verdun: My Fight for France* (Philadelphia: Dorrance, 1940), pp. 158–59.
3. *Congressional Quarterly Weekly,* Vol XXV, August 4, 1967. p. 1351, and August 18, 1967, p. 1627.
4. U.S., Congress, Senate, Committee on the Judiciary, Subcommittee on Separation of Powers, *Panama Canal Treaties: U.S. Senate Debate 1977-78,* 95th Congress, 1978, Part 1, pp. 4-9. (Hereinafter referred to as *Panama Canal Treaties.*)
5. U.S., Congress, Senate, Committee on Foreign Relations, *Senate Debate on the Panama Canal Treaties: A Compendium of Major Statements, Documents, Record Votes and Relevant Events,* 96th Cong., 1st sess., February 1979, pp. 73-74. (Hereinafter referred to as *Senate Debate.*)
6. In August of 1978, the author interviewed people involved with the treaty in the State Department and Senate staffs of over 20 Senators in Washington, D.C. As most of them preferred not to be quoted, I will merely use the reference of "Interviews" throughout this paper.
7. Ibid.
8. Bunau-Varilla, *From Panama to Verdun,* p. 159; Walter LeFeber, *The Panama Canal* (expanded ed.) (New York: Oxford University Press, 1979), pp. 34-46.
9. U.S., Congress, Senate, Committee on the Judiciary, Subcommittee on Separation of Powers, *The Proposed Panama Canal Treaties: A Digest of Information,* 95th Cong., 2nd sess., 1978, p. 165.
10. U.S., Congress, Senate, Committee on Foreign Relations, *A Chronology of Events Relative to Panama Canal,* 95th Cong., 1st sess., 1977, p. 29.
11. *New York Times,* May 16, 1978, p. 20.
12. *Washington Post,* September 4, 1977, p. A-3; September 7, 1977, pp. 1, 12.
13. *Senate Debate,* p. 190.
14. Ibid., p. 97.
15. Ibid.
16. Ibid.
17. U.S., Congress, Senate, Committee on Foreign Relations, *Hearings Before the Committee on Foreign Relations on the Panama Canal Treaties,* 95th Cong., 1st sess., 1977. (Hereinafter referred to as *Hearings.*)

18. Ibid., Part I, p. 11.
19. Ibid., Part III, pp. 126–42.
20. *Senate Debate*, pp. 292–342.
21. Ibid., p. 6.
22. The reader will discover that some of the data, the conditions and the occurrences reported in this chapter are similar to some of those reported by Cecil Y. Crabb & Pat M. Holt in their chapter on the Panama Canal Treaties in *An Invitation to Struggle: Congress, the President and Foreign Policy*, Washington, D.C.: CQ Press, 1980. Because we were looking at similar data for reasons not dissimilar, it is not too surprising that through mutually independent research we would use some of the same facts and activities. I have included references to their work where similarities occur despite the fact that I did not use their book in the research and writing of this chapter.
23. U.S., Congress, Senate, Committee on Foreign Relations, *Panama Canal Treaties: Report*, 95th Cong., 2nd sess., February 3, 1978, pp. 5–6. (Hereinafter referred to as *Senate Report*.)
24. Ibid., pp. 3–4, emphasis added.
25. U.S. Congress, *The Congressional Record*, 95th Congress, 2nd sess., February 1978, p. S-1498.
26. *Senate Debate*, p. 11.
27. For a different treatment of the DeConcini reservation problem see Cecil V. Crabb and Pat M. Holt *Invitation to Struggle: Congress, the President and Foreign Policy*, Washington, D.C.: CQ Press, 1980, pp. 78–80. And see Thomas M. Franck and Edward Weisband *Foreign Policy By Congress*. (New York: Oxford University Press, 1979), pp. 275–286.
28. Interviews.
29. "Panama Canal Treaties: Major Carter Victory," *Congressional Quarterly Almanac*, 1978, p. 393.
30. Interviews.
31. Ibid., pp. 398–99.
32. Interviews.
33. Ibid.
34. *Senate Debate*, pp. 374, 407.
35. Ibid., pp. 469, 548.
36. *Panama Canal Treaties*, Part II, pp. 3818–20.
37. David M. Maxfield, "Sarbanes: The Quiet Worker in the Canal Debate," *Congressional Quarterly Weekly*, April 22, 1978, p. 953.
38. Ibid.
39. U.S., Congress, Senate, *Report of Delegation Studying the Panama Canal Treaties and Other Matters of Interest to the U.S. in Latin America*, 95th Cong., 2nd sess., Senate Document 95-80, 1978.
40. *Hearings*, Part II, pp. 193–204.
41. Thomas J. McIntyre, *The Fear Brokers*, (New York: Pilgrim Press, 1979), p. xii.
42. James W. Symington, "The Canal: Use Not Territory is the Issue," *Washington Post*, September 2, 1977, p. A-27.

43. McIntyre, *The Fear Brokers,* pp. 122–23, 389.
44. Ibid., p. 48.
45. "Panama Canal Treaties: Major Carter Victory," pp. 388–399.
46. Bernard Roshco, "The Polls: Polling on Panama—Si, Don't Know; Hell no!" *Public Opinion Quarterly* 42 (1978): 551–62.
47. See Crabb and Holt, op. cit. pp. 82–85.
48. *Congressional Quarterly Weekly,* April 28, 1978, p. 806.
49. Ibid., May 26, 1979, p. 1008.
50. Article in newspaper, *Matatino,* July 16, 1979, pp. 8-a, 9-a.
51. Interviews.
52. *New York Times,* July 31, 1979, p. 5.
53. Interviews.
54. Ibid.
55. Panama Canal Treaties, Part II, p. 3643.
56. *Congressional Quarterly Weekly,* March 4, 1978, p. 563.
57. Ibid., p. 678.
58. Adam Clymes, "Canal Pact Support Still Short of Goal," *New York Times,* March 15, 1978, p. 6.
59. Ibid.
60. Martin Tolchin, "White House Woos Holdouts on Canal," *New York Times,* March 14, 1978, pp. 1, 7.
61. "Carter's Panama Triumph—What it Cost," *U.S. News and World Report,* March 27, 1978, pp. 27–28.
62. *Time,* March 27, 1978, p. 8. Also Crabb and Holt, *An Invitation to Struggle,* pp. 80–82.
63. Interviews.
64. Hedrick Smith, "After Panama, More Battles," *New York Times,* April 20, 1978, pp. 1, 8.
65. Ibid.
66. James Reston, "Carter's Nightmare," *New York Times,* April 21, 1978, p. 27.
67. Franck and Weisband agree partially with my conclusions. They also conclude that the President has to work closely with congressional leadership and staff. But we disagree on the strength of Senate leadership and we disagree on the issue that the President needed to get the Congress more involved in the treaty negotiations. My findings indicate that the administration attempted this time and time again, but that Congress refused to give anything but negative input throughout the whole process. Little of a constructive nature was given by Congress during the whole 12 years of negotiations.

Chapter 5
Congress as Trojan Horse? The Turkish Embargo Problem, 1974–1978
Keith R. Legg

Henry Kissinger assigned major responsibility for the embargo on military assistance to Turkey to the activities of the Greek-American lobby. Orchestrated by the Foreign Ministry in Athens, Greek-American and others sympathetic to them had mobilized congressional support to further Greek rather than American interests.[1] This is a one-dimensional explanation. Could a handful of Greek-Americans really be responsible for a prohibition on military assistance to a NATO ally in the face of the almost unanimous disapproval of Democratic and Republican congressional leadership, a determined President, as well as a prestigious and calculating Secretary of State? Clearly, the issues were far more complex, the number of interested parties far greater, the stakes far higher, and the perceptions of interest more divergent than Secretary Kissinger's explanation suggests.

The narrow issue of the embargo stemmed from a provision common to agreements between the United States and the recipients of our military assistance—namely, that military equipment we supplied could not be used for aggressive purposes. If violated, this provision directed the President to terminate further assistance.[2] This statutory language engendered little or no discussion when originally included in military assistance authorizations. The question of what precisely constituted aggression has remained cloudy, but the existence of this provision has been used to urge restraint on recipient states with foreign policy goals requiring military action.

This narrow issue can be further subdivided: Why was the administration unwilling to carry out provisions of existing legislation? How were the majorities obtained to force unwanted action on the executive?

The narrow issue led ultimately to the larger institutional issue of executive-legislative relations. Congressional proponents of the embargo on arms to Turkey viewed the issue as one of executive dereliction—the law must be observed. The administration, particularly Secretary of State Kissinger, viewed the embargo legislation as an infringement by Congress on the foreign policy prerogatives of the President, and on the ability of the United States to conduct a rational foreign policy. The strategies utilized by the executive branch to influence the outcome of the narrower issue had the effect of escalating the conflict to the institutional level.[3] At that level, a heterogeneous coalition, led by those representing the Greek-American lobby, could thwart administration preferences and enact the embargo. Eventually, as the personal and political factors that pushed the conflict to the institutional level receded in importance, the coalition weakened and the embargo was lifted.

This chapter is divided into three sections: (1) the participants, their goals and capabilities; (2) the conflict; and (3) the aftermath and conclusion.

CHRONOLOGY

July 15, 1974	Government of Archbishop Makarios in Cyprus is overthrown by coup supported by military government of Greece.
July 20, 1974	Turkish troops invade northern part of Cyprus justifying intervention under 1960 Treaty.
July 22, 1974	Cease-fire on Cyprus.
July 23, 1974	Greek military government collapses, former Prime Minister Karamanlis heads new civilian government.
August 8, 1974	President Nixon resigns.
August 14, 1974	Turks proceed to extend occupation of Cyprus to include nearly 40 percent of the island.
August 15, 1974	Rep. Brademas proposes ban on military assistance to Turkey in meeting with Secretary Kissinger.
September 25, 1974	House of Representatives votes 307–90 for cut-off in military aid.
October 1, 1974	Senate approves by 57–20 vote cut-off in military aid for Turkey.

October 14, 1974	President Ford vetoes spending authorization bill including cut-off in Turkish military aid.
October 17, 1974	President Ford vetoes second authorization bill including cut-off in Turkish military aid. Later the same day, he signs bill that includes postponement of aid cut-off until December 10, 1974.
December 31, 1974	President Ford signs military and economic assistance bill that defers aid cut-off to Turkey until February 5, 1975.
February 5, 1975	Embargo on military aid to Turkey goes into effect.
April 2, 1978	President Carter, reversing previous position, urges end of arms embargo on Turkey.
July 26, 1978	Senate action repeals embargo.
August 2, 1978	House votes end of the embargo.
September 27, 1978	President Carter lifts embargo on arms aid to Turkey.

THE PARTICIPANTS

Participants need to be delineated at several levels. At the "state as actor" level, states are perceived as having capabilities, responsibilities, and goals, and as taking actions. Yet, this level obscures the complexity of the foreign policy process. Organizational conflicts, personal ambitions, and bureaucratic routines are largely ignored. Yet, these aspects of the foreign policy process, when perceived by the Greeks and the Turks, may acquire a substance, even a coherence and rationality. Because of this, the foreign policy process itself may produce consequences unanticipated by American officials. Similarly, policymakers in the United States, both in the executive and Congress, fail to perceive the internal complexities of the foreign policy process in Greece and Turkey, and they confuse process with reality.

United States policy in the Eastern Mediterranean is primarily a means for achieving the larger foreign policy goals of East-West stability. Greece and Turkey, as NATO allies, are assumed to share our interests. However, conflicts between Greece and Turkey, especially over Cyprus, have complicated achievement of our goals. The "balanced" nature of American responses to these quarrels—regardless of the particular instance of the internal pressures—exacerbated the problems further.

For Greece, NATO has been important as a symbol of membership in the "West." More important than involvement in NATO was the tie to the United States. Traditionally, Greek foreign policy aims have been realized through attachment to a single great power. This arrangement permitted the great power "patron" considerable influence, both direct and indirect, in the policy process of its Greek "client."[4] In return, Greece expected support to further historic Greek interests. The major goal was the "megali idea," a plan for the inclusion of all Greeks into the modern Greek state. Since Greek goals required changes in the status quo, great power assistance was crucial. Historically, the major antagonist in this quest has been the Ottoman Empire and its successor, Turkey. Some ethnic Greeks remain in Northern Epirus (part of Albania), and in Turkish Istanbul, but the major target has been the island of Cyprus with a population 80 percent Greek. It is Turkey, supporting the Turkish minority on the island, that has prevented the smooth inclusion of the Greek Cypriots into the Greek state. In the past decade, another point of contention with Turkey had surfaced—claims and counterclaims over territorial waters and the sea bed in the Aegean. The real obstacle to achieving Greek foreign policy goals was Turkey—historical rival and fellow member of NATO. The Soviet Union, the adversary assumed by the institutions of collective defense, was not a paramount concern.[5]

As in past times, the interests of Greece were not necessarily paramount for the great power patron. Once again, Greece, the loyal client, felt betrayed as her interests were sacrificed or ignored by the United States. Turkey, in the perceptions of Greeks, might also be a dependent of the United States; but Greece, because of cultural ties, greater loyalty, and prior intimacy, deserved American beneficence more than Turkey. And, because of this dependence, the United States was expected to force Turkish acquiescence to Greek goals.

For Turkey, bilateral ties to the United States were also more important than NATO membership. The Turks, heeding the call of the United Nations, had sent significant forces to aid the United States in the Korean War. The United States had also been permitted to establish a network of intelligence gathering bases on Turkish soil and to keep nuclear weapons and delivery systems there. NATO membership came after a pattern of bilateral relationships had been established. For the Turks, this affiliation was due less to a perception of a Soviet threat than as an affirmation of Turkey's status as a modern, Western state. The achievements of Ataturk—secularization, economic and political modernization—were recognized.

To further economic development and maintain national security, Turkey needed continued assistance from the United States—and NATO membership facilitated this. The other major foreign policy problem concerned the Greeks: the Turks could not permit the application of a "Greek" solution to Cyprus for nationalist as well as strategic reasons. Later, the controversies over the Aegean further complicated relations.

Turkey, unlike Greece, did not view relations with the United States as those of a client with a patron. Relationships were far more balanced with advantages accruing quite equally to each side. The United States paid attention to the force of Turkish nationalism and, more important, the decision making structures in Turkey were not penetrated by Americans. American policies were not expected to further specifically Turkish interests. On the other hand, American policies that impinged on Turkish interests could provoke a response that affected our own.

The Cyprus Problem

The major cause of antagonism between Greece and Turkey is Cyprus. This island, close to the coast of Turkey, has a population of 600,000, of which 450,000 are Greek and 150,000 Turkish. American responses—and nonresponses—to recurring crises there have strained our relations with both countries. Cyprus gained international visibility in the 1950s with the demand of the Greek Cypriots for *Enosis* (union) with Greece. The island, originally under Ottoman domination, had passed to British administration in 1878, and to British ownership in 1914. The British merely ruled, giving considerable autonomy to the two ethnic-religious communities, and little thought to future development. The two ethnic communities looked to Greece or Turkey for guidance and assistance; the development of a common Cypriot nationality was not promoted.

By the late 1950s, the terrorist campaigns of the Greek Cypriots of *EOKA* [Ethnike Organosis Kypriakou Agonos (National Organization of Cypriot Fighters)] had convinced the British to withdraw. The same campaigns had convinced Turkish Cypriots and the Turkish government that union of Cyprus with Greece would be a disaster. They preferred partition. Consequently, the territorial aspirations of Greece and the demands of Greek Cypriots for *Enosis* were thwarted as were Turkish hopes for partition. Ultimately, Britain, Greece, and Turkey signed the Zurich and London agreements of 1959 which made them joint guarantors of an independent Cyprus. The compromise was acceptable to the United States because it brought stability to the region and reduced the tension between our Greek and Turkish allies.

The Cyprus Constitution of 1960 was a cumbersome arrangement that gave the Turkish minority an effective veto on government fiscal decisions, on defense and foreign policy. Archbishop Makarios, heavily involved in the *EOKA* movement and exiled by the British, returned to become president of Cyprus. The leader of the Turkish community became the vice-president. Stalemate ensued and, when President Makarios tried to alter the Constitution in 1963, armed clashes erupted that were ultimately quelled by a U.N. Peacekeeping Force (which remained until the Turkish invasion of 1974). Henceforth, the Republic of Cyprus governed only Greeks; the Turkish communities responded to their own leaders. Talks between Greek and Turkish leaders did resume in 1968, but little progress was made toward a solution.

The quest for solutions was complicated because a split developed between Archbishop Makarios and his followers who saw advantages in independence and nonalignment, and the government in Athens. The Greek government, at this point a military dictatorship, sought the popular support that incorporation of Cyprus into the Greek state would bring. Local Cypriot allies included those uncomfortable with the Archbishop's sometime support from the Cypriot left and his flirtations with the Soviet Union and left-leaning Third World countries. In addition, the most extreme anti-Turkish elements occupied prominent places in the anti-Makarios group. From 1969 to 1974, the quarrel intensified and several attempts were made on the life of Makarios by a new guerrilla organization, *EOKA B*. In July 1974, a coup by this group, backed and orchestrated by the Athens government, took over the government of Cyprus. At this point, the Turks invaded the northern part of the island and the Eastern Mediterranean was at the point of war. The military junta in Athens recalled a popular civilian ruler from exile and withdrew to the barracks. Archbishop Makarios returned to lead the Cypriot state. However, United States activities in trying to forestall the crisis, and the outcome of the crisis itself, were to bedevil American policymakers for several years to come.

Confounding Factors Within Greece

Greeks expected the United States to further Greek interests. Moreover, they assumed that little could happen inside Greece that was not instigated by or at least acceptable to the American "patron." The pattern of domestic politics in the postwar period reinforced this view. Our efforts to maintain the priority of NATO, and with it Greek-Turkish cooperation, in light of events on Cyprus were misunderstood. The closeness of American officials to military and economic elites, as well as to conservative, traditional politicians and the monarchy, created further problems. It was assumed that the United States either determined or approved domestic policies that encouraged economic inequality, illegal electoral manipulations, and the continued exclusion of left-wing Greeks from political participation.

These internal pressures produced a new center government led by George Papandreou and his American educated son, Andreas, in 1964. Although hardly radical in domestic legislation, this government was viewed as disruptive of the status quo—particularly in regard to defense and foreign policy. This government was under continual pressure, some undoubtedly instigated by the United States since the policies of Andreas were viewed as a threat to NATO. In July 1965, the King, viewed as pro-American, forced the resignation of the Papandreou government. For the next two years, various conservative and

caretaker governments attempted to govern in the face of a tumultuous political situation, and amid increased questioning of the role of the United States
in Greek politics.

An election scheduled for April 1967 was to resolve the crisis—most likely
in favor of the Papandreous. The military, in the form of a coup organized
by crucially-placed but middle-rank officers, intervened to prevent the election
and take over the government. The consequent military dictatorship, with
some changes in personnel, lasted until the Cyprus fiasco of 1974. In the eyes
of most Greeks, American connivance was necessary, not only for the down-
fall of the Papandreous, but for the coup and the very survival of the military
dictatorship.

United States action lent credence to this view. After a short interlude,
high American officials restored Athens to their itineraries. Every visit gave
visible evidence of American support. Presumably, American priorities for
NATO and for facilities to support possible intervention in the Middle East
encouraged this "business as usual" policy. However, from the Greek perspective
these arguments seemed suspect. Although an arms embargo was imposed
shortly after the coup and lasted until 1969, it prevented the flow of major
weapons, those that might strengthen Greek military forces in their NATO
role, but continued the flow of small arms and other equipment useful for
internal security. Moreover, the Colonels, after an abortive counter-coup
attempted by the King—one that resulted in the loss of his throne—began a
systematic retirement of many of the most experienced senior officers, thus
further weakening Greek forces in NATO. Moreover, the extreme nationalism
fostered by some prominent members of the junta undermined relations with
Turkey.

The military dictatorship, in the face of increasing internal dissent, adopted
more coercive policies, and itself moved in more secretive and reactionary
ways. The decision to invade Cyprus and overthrow the Makarios government
was clearly an attempt to save the military regime through a tremendous
foreign policy success. Even though popular opinion implicated the United
States in all Greek policy, our access to the actual decision makers in Greece
diminished and even disappeared. The decision to intervene in Cyprus was
taken without American knowledge, much less acquiescence.

The failure of the venture in Cyrpus brought a collapse of the military government; Constantine Karamanlis, the popular conservative prime minister of the
1950s and 1960s, was summoned from exile in 1974, his leadership was re-
affirmed by elections, and civilian government was restored. However, the old
relationships, the multiplicity of ties that had connected Greek officials and
institutions to their American counterparts, were not to be restored. The old
officer corps that identified professionally with NATO had been drastically
altered by retirements, resignations, and dismissals during the dictatorship.
More important, the military as an institution was no longer in a position to

veto civilian policies in defense and foreign affairs. The political spectrum itself had increased and even the character of politics had been altered. The pro-American monarchy was gone. The Left was now respectable—or at least accepted as a legitimate participant. Andreas Papandreou now led a significant party advocating what amounted to a nonaligned international position for Greece. Patron-client relationships, the basic mode of organization for traditional politicians, were reduced in effectiveness. Popular opinion counted for more and imposed constraints on official action. Although constitutional government was restored, the institutions were probably less important than the popularity of Karamanlis himself. The United States was viewed as responsible for the military dictatorship, for not halting the military move on Cyprus, and for not preventing the Turkish "counter" invasion of the island.

Greek elites, anticipating membership—later made final—in the European Economic Community, now looked to Europe for economic and political support. One of the first acts of the new civilian government was the withdrawal of Greek forces from the operational control of NATO. Greek military facilities, particularly air and naval facilities, were no longer automatically available for American use. The failure of the United States to restrain the Turks, added to the American involvement and apparent support for the military dictatorship, created tremendous popular and elite pressures for such measures. The Greek government, no longer a client with a single patron, found itself in a position to bargain with the United States. More important, through a set of unusual circumstances, the Greek government now found itself with a new arena for seeking foreign policy goals—the United States Congress.

Confounding Factors Within Turkey

Turkish politics also underwent considerable change in the 1960s and 1970s. American interests, or those of NATO generally, no longer received automatic priority. The modernizing autocracy of Ataturk and his successor gave way to a competitive party system in the 1950s. Despite electoral violence, corruption, misplaced and mismanaged economic policies, democracy continued. The Turkish military, acting as national guardian rather than alternative government, intervened from time to time, the latest in 1980, to restore faltering public order, or to interrupt the excesses of civilian politicians.

The Turkish political spectrum was progressively expanded from the two party dominance of the 1950s to include additional parties on both left and right. Politics was not only more fragmented, making leadership dependent upon sometimes fragile parliamentary coalitions, but polarized as well. The Republic Peoples Party headed by Premier Bulent Ecevit had a center-left orientation and responded to popular sectors critical of American policy. The other major figure, Suleyman Demirel, leading the Justice Party, had to deal with several conservative and religious-oriented parties to the right.

American foreign policy and its consequences were integral parts of domestic political controversy. The left perceived American interventions and preferences as detrimental to Turkish interests. The revivial of Islamic fundamentalism also brought with it calls for a reorientation of Turkish foreign policy. Moreover, American policy itself, particularly the desire to contain the Cyprus crisis of 1963-64 through rather heavy-handed pressure, was not forgotten. Later efforts to combat the American domestic drug problem through alterations in Turkish agricultural policy (a subsidy program to prohibit and control the cultivation of opium poppies) were viewed by many Turks as blatant intervention. At the same time, questions about the consequences for Turkey of American defense and deterrent strategy were tied to the obvious deterioration of the Turkish military forces. Further, the attraction of Europe and other regional ties increased as the scale of American economic and military assistance declined.

The Turks, like the Greeks, found themselves with foreign and domestic priorities that did not coincide with those of the United States. Moreover, American requirements for intelligence gathering facilities gave the Turks significant bargaining capability.

THE 1974 CYPRUS CONFLICT

The failure to defuse this crisis underlined the changed relationship of the United States with its NATO allies. Clearly, the national goals of Greece and Turkey took priority over American goals of preserving NATO or gaining political stability in the Eastern Mediterranean. Moreover, the long-term consequences of this failure further weakened the American position in the region.

The United States, forewarned of the Greek-sponsored plan to overthrow Archbishop Makarios and install a pro-*Enosis* government of Cyprus, tried to intervene. The United States was fully aware that the consequences of such action would include Turkish military action. However, those running the Greek government—at this point, the head of the military police was paramount—were purposely isolated from American diplomatic activity. And for their part, the Turks—Premier Ecevit—were unwilling to follow the American calls for restraint that had been heeded on other, somewhat similar occasions.

The plan proceeded: On July 19, Greek-led forces of *EOKA B* overthrew Makarios, installed Nikos Sampson, and invaded certain Turkish Cypriot enclaves. The Turks, acting as a guarantor power under the 1959 agreements establishing an independent Cyprus, landed an invasion force in northern Cyprus on the 20th. For several days, clashes occurred between Greek and Turkish troops on Cyprus, and the two countries themselves were on the verge of war. At this point, the military leaders in Athens, before turning the Greek government over to civilians, ordered a cease-fire on Cyprus. Sampson was replaced by the legal vice-president (Makarios had fled to London) and talks proceeded among the guarantor powers.

The efforts to settle the crisis ran aground quickly. Greek Cypriots were not in complete accord with decisions made for them by the new Greek government, and the Turkish government was unwilling to give up the leverage of military occupation without some guarantees about ultimate solutions. At that point, on August 14, the Turks moved to extend their occupation to include nearly 40 percent of the island.

The Turks now clearly occupied the territory of the legal government of Cyprus. This action created an enormous refugee problem, as thousands of Greeks fled from Turkish occupation and, more important, produced international condemnation. The Turks, whose initial invasion could be justified, had seized the opportunity to impose a solution to the Cyprus problem, and thus gain domestic credit for an enormous nationalist victory. Greece, whose military government had provoked the crisis, not only rid itself of an undesirable government, but assumed the role of injured party.

THE UNITED STATES AND THE AFTERMATH OF THE CRISIS

The Cyprus crisis of 1974 clearly demonstrated that American priorities for stability in the Eastern Mediterranean and the preservation of NATO were not shared by Greece and Turkey. Greeks resented our failure to restrain the junta and prevent the Turkish response. Their response was to leave the military structure of NATO. The Turks resented our efforts as well. However, on the surface, the American "failures" had not necessarily produced an impossible situation. An undesirable regime had been replaced in Greece. A Turkish government beset by economic problems had scored a great nationalist victory. The occupation of northern Cyprus by the Turks had created a de facto situation of apparent stability, for they were unlikely to withdraw. Perhaps American interests in stability could now be served. Perhaps Greece and Turkey would now cooperate to serve the larger interests of regional stability. This hope simply ignored the distrust of Greeks and Turks for one another, their perceptions of American policy, and their likely response to it.

This chain of events coincided with the unfolding of the Watergate affair and the resignation of President Nixon, and added to the growing disenchantment with the strategies and policies of Secretary of State Kissinger. A small number of congressmen, prominent Greek-Americans, and intellectuals had consistently attacked the Greek military junta and American policies toward it. The House Subcommittee on European Affairs headed by Congressman Benjamin Rosenthal was the focus of this activity in Congress.[6] Their efforts to alter American policy toward the military regime in Athens had been largely unsuccessful. The Cyprus crisis, resulting in the collapse of the Greek military dictatorship, provided a new issue—the illegal Turkish occupation of Cypriot territory. Moreover, American action during the crisis, largely the private diplomacy of Kissinger, was judged to be ineffective. American efforts to halt the Greek sponsored coup, as well as the initial Turkish invasion and subsequent advance, seemed weak. To make matters worse, Turkish officials seemed pleased with the results of American policy. Atonement for American complicity with the Greek military dictatorship and acquiescence in Turkish agression could come with the reversal of the consequences of these irrational acts: namely, the withdrawal of Turkish troops from Cyprus.

Quite understandably, Greek-Americans—or other officials with close ties to Greek-Americans—were quick to advocate this position. Greek-Americans, although small in numbers, were well organized, most notably in the American Hellenic Educational Association (AHEPA). Throughout the post-war period, active Greek-Americans had exerted political pressure on behalf of Greek interests. Greek-Americans had become more prominent in American politics. The former vice-president, several state governors, representatives, including the majority whip, and several influential congressional staff members were Greeks. Although split on the issue of attitudes toward the Greek military regime, they were united in opposition to Turkey. In addition, the controversy surrounding American support for the Greek military regime had attuned other influential members of the House and Senate to Greek affairs, and in this case, to the Greek cause. Others, with more general antagonism to administration foreign policy, joined.

The first proposal to ban military aid to Turkey seems to have been made to Secretary Kissinger by the Democratic whip, Representative Brademas, on August 15, before the Turks had completed their second advance. From Secretary Kissinger's perspective, these advocates were merely instruments of the Greek foreign office. Such an analysis ignored the continuity of the criticism and the independence of the critics. Secretary Kissinger viewed foreign policy-making as a prerogative of the executive branch. However, the traditional arguments buttressing such a position—superior information, ability to plan, speed of implementation—were all weakened by the Vietnam experience and scarcely strengthened by American activities during the Cyprus crisis. Ordinarily, American foreign policies are not altered by the criticism of a few congressmen. In this case the general antipathy to the administration as well as hostility to Kissinger created an unusual situation. The responses of the Secretary of State furthered the interests of the critics. At a news conference Kissinger was asked about the requirement of the military assistance acts for an embargo on military aid to countries usuing U.S. supplied equipment for aggressive purposes. The Secretary professed ignorance of the application of this provision to Turkey and promised a legal analysis of the question.[7]

This analysis was completed, but withheld for some seven months. Only a State Department "leak" brought the question into the open. It seemed a transparent attempt to evade clear provisions of the law. The provision had been used to inhibit Turkish plans during the Johnson administration, but it had not been used against the Israelis and was not applied to the Greeks who apparently used NATO supplies on Cyprus. For the Secretary, the decision was clearly political; subterfuge and delay were necessary because Turkey, crucial to our larger security interests in the Eastern Mediterranean, was not likely to succumb to available American pressures. However, in the American political context of the mid-1970s, such a course invited calamity. The failure of the administration to uphold the law by terminating military assistance to Turkey was linked to other alleged executive violations: impoundment, FBI and CIA illegalities, and Watergate itself. The narrow and parochial foreign policy issue could now join with others. The way was open for a dispute over Kissinger's policies and methods. Those congressmen interested in an embargo on arms to Turkey now had many potential recruits to the cause. Moreover, the fact that this was a complex yet narrow issue confined discussion to the limited "attentive" public. Constituency pressure, except for Greek-Americans, was likely to be limited. However, this factor was significant. The Greek government made significant efforts to mobilize prominent Greek-Americans to exert pressures on Congress, the administration, and even the mass media.[8] Greek-Americans were found in both parties, and often were significant campaign contributors. The embargo was the one issue on which they were likely to press for a congressman's vote.[9]

Congressional Initiatives and Administration Response

Congressional initiatives to cut military aid to Turkey did not begin with the Cyprus crisis of 1974. Indeed, relations between the United States and Turkey had deteriorated at least since the early spring of 1974. In 1972, Turkey cooperated with the United States in an effort to halt the international drug traffic that led from the Turkish opium poppy farmer to the United States. We provided funds to compensate farmers for not growing poppies—and also to encourage the development of new sources of income. For a variety of reasons, Turkish farmers did not like the arrangement or its administration. The intervention of the United States in a matter perceived to be explicitly domestic was politically uncomfortable for the Turkish government. Consequently, the Turkish government decided to terminate the arrangement with the United States.

American reactions, both administrative and congressional, were strong. State Department officials noted that economic aid tied to a ban on opium poppies would be lost. Our ambassador to Turkey was called home for consultations. Congressmen, especially those from urban districts, were particularly incensed. Congressman Rangel (D.-N.Y.) argued that Turkish noncooperation in banning the international drug traffic required a termination of all aid.[10]

By July, a resolution calling for a cutoff of military assistance to Turkey, co-sponsored by 238 congressmen, had been introduced in the House of Representatives.[11] Although the crisis erupted in Cyprus in mid-July, the concern of Congress remained the drug traffic. The House of Representatives voted on August 6 to urge that foreign aid to Turkey be cut off unless safeguards were devised to prevent the smuggling of Turkish heroin. Even after Turkey moved to occupy more of Cyprus in mid-August, the House of Representatives, still concerned with poppy growing, amended legislation concerning the Export-Import Bank to ban further business with Turkey. A similar action pending in the Senate urging President Ford to cut off military aid was approved 64 to 27.

The Turkish government appeared to see the issues separately at first; that is, the American responses to the decision to lift the ban on poppy growing were seen as economic, expected and accepted. However, as the temperature of Greek-Turkish relations rose over Aegean Sea issues during the summer, and Cyprus broke, Turkish governments had to consider a popular opinion that contained significant elements of anti-Americanism and did not differentiate between congressional and administrative opinion. Turkish government leaders themselves were caught unprepared for the congressional action. No Turkish government could appear to be moved to concession by American legislative pressure.

The interaction of Congress and the executive had impacts, often unintended, elsewhere. Greece was clearly interested in the embargo on Turkish arms. The United States Congress linked the lifting of the embargo to progress toward a Cyprus settlement. Obviously, the Greeks themselves had no similar leverage. The legislation was phrased in such a way as to give the Greeks, or the Greek Cypriots, an ability to monitor conditions that would lead the President of the United States to lift the embargo on arms to Turkey. Greece and its supporters in the Congress clearly overestimated the leverage provided by the embargo, underestimated the interest of the executive branch and other NATO countries evading it, and ignored political realities within Turkey. There was an adverse impact on two parallel sets of negotiations—first, those concerning Cyprus that were occurring on several levels, and second, the discussions between Greece and Turkey over the various Aegean Sea issues.

From the late summer of 1974 until the summer of 1978, three administrations wrestled with the problem of the Turkish embargo. At first Secretary Kissinger and the leadership in Congress, both Democratic and Republican, clearly misjudged the sentiments of the rank and file membership. The September vote in the House, 307 to 90 in favor of a cutoff in military aid until "substantial progress" had been achieved toward a Cyprus settlement, along with a postponement of the foreign aid bill in the Senate because of a likely defeat without a similar ban, indicated the congressional mood. Majorities of both parties were in favor of the embargo, although the Republicans made up a more substantial portion of the opposition to it. Some congressional hostility to Turkey remained because of the drug issue but, more important, some members found their Greek constituents, often prominent campaign contributors, pressing for a cessation of military aid. The intensity of Greek-American activity increased with the establishment of the American Hellenic Institute in the late summer of 1974 and its lobbying arm, the American Hellenic Institute Public Affairs Committee (AHIPAC) some months later. These organizations joined the older Greek-American organizations such as AHEPA in orchestrating grass roots pressure on congressmen each time the executive branch proposed to weaken or abolish the embargo. In addition, the new organizations sought to mobilize support for the Greek position from a wider "attentive" public including academicians and other opinion leaders. They also sought support from other ethnic groups such as Armenians and Jews with traditional anti-Turkish biases. Turkish-Americans were scarce and poorly organized; consequently, the little active counter-pressure came from general interest groups with security concerns. The regional Turkish-American groups did not join at the national level for purposes of "presenting a more balanced view of Turkey and the Turkish people" until December 1979, after the embargo issue had disappeared. Despite these constituency pressures, however, the embargo itself was not a really crucial issue for most members.

Administration strategy merely increased congressional resolve—for example, attempts to delay the foreign aid legislation and operate on a continuing resolution were seen as efforts to evade congressional intent. The White House position then shifted toward trying to get qualifying language in the legislation that would give the President greater flexibility in lifting the embargo. But regardless of the qualifying language, the President would be sure to find his assessment challenged by spokesmen for Greece or the Greek Cypriots. As that strategy failed, the President vetoed the stop-gap spending measure with the restrictive language. Later, both Senate and House approved a new resolution to continue military aid to Turkey until December 10, provided Turkey observed the Cyprus cease-fire and neither increased its fire on Cyprus nor transferred U.S.-supplied military equipment there. Ford signed, but with displeasure. The debate on the regular foreign aid authorization bill continued, and finally passed both houses with a provision permitting continued military aid to Turkey until February 5. Again, the President signed but with objections. The "Greek lobby" had succeeded.

The Ford administration, apologetic to the Turks, immediately began to pressure Congress to lift the ban or to alter the time of its application. These actions further intensified legislative resistance. For example, the Defense Department, just days before the February 5th cutoff date, announced plans to sell Turkey some $230 million in tank equipment. Secretary Kissinger, playing the role of broker between the Turks and Congress, tried to secure concessions from the former in order to convince the latter to alter the ban.

Instead, the Turks responded with threats to close the American bases and the Congress sensed that Kissinger was continuing to "tilt" toward the Turks. Efforts to lift the ban, which now included $78 million worth of equipment already paid for, were rejected. The Turks not only did not respond with concessions on Cyprus, they began to limit American military activity in Turkey.

The retaliatory action of the Turks was sufficient to erode previous majorities in the Congress. By May, the Senate had narrowly voted to resume military aid to Turkey. The House was much less agreeable. However, six months after the embargo was put into effect, it was altered to permit the Turks to receive arms aid previously contracted plus access to military sales. Only military assistance grants remained prohibited. Clearly, the embargo had not induced Turkish concessions on Cyprus, nor had it facilitated direct Greek-Turkish dialogue on other outstanding issues. Even in practical terms, the flow of military goods had been little affected. On the other hand, several of the most sensitive American installations continued to operate.

The major consequence was a reexamination by Turkey of its ties to the United States. From the Turkish perspective, a loyal ally should not suffer the indignities of an embargo, even a partial or symbolic one. If NATO was important to the United States, then the United States would have to finance, or assist in financing, the modernization of the Turkish armed forces. The precarious economic condition of Turkey precluded such an ambitious program. If the United States refused, then friendlier ties would have to be cultivated with the USSR and Eastern Europe, and Turkish forces would have to be redeployed to meet the real threat—Greek forces in the Aegean.

Regardless of common NATO membership, the Turks had considerable bargaining power because of the 26 American military installations. Recognition of this reality prompted the Ford administration to push for inclusion of grants to Turkey in the regular foreign aid authorization legislation for fiscal year 1976.

More important, negotiations were occurring with both Greece and Turkey for renewal and renegotiation of the agreements concerning American bases in the two countries. The new joint defense agreement with Turkey was unveiled first. It called for $1 billion in grants and aid to Turkey over a four year period and the reopening of the 26 American bases. This announcement simply gave new life to the embargo controversy.

The Greek government responded by suspending negotiations on a bases agreement with the United States. From the Greek perspective, this agreement reduced or eliminated pressure on the Turks to make concessions on Cyprus; it also would alter the military balance in the Aegean. This agreement, since it made no effort to nudge Turkey toward concessions on Cyprus, and because of its timing, gave renewed strength to the pro-embargo coalition in Congress. Perhaps in recognition of this, President Ford delayed sending the agreement to Congress until June. However, it was clear that no immediate action was likely to occur. Some congressmen were opposed, others felt that a companion agreement with the Greeks should be considered at the same time. Further, in the summer and fall of 1976, Greece and Turkey appeared to be on the verge of war because of controversy over oil exploration activities in the Aegean. The announcement by the Ford administration in September of its intention to sell Turkey F-4 jets, anti-tank missiles, Sparrow air-to-air missiles, spare parts, and services for $125 million was hardly fortuitous. Moreover, when it was clear that the transaction could not be cleared through the Foreign Military Sales program of the Defense Department because of the embargo, the State Department encouraged the Turks to buy military equipment, particularly the F-4 jets, directly from commercial suppliers.[12]

President Ford's attempt to secure congressional approval of the agreement with Turkey was reversed by President Carter in January 1977. Instead, a flurry of special missions to Greece and Turkey were initiated. The result was a decision to seek a further relaxation of the embargo in fiscal year 1978, increasing to $175 million the ceiling on arms sales to Turkey, rather than approval of the bases agreement. This proposal, eventually passed by the Congress despite considerable opposition, engendered disappointment in Turkey.

Ultimately, the Turkish government began to pressure the Carter administration to push for congressional approval of the bases agreement, hinting that American military forces in Turkey would be asked to leave if approval was not forthcoming. This chain of events was given greater significance by a change of government in Turkey. The new government seemed oriented toward wider contacts with the USSR and the Arab countries, as well as finding other sources for needed military equipment. Premier Ecevit argued that the Carter administration, by waiting for progress in Cyprus (essentially awaiting Greek Cypriot responses to Turkish proposals) simply encouraged the Greek Cypriots to harden their position. The Carter administration, sensing the frustration of the Turkish government—and the possibility of a defection from NATO—began a flurry of diplomatic activity that ended with the decision to ask Congress for an end to the arms embargo as well as passage of a revised bases agreement, all without waiting for concessions on the Cyprus question.

The reaction was predictable. The Greek government expressed its displeasure. Congressional supporters of the embargo prepared to defeat the administration proposals. The Turks applied pressure by engaging in symbolic exchanges with the USSR and Eastern Europe. The Greeks and the Greek Cypriots rejected Turkish proposals for settlement, thus implying that further concessions were mandatory. The Carter administration, by now fully aware of the possibility of congressional defeat for its proposals, as well as the consequences of defeat, made repeal of the arms embargo the "highest foreign policy" priority and began a major drive for passage. The arguments were straightforward: NATO and the United States could not afford to lose Turkey as an ally; Turkey's defense forces required modernization that only American military aid could ensure; and, finally, congressional insistence on Turkish concessions on Cyprus had not had the desired effect, and would only ensure a further deterioration in Turkish-American relations.

First the Senate, in a 57-42 vote, and then the House of Representatives, in a 208-205 vote, repealed the embargo on American military assistance. When finally signed by President Carter in September, the only concession to the "Greek lobby" was a requirement for the President to certify that Turkey was acting in good faith to resolve the Cyprus dispute before Congress approved military assistance. Although no action was taken on the bases agreement, Turkey agreed to reopen the four bases used by the United States for intelligence operations. As relations between the United States and Turkey improved, those between Greece and the United States deteriorated.

Administration Argument and Congressional Action

Congressional initiative produced the embargo on military assistance to Turkey, and congressional recalcitrance, particularly in the House of Representatives, maintained it for nearly four years. The Greek lobby itself could not have held such a coalition together for that length of time. The factors that contributed to initial support—hostility to Kissinger, excesses of the Nixon administration, pressure from Greek-American constituents, and hostility to Turkey over the drug issue—clearly declined in salience. Yet the arguments offered by the executive branch for removing or mitigating the embargo rarely had much effect. Eventually, President Carter led an all-out campaign to lift the embargo, but it is difficult to determine whether this campaign or other more idiosyncratic factors produced the desired outcome.

From the first, spokesmen for the executive branch maintained that the embargo would not be effective in pushing the Turks toward concessions on Cyprus. This was eventually viewed, especially by pro-Greek congressmen, as a self-fulfilling prophecy. The executive branch, particularly President Ford and Secretary Kissinger but President Carter and Secretary Vance as well, made clear to the Turkish government their displeasure with the embargo. The administration positions in the recurring conflicts over "escape clause" language in the proposals for mitigating the embargo leave no doubt about sentiments. The bill signed by President Carter charged him with merely certifying "Turkish good faith" in bargaining on Cyprus.

It can also be argued that this embargo was ineffective because arms continued to flow. In fact, the arms embargo during the early years of the military regime in Greece had little effect on progress toward democratization, at least in part because the embargo was violated. Successive attempts to permit sales of military equipment were successful. Moreover, Turkey had access to other sources of supply—Italy, the Federal Republic of Germany, and to U.S. military equipment through NATO's Maintenance and Supply agency. In fact, Turkish arms imports increased throughout the period and the proportion of the Turkish budget devoted to the military increased dramatically. Consequently, the embargo may have prevented a complete modernization of Turkish forces, but surely did not interfere with their effectiveness on Cyprus.[13] The real effect of the embargo, and perhaps the real intention of the Greek foreign office, was to prevent an alteration of the balance of forces in the Aegean Sea.

Ordinarily, incantations of collective security and the preservation of NATO have been sufficient to ensure congressional compliance with administration desires.[14] Certainly, such arguments have been commonplace in our efforts to restrain the internecine conflicts of the Greeks and Turks. Given the place of NATO in the architecture of American foreign policy, it is not surprising that any alteration in existing relationships is viewed with hostility and alarm. Greece and Turkey, despite parochial quarrels, must give their priorities to collective security and NATO. NATO-related legislation must not be the instrument for other goals. Allies, if they are committed to NATO and collective security, are not supposed to engage in activities that undermine it. On the other hand, if collective security is genuine, the United States should not impose an arms embargo on her allies or allow their forces to become ill-equipped.

The fact that the Greeks or Turks do pursue goals that conflict with the interests does raise some serious questions. Greece and Turkey were added to NATO after its formation as part of the general effort to contain communism on all fronts. For both countries, the tie to the United States was more important than the principle of collective security. Moreover, the strategic problems of Greek and Turkish membership have been minimized. The southern flank, consisting of Greek, Turkish, and some Italian forces, is quite separate from the crucial central front. Most strategies assume a conflagration on the central front; and this means, since forces would be difficult to transfer, that the mission of the southern flank is primarily a holding action. The terrain of the southern flank makes serious military activity—other than in conjunction with a main event elsewhere—extremely unlikely.

Furthermore, even within the southern flank, geography makes deployment of forces from one sector to another virtually impossible. (The three areas of deployment are eastern Turkey, Greek and Turkish Thrace, and northeast Italy.) It might be argued that American policy implicitly recognized the minimal importance of Greece and Turkey to NATO. At the outset of the military regime in Greece, the U.S. embargo included heavy military equipment but not the small arms and other supplies useful for internal security purposes. If the Turkish military contribution to NATO (which, in terms of numbers, is impressive) is really crucial, how could the United States permit such deterioration over so many years? If these countries are really not essential to NATO, then the embargo could be considered an appropriate policy instrument. However, such a position would legitimize the attempts of both

Greece and Turkey to influence American policy through indirect congressional pressure or diplomatic bargaining.

The argument stressing the importance of NATO and collective security or guidance for our policy toward Greece and Turkey was joined by other arguments focusing more narrowly on American Middle East interests. Arguments couched in terms of NATO were careful to accord Greece and Turkey equal weight in the alliance. In fact, this emphasis on balance in terms of support or displeasure had created hard feelings in 1956 and 1964 during past outbreaks of Greek-Turkish hostility. However, depending on the issue, the importance of one country or the other could vary. Our need to use Greek naval and air facilities justified lifting the embargo against the Greek military junta. Now, identical arguments for naval and air facilities plus bases used for gathering intelligence on the Soviet Union were used to justify lifting the embargo on the Turks. Actually, American use of facilities in both Greece and Turkey for other more narrowly NATO purposes had been increasingly restricted. Neither Greece nor Turkey saw their interests in the Middle East— particularly in regard to the Arab-Israeli question—as identical to ours. We would not be able to use these facilities to aid the Israelis in another conflict. Both national security and NATO arguments contained contradictions and flaws; they may not have impressed congressmen unequipped with the traditional East-West focus of American foreign policy.[15]

In this case, since the problem was Turkey, administration spokesmen indicated that in a forced choice, Turkey was more crucial on strategic grounds. By the late 1970s, Turkey may have been more crucial on political grounds as well. Greek forces remained outside the operational control of NATO; the bases agreement had not been renegotiated; the Greek military had lost its preeminent position; and domestic political forces were increasingly critical of the United States.

What factors account for the reversal of congressional sentiment? The embargo was narrowly repealed, by three votes in the House and seven in the Senate. The Senate had changed its position months after the passage of the embargo, largely persuaded by national security arguments. It can also be suggested that constituency pressures from Greek-Americans were less compelling. An analysis of votes in the House of Representatives is interesting mostly because of what is not revealed. Despite the intense campaign by the White House to influence members new to Congress since the 1974 embargo, about 60 percent of them, irrespective of party affiliation, voted to continue the embargo. The only clear division among new members occurred along urban-rural lines: 68.2 percent of the urban were in favor, compared to 37.8 percent of those representing rural districts.

Table 5.1 indicates the general shift among representatives voting on both the original 1974 roll-call and the 1978 one that resulted in repeal of the embargo. The original enormous pro-embargo vote shifted into a narrow anti-

Table 5.1. Representatives Voting in 1974 and 1978.

	1974 Vote		1978 Vote	
	Pro-Embargo	Anti-Embargo	Pro-Embargo	Anti-Embargo
Democrats N 142	84.5%	15.5%	47.2%	52.8%
Republicans N 99	72.7	27.3	38.4	61.6
Urban N 166	86.1	13.9	51.8	48.2
Nonurban N 75	65.3	34.7	25.3	74.7

Table 5.2. Representatives Voting in 1974 and 1978.

	1974 Vote		1978 Vote	
	Switchers For Embargo, For Repeal N=92	Solids For Embargo, Against Repeal N=100	Solids Against Embargo, For Repeal N=44	Switchers Against Embargo, Against Repeal N=5
Democrats	58.7%	66.0%	47.7%	20.0%
Republicans	41.3	34.0	52.3	80.0
Urban	65.2	83.0	45.5	60.0
Nonurban	34.8	17.0	54.5	40.0

embargo vote. Republicans, originally less pro-embargo, were slightly more anti-embargo, suggesting that party affiliation of the President made little difference. Representatives from nonurban districts were also much less pro-embargo in 1974 and considerably more anti-embargo in 1978. This contrast with urban congressman suggests a lingering effect of the drug issue as well as Greek-American constituency pressure in urban districts. This is borne out by the data presented in table 5.2. The 92 switchers (for embargo, for repeal) made the difference in the final outcome. Both parties were represented in rough proportion to their strength. Since there are more urban than rural districts, the high proportion of urban switchers is to be expected. Those solid for the embargo are disproportionately Democrats from urban districts. Conversely, those most consistently pro-Turkish are more likely to be Republican and nonurban.

Table 5.3 examines further the question of what category of representative provided the winning edge for repeal of the embargo. In this case, the representatives were placed into two categories, those serving from three to six terms and those serving seven or more terms. Urban Democrats with considerable seniority made up the greatest number of those who switched positions from 1974 to 1978. Presumably, such individuals would have less to fear from constituency pressure. More important, however, they are the most likely to have viewed the embargo issue as part of the larger issue of institutional conflict. It is also interesting that the core of solids was drawn from the same

Table 5.3. Representatives Voting in 1974 and 1978.

	1974 Vote				1978 Vote			
	Switchers For Embargo, For Repeal		Solids For Embargo, Against Repeal		Solids Against Embargo For Repeal		Switchers Against Embargo Against Repeal	
	N=50	N=42	N=53	N=47	N−20	N=24	N=3	N=2
Terms in House	3−6	7+	3−6	7+	3−6	7+	3−6	7+
Democrats								
Urban	26%	57.1%	52.8%	72.3%	10%	29.2%	33.3%	−
Nonurban	20	16.7	3.8	4.2	35	20.8	−	−
Republicans								
Urban	34	14.3	28.3	12.8	20	29.2	−	100.0
Nonurban	20	12.0	15.1	10.6	35	20.8	66.7	

category of congressmen, urban Democrats with seven or more terms of service. Apart from senior urban Democrats, little pattern emerges from the roll-call analysis. This lends support to the possiblity that some members acted in accordance with the "balance" doctrine of the State Department. They may have joined with the Senator who remarked, "Last time I voted for Greece, this time I will vote for Turkey."

American Foreign Policymaking and the Embargo Problem

The major American policies toward Greece and Turkey, the Truman Doctrine and the inclusion of the two states in NATO, were "global" responses to a perception of threat from the Soviet Union. There was little knowledge or understanding of internal politics in either country and little thought to conflicts between them. When internal conditions, particularly in Greece, evoked critical comment about the internal effect of a proposed policy, the specific issue was generally elevated to a general issue of NATO security requirements. When conflicts did erupt periodically, mainly over Cyprus but more recently over Aegean Sea issues, American responses have been hasty and ad hoc. Justifications have been invented and rationales offered to satisfy the critics of the moment. Little attention has been given to future consequences of our actions. Similar arguments have been used to support opposing positions. These inconsistencies and lapses are less significant at home because policy toward Greece and Turkey is a minor concern. However, these lapses and inconsistencies loom large in the minds of the foreign policymaking elites in both Greece and Turkey, and even in the minds of citizens at large.

NATO and collective security were clearly less important to either Greece or Turkey than were ties to the United States. We obscured the difference in our relations with these countries and in our own perceptions. Thus, the misperceptions about NATO relationships created extravagant notions of American friendship and power in Greece and Turkey. And similarly extravagant notions in the Congress about collective security and American power created unrealistic expectations about the willingness of Greece and Turkey to acquiesce in American goals. The framework of American foreign policy based on Soviet-American relations was simply inappropriate for understanding and solving the foreign policy problems in the Eastern Mediterranean.

The top reaches of the American foreign policymaking establishment, preoccupied with general problems of East-West relations, have had little time for examination of policies at the periphery. When peripheries do gain attention, it is at times of crisis. At these times, deep knowledge and calculations of long-term interests are rarely central to the decision. Instead, top policymakers are judged on short-run success—on ability to surmount crises. The Nixon administration adjusted to the crises brought on by the Greek military dictatorship by adopting a business-as-usual attitude. Initial "success" was costly in the long run. Secretary Kissinger found success elusive in the Cyprus crisis of 1974, and his successors had no better luck.

These policymakers, since they are often drawn to the top policy positions from outside the foreign policy bureaucracy, rarely have to accept the future consequences of their decisions. Those in the bureaucracy not only find their expertise and experience ignored, particularly when it involves the peripheries, but find their personal and career futures jeopardized by policies in which they had little part.[16]

The complexity of relations with any state, involving as it does so many separate parts of the government, provides many opportunities for misperceptions. Decisions emanating from a particular part of the government, although in reality simply the products of bureaucratic processes, are interpreted by the elites and public of affected states as decisions taken at the highest levels. For example, the decision of the U.S. Navy to utilize Piraeus as a "home port" for the Mediterranean fleet was certainly not a product of much thought for long-term consequences.[17] The Greek public viewed the decision as another instance of American support for the military regime; indeed, the home porting arrangements were one of the first casualties of the restored democray. Uncoordinated actions, all taken in the name of the United States, were consistently given unintended meanings by both Greeks and Turks.

The entrance of the Congress into more detailed supervision of foreign policy makes some of these problems more serious. The complexity of the legislative processes is not understood by either elites or publics in other countries (or perhaps in our own). Decisions that are basically minor for most congressmen are of great importance to the foreign states. Irreverent and sometimes insulting remarks get transmitted abroad. The legislative processes—with numerous opportunities for defeat but fewer for victory—are confusing for foreign observers whose political life may depend on American action. Legislative timetables are not conducive to smooth foreign relations.

As Congress requires additional certifications, notifications of intent, and other positive responses from the administration before specified foreign policy activities commence, the opportunity for bureaucratic missteps increases. The regular bureaucratic processes produce letters and documents and send them on to Congress. In the case of the Turkish embargo, several of these routine notifications arrived at inopportune times, disrupting Greek-Turkish negotiations, or suggesting to Congress administration duplicity or deceit. In other instances, the notifications to Congress occur after the negotiation with the foreign government is complete. An adverse congressional reaction complicates, often unnecessarily, the relations. On the other hand, the oversight role of Congress may be weakened because these notifications and letters of intent may go to committees sympathetic or uninterested in the policy instead of the legislators really knowledgeable about the problem.

Congress was not successful in resolving the Cyprus dilemma, but the administration had not been particularly successful prior to congressional intervention either. In this case, congressional involvement clearly prolonged the problem and, in prolonging, seemed to worsen it. Analysis of foreign policy-making, whether in the rarified heights occupied by policymakers or through regular bureaucratic processes, rarely finds complete rationality. For congressional involvement, additional problems arise. Perhaps most serious from the analyst's point of view is the fact that many congressional participants in detailed yet crucial decisions were uninformed and uninterested in the problem. Foreign policy decisions, despite the different context, were taken on the basis of "usual politics" considerations. As Representative Symington remarked, "If the 535 member Congress thinks its collective wisdom is all that is necessary to break the deadlock [over Cyrpus], it engages in a presumption commensurate with its size."[18]

In domestic legislation, compromise may be the preferred outcome. In foreign policy, public compromise is the function of negotiation, not the formulation of bargaining positions. Moreover, the issue was whether to have an embargo or not, hardly an issue on which compromise was possible. And finally, the legislative process is simply not suited to the needs of diplomatic negotiation, nor is it a substitute. Congress, through a series of deadlines, combinations of inducements and threats, and parliamentary maneuvering, attempted to influence the behavior of the Turkish government. Although such strategies might work in domestic political struggles, they merely increased Turkish intransigence. Moreover, such actions seemed to give the Greek government an inflated view of its leverage over American policy. The skills of negotiation, the recognition of nuances, of the importance of timing and of symbolic considerations are not part of the congressional repertoire, at least in the realm of foreign affairs. In this case, congressional involvement did not resolve the inadequacies of executive branch policy, but escalated the problem and prolonged it instead.

NOTES

1. Laurence Stern, *The Wrong Horse: The Politics of Intervention and the Failure of American Diplomacy* (New York: Times Books, 1977), p. 141. Stern provides a detailed and convincing accunt of the Cyprus crisis of 1974. The Cyprus crisis was only one of a number of incidents demonstrating and contributing to the mutual antagonism of Secretary Kissinger and the Congress.

2. See P.L. 87-565, Pt. II, Sec. 201(a), *76 Stat. 259* (1962), amending the Foreign Assistance Act of 1961 by adding Subsec. 505(d), *22 U.S.C.A.* Sec. 2314(d) and *22 U.S.C.A.* Sec. 2302 (1975 Suppl.). There is an extensive discussion of the legal issues raised by the Turkish invasion and occupation of Cyprus, although from a pro-Greek perspective, in A. A. Fatouros, "How to Resolve Problems by Refusing to Acknowledge They Exist: Some Legal Parameters of Recent U.S. Policy Toward Greece and Cyprus," in *U.S. Foreign Policy Toward Greece and Cyprus,* edited by Theodore Couloumbis and Sallie Hicks (Washington, D.C.: Center for Mediterranean Studies and American Hellenic Institute, 1976), pp. 20–48.

3. See Richard Haass, *Congressional Power: Implications for American Security Policy,* Adelphi Papers Number 153 (London: International Institute for Strategic Studies, 1979).

4. This problem is discussed extensively in Keith Legg, *Politics in Modern Greece* (Stanford, Calif.: Stanford University Press, 1969), Chapter 3.

5. The major points of contention between Greece and Turkey are thoughtfully set forth in Andrew Wilson, *The Aegean Dispute,* Adelphi Papers Number 155 (London: International Institute for Strategic Studies, 1979).

6. In the House of Representatives, the leaders of the Greek lobby were John Brademas, the Democratic Whip; Lester Wolff, Don Edwards, Benjamin Rosenthal, and Donald Fraser. In the Senate, the major supporters of the embargo were Thomas Eagleton, Claiborne Pell, and Paul Sarbanes (earlier a member of the House). In addition, several congressional staff members, Brademas, Sarbanes, and Pyrros, are of Greek descent.

7. Stern, *The Wrong Horse,* pp. 142–49.

8. Herbert J. Gans, *Deciding What's News: A Study of CBS Evening News, NBC Nightly News, Newsweek and Time* (New York: Vintage Books, 1980), p. 347.

9. Morton Kondracke, "The Greek Lobby," *The New Republic,* April 29, 1978, pp. 14–16.

10. See the remarks of Representative Rangel reprinted in "Controversy Over the Cutoff of Military Aid to Turkey," in *Congressional Digest,* 54 (April 1975): 124.

11. The chronology and details of the debate on the Turkish embargo are drawn from the *New York Times* and the *Congressional Record.*

12. General Accounting Office, *Report to the Congress: What Would be the Impact of Raising or Repealing the Commercial Arms Sales Ceiling?* January 4, 1980, p. 14.

The Turkish Embargo Problem 131

13. The Turkish military budget actually incrased, in constant dollars, from $1,270 million in 1974, to $1,640 million in 1975, to $2,230 million in 1976. Arms imports amounted to $235 million in 1973, $232 million in 1974, $238 million in 1975, and $291 million in 1976. See data in *World Military Expenditures and Arms Transfers, 1967-1976* (Washington, D.C.: United States Arms Control and Disarmament Agency, 1978), p. 65. See also Christopher J. Deering, "The Turkish Arms Embargo: Arms Transfers, European Security, and Domestic Politics," paper presented at the 1980 Annual Conference, International Studies Association, Los Angeles, California, March 1980. Deering presents data on p. 11 showing U.S. arms transfers of $180.3 million in 1973, $199.5 million in 1974, $174.9 million in 1975, $116.8 million in 1976, $49.0 million in 1977, and $175.1 million in 1978.

14. John C. Campbell, "The Mediterranean Crises," *Foreign Affairs* 53, (4), (July 1975): 605-24.

15. These arguments are set forth in various testimony found in *Greece and Turkey: Some Military Implications Related to NATO and the Middle East*, prepared for the Special Subcommittee on Investigations of the Committee on Foreign Affairs, by the Congressional Research Service, Library of Congress, February 28, 1975. See also, *The Military Aspects of Banning Arms Aid to Turkey*, Hearing before the Committee on Armed Services, United States Senate, 95th Congress, Second Session, June 28, 1978; and the *United States-Turkish Defense Cooperation Agreement*, Hearings before the Committee on Foreign Relations, United States Senate, 94th Congress, Second Session, on S. J. Resolution 204, September 15, 1976.

16. For a contrast in bureaucratic decision making, see Chihiro Hosoya, "Characteristics of the Foreign Policy Decision-Making System in Japan," *World Politics* 26 (3), (April 1974): 353-69.

17. Thomas Keagy and Yiannis P. Roubatis, "Homeporting with the Greek Junta: Something New and More of the Same in U.S. Foreign Policy," in *U.S. Foreign Policy Toward Greece and Turkey*, pp. 49-66.

18. "Controversy Over the Cutoff of Military Aid to Turkey," p. 127.

Chapter 6
Economic Sanctions Against Rhodesia*
Stephen R. Weissman and Johnnie Carson

For more than a decade, United States participation in United Nations economic sanctions against Rhodesia, Great Britain's rebellious white-led colony, was a subject of political controversy both within and between the executive branch and Congress. First imposed by Executive Orders in 1968, the sanctions were partially lifted by an Act of Congress in 1971, and then reimposed by the legislators in 1977. Twice in 1979 the Senate voted to lift all sanctions, but the House of Representatives failed to go along. Finally, in December 1979, as the British were on the verge of success in their diplomacy of negotiating a political agreement among the major black and white political groups for a peaceful transition to independence, President Carter, with the support of both houses, joined Britain in lifting sanctions.

This chapter focuses on the last year of U.S. sanctions when the President was often hard pressed to hold the line against congressional attempts to resume normal economic relations with Rhodesia. The interplay among the executive branch, the House, and the Senate in this period revealed much about contemporary constraints on coherence in U.S. foreign policy, particularly in that large middle group of cases which do not attract the sustained interest of millions of voters and hundreds of congressmen, but are not so submerged that hardly anyone outside of the executive branch is prepared to discuss them.

BACKGROUND

A brief review of the recent history of U.S.-Rhodesian relations may be useful in contributing to a greater understanding of subsequent developments.

---

*This is a purely personal analysis by the authors of this historical case and does not necessarily reflect the views of any members of the Subcommittee on Africa.

In November 1965, the white settler-dominated government of Southern Rhodesia unilaterally declared its independence from Great Britain after nearly three years of unsuccessful negotiations, during which representatives of the 5 percent white minority refused to accede to British conditions for decolonization including "unimpeded progress to majority rule" for the 95 percent black majority. At Britain's request, the U.N. Security Council imposed partial mandatory economic sanctions on the Rhodesian government in 1966 and comprehensive mandatory sanctions in 1968. These Security Council resolutions were implemented in the United States by Executive Orders issued by President Lyndon Johnson under the authority of the U.N. Participation Act of 1945.

In 1971, though, Congress responded to pressure from the U.S. ferrochrome and stainless steel industries, which believed themselves disadvantaged by lack of access to low-priced Rhodesian chromium, by passing the (Senator Harry) Byrd Amendment to the 1972 Military Procurement Act. The Byrd Amendment weakened sanctions considerably by permitting the United States to import chromium and other "strategic and critical materials" from Rhodesia. Its passage was also facilitated by a show of indifference from the Nixon White House which was less sensitive to black African concerns than its predecessor.

With the demise of Portugal's African empire, the victory of Soviet and Cuban-assisted nationalist guerillas in the Angolan civil war, and escalating attacks by Soviet and Chinese-armed Rhodesian guerillas supported by neighboring "Front Line" states (Mozambique, Zambia, Botswana, Tanzania and Angola), the Ford administration switched gears in 1976, calling strongly for repeal of the Byrd Amendment and rapid progress toward majority rule in Rhodesia.

Early in 1977, the Carter administration succeeded in persuading Congress to repeal the Byrd Amendment. The President's way was eased by rampant disillusion among ferrochrome industry lobbyists who had discovered that the Byrd Amendment let in more ferrochrome than raw chromium, thereby helping to bankrupt half of the remaining U.S. ferrochrome companies. Later in the year, Great Britain and the United Stated proposed a detailed "Anglo-American Plan" for a peaceful settlement, including a 100 seat National Assembly with 20 members to be especially elected by their parliamentary colleagues to represent minority (i.e., white) interests; safeguards for white property along with a projected Western Zimbabwe Development Fund to help a black government buy out unutilized white land; and a free and impartial independence election presided over by a British Commissioner supported by a U.N. peacekeeping and monitoring presence.

Rhodesia's Prime Minister, Ian Smith, responded during 1978 with his alternative "Internal Settlement" which was supported by three major black leaders who promptly joined him in a new interim administration. The Internal Settlement had a 100 member Assembly too, but 28 of these would be selected by white voters or nominated by outgoing white parliamentarians. The provision for land acquistion was more restrictive than that of the Anglo-American Plan and it also lacked the financial backing of Western donors. Other parts of the Internal Settlement guaranteed white control of the civil service, police, judiciary, and defense forces through white-dominated "independent commissions" for each of these institutions. And the above provisions were not to be changed for *at least* 5 to 10 years. A free and fair independence election was promised, but it would be supervised by the existing authorities, not outsiders. The Internal Settlement was rejected by the overwhelming majority of ZAPU (Zimbabwe African People's Union) and ZANU (Zimbabwe African Nationalist Union), the historic nationalist opposition which provided the political core of the "Patriotic Front" guerilla coalition.

THE CASE IN BRIEF

Throughout 1979, the Carter administration was faced with the need to defend its sanctions policy against powerful challenges from Congress. In the end, it withstood the opposition partly because of the executive's natural advantages in dealing with Congress: its ability to threaten use of the veto which can only be overridden by a two-thirds vote in each house, its superior organizational capacity, and its political credibility and clout with congressmen and interest groups—especially those associated with the President's party. Yet, despite these advantages, the Senate went ahead and lifted sanctions while the House did not. Had the House gone along with the Senate, even a presidential veto might not have saved sanctions for long. In the first place, the Rhodesian government might have been encouraged to continue the war rather than come to the conference table as it did in late 1979. In the second, an administration that was preoccupied with a number of serious policy and political problems might not have been willing to persist very much longer in its drive for a negotiated settlement. Therefore, in order to explain the President's success it is necessary to understand why the Senate voted one way and the House another.

It is not readily apparent that any broad political differences between the two chambers or any innate differences in the way they relate to the executive account for their varying positions on Rhodesian sanctions. Rather, the most significant factors were:

1. The existence in the House of a substantial group of black and white liberal congressmen, several of whom were strategically placed on the Foreign Affairs Committee, who were strongly committed to the administration's Southern Africa policy and willing to mobilize existing and potential interest groups for joint lobbying activities; and the lack of an equivalent group in the Senate.

2. The more disciplined procedures of the larger body, such as rules favoring the use of established internal organizational channels and prohibiting "nongermane" debate, which discouraged efforts to lift sanctions at politically op-

portune moments; and the freer, more club-like organizational style of the Senate which was, therefore, more vulnerable to such attempts.

3. The executive's own lack of consistent leadership on the issue—due to a cautious legislative style and a reluctance to "unleash the dogs" on an important but second ranking issue—which permitted the opponents of sanctions in both houses to build up momentum; and the aforementioned qualities of the Senate environment which meant that the impact of any executive weaknesses would be felt most strongly there.

THE BASIC ISSUES AND THE CASE-JAVITS COMPROMISE

It was the view of the Administration and its liberal supporters that sanctions should not be lifted until the Internal Settlement government negotiated a political settlement with its Patriotic Front and "Front Line" state adversaries—preferably including an impartially-administered election—and the country thereby achieved internal stability and international recognition. This position was consistent with liberals' support for racial equality. In addition, it was based on its supporters' assumptions that:

* the Patriotic Front's nationalist drive for a black-dominated government was a powerful political force that could not be repressed by military might;
* the United States could not afford, either politically or economically, to antagonize Africa and much of the Third World by appearing to oppose black self-determination in Rhodesia;
* a continuation of the conflict would open up increased opportunities for Soviet and Cuban influence in Rhodesia and Southern Africa generally;
* a negotiated political solution would be a helpful precedent for the resolution of similar conflicts in the remaining white minority redoubts of Namibia and South Africa.

On the other side, conservative critics asserted that, by maintaining sanctions against Rhodesia until there was a negotiated settlement, the United States was implicitly supporting the Patriotic Front and giving it a veto over political arrangements within Rhodesia. The Internal Settlement was an appealing recipe for many who held reservations about unlimited black rule in Africa. Also, the critics assumed that:

* the Internal Settlement could ultimately prevail if sanctions were dropped and it obtained Western recognition and assistance;
* the administration was too attentive to those African and Third World countries which tended to support Soviet and Cuban policies, and failed to exploit the economic pragmatism and anticommunism of others who would be impressed by a strong U.S. stand against sanctions;

- the Patriotic Front was led by Marxist terrorists and supported by communist countries; therefore concessions to the Patriotic Front would strengthen communist and terrorist influence in Rhodesia and Southern Africa;
- rather than creating a precedent of a negotiated settlement with communist-aided guerillas, the United States should favor government-led reforms in Namibia and South Africa.

In Congress, the first confrontation between these forces during the Summer of 1978 had produced the "compromise" Case-Javits Amendment in the Senate which was quickly enacted into law with minor changes. Under the Case-Javits approach, the United States would no longer enforce sanctions if the President determined that:

1. the government of Rhodesia has demonstrated its willingness to negotiate in good faith at an all-parties conference, held under international auspices, on all relevant issues; and
2. a government has been installed, chosen by free elections in which all political and population groups have been allowed to participate freely, with observation by impartial, internationally-recognized observers.[1]

The administration supported the Case-Javits compromise because conservative efforts to lift sanctions entirely had failed by only 6 votes in the Senate and 52 in the House. Moreover, the amendment bought the President time and preserved his flexibility by allowing for a presidential determination regarding the conditions for lifting sanctions. Nevertheless, the language of the amendment tended to subtly shift the focus of political discussion about Rhodesia away from the overall political-military situation and U.S. foreign policy interests and toward the Internal Settlement government's willingness to negotiate with its adversaries and its actual conduct of a free and fair election. After October 1978, when the leading figures in the Internal Settlement journeyed to America and publicly pledged to attend a conference with the Patriotic Front, the election issue rose to the fore.

Round One: Should Congress Send Observers to the Internal Settlement Election?

Senate Action. The Chairman of the Senate Foreign Relations Committee's Africa Subcommittee was George McGovern, a supporter of the administration's Southern Africa policy. McGovern was convinced that the forthcoming Internal Settlement election was "unlikely" to meet the Case-Javits criteria of freedom and fairness "given the hostilities taking place and the fact that the election will not be supervised by a neutral administration." But he knew that several conservative groups were planning to observe the election and that its evaluation was bound to be controversial. Since, in McGovern's view, the administration had failed to effectively counter growing "anticommunist, antiterrorist and anti-administration" perspectives in Congress, he doubted that the President alone could issue a politically credible determination that the Rhodesian government had not met the Case-Javits criteria.[2] Thus, as a political tactic, he introduced a concurrent resolution providing for Congress to send a team of 25 to 50 "impartial professionally qualified observers recruited from private life" to monitor the election and report on whether it was free and fair. The observers were to "scrutinize the electoral laws and survey the electoral process" and report on whether all population and political groups had an opportunity to "participate fully" as well as on the extent to which guerilla activities or voter boycotts affected the level of participation.[3] McGovern succeeded in persuading Senator S.I. Hayakawa to cosponsor the resolution, although Hayakawa was a conservative opponent of the administration's policy. Unlike McGovern, Hayakawa believed that impartial observers would probably conclude that the election constituted a "realistic" measurement of black political opinion in Rhodesia. While the resolution provided for House and Senate leaders to pick the cochairmen of the observer team (who would, in turn, choose the remaining members), it was expected that McGovern would nominate one cochairman and Hayakawa the other. As plans developed, one of the cochairmen was to be a constitutional lawyer and the other an election analyst and the remaining members of the team were to be mostly lawyers and election officials with little African experience.

Consistent with the increased centralization of the Foreign Relations Committee under Chairman Frank Church, the full Committee held hearings on the McGovern-Hayakawa Resolution. Among the witnesses, black and liberal church groups were highly critical of the observers idea. Reverend Jesse Jackson (President of Operation PUSH, a major civil rights and educational development organization), Randall Robinson (Executive Director of TRANSAFRICA, a two-year-old Washington lobby on African and Caribbean issues supported by the Congressional Black Caucus and a cross-section of civil rights leaders and elected black officials), and Sister Janice McLaughlin (from the Washington Office on Africa, a Protestant church-supported lobby for black self-determination in Southern Africa) all maintained that the dispatch of even congressional observers would constitute de facto U.S. recognition of the Internal Settlement and hinder future U.S. efforts to mediate the conflict. They questioned the need to observe the election process itself since the Rhodesian Constitution gave each white vote ten times the weight of each black one, preserved white control over major policy areas, and was approved in a whites-only referendum. They also pointed out that 85 percent of the country was under martial law, the internal political arms of the Patriotic Front were banned, and there was widespread political intimidation by private political armies, security forces, and white employers. Sister McLaughlin argued that the observer team could have precisely the opposite effect from that which McGovern desired.

I think that sending observers focuses attention on the mechanics rather than the substance of democracy in Zimbabwe. I also believe observers would see very little. If they are protected by the Rhodesian security forces no African will speak freely to them. . . . Also the internal government will be on its best behavior. . . . Without an awareness of what has been taking place in the previous months, the observers could well come away with a false picture.[5]

On the other hand, two Washington-area professors and a journalist testified in favor of the proposal, but not without reservation. For instance, Professor Michael Samuels of Georgetwon University stated that congressionally-appointed observers would countervail the "preconceived bias" of private observers toward the Internal Settlement and cause "much less damage" to a future U.S. mediating role than official administration ones would. However, he questioned the "wisdom" of a unilateral effort and sought to encourage an interparliamentary delegation.[6] Professor Ralph Goldman of American University Law School advised the Committee on the mechanics of observing foreign elections but confessed "grave misgivings" about the technical difficulties and dangers of the Rhodesian mission.[7]

The administration's position, expressed by Assistant Secretary of State for African Affairs Richard Moose, was ambiguous. First, Moose restated the administration's policy of seeking an internationally-supervised election to end the war. He then noted that the Internal Settlement's election would be conducted under a constitution which gave whites disproportional power and had been approved by only white voters, amidst the violent atmosphere of war and martial law, and without the participation of the Patriotic Front. He suggested that it was not "unreasonable to question" whether the new government would obtain internal and external backing. Moose went on to say that the administration had decided not to send official observers to the election in order to preserve its potential mediating role and avoid raising expectations in the Rhodesian capital. But, after noting that there was "some carry-over" of these objections even to congressional observers, he concluded, "We certainly respect the right of the Congress to inform itself whatever way it sees fit about the proceedings that are under way" and "We will certainly take into account any report [the observers] make."[8] There was no effort to either formally discourage Congress from sending an observer delegation or to work informally behind the scenes to oppose the McGovern-Hayakawa resolution.

The Administration's ambivalence was compounded of fear that congressional observers might focus on the mechanics rather than the structure of the elections and have a political impact that could lock the administration into a favorable verdict and cautious concern that the administration not look biased against the Internal Settlement, undermining the credibility of an eventual negative determination. Another reason for caution was the fact that the Rhodesian issue was considered less important than such other foreign policy controversies as the Panama Canal and SALT and, therefore, had less of a claim on the administration's resources.

At its decisive "mark-up" on March 14th, the Foreign Relations Committee voted 8-1 (with 6 absences) to report the resolution favorably to the Senate. Senator Charles Percy, the lone dissenter, raised questions about apparent recognition of the Internal Settlement and difficulties in effectively monitoring the election. McGovern and Hayakawa responded by pointing out that the resolution included a formal disclaimer of any such endorsement, and that the observer team could spot massive intimidation and had been promised free access to the territory by the Rhodesian government. Senator Jacob Javits, the ranking Republican on the committee, strongly defended the proposal on narrow, legalistic grounds as an "implementation" of the Case-Javits Amendment in the absence of executive observers. During the discussion, an administration spokesman "clarified" the administration's position, saying it was "neutral" on observers as far as Congress was concerned. Chairman Church, who had earlier wondered whether sending observers was not "an idle exercise" since the administration considered the Internal Settlement illegitimate, now concluded that, if Javits was for the resolution as a follow-up to the Case-Javits Amendment, he was too. Senator Edmund Muskie indicated he was impressed by the arguments on both sides. He said he would support the resolution "today" but "might not later."[9]

The floor debate on the McGovern-Hayakawa resolution followed the lines of the previous discussions. The opposition was led by Senator Paul Tsongas, a liberal former Peace Corps volunteer in Ethiopia, who was joined by Percy, Senator Edward Kennedy, and a few other liberals. In the end, a powerful coalition of ideologically disparate Senators backed the resolution, which passed 66-27.

House Action: A nearly identical proposal was introduced in the House by Representative William Carney, but it was quickly apparent that the legislative environment was very different. The key forum for discussion of the observers resolution was the House Foreign Affairs Committee's Subcommittee on Africa, not the full committee as in the Senate (Chairmen Clement Zablocki ran the Committee in a more decentralized fashion than Church). The new Chairman of the Africa Subcommittee, Stephen Solarz, a liberal New York City Democrat, was highly skeptical about the substance of the proposal and aware that three of his five Democratic colleagues on the Subcommittee would be strongly opposed. These were Congressmen Charles Diggs, Cardiss Collins, and William Gray, members of the Congressional Black Caucus who had gravitated to the Africa Subcommittee. None of the members of the Africa Subcommittee were strong conservatives like Hayakawa and Jesse Helms on the Foreign Relations Committee. Solarz scheduled extensive hearings on Rhodesia with both administration and private witnesses so that the observer issue was more firmly embedded in the context of the overall Rhodesian political situation and U.S. interests in the region than it had been in the Senate Committee. Finally, Solarz hosted an informal reception for African ambassadors from countries of varying ideological stripes; all those present, including two of the subcommittee's three Republicans, were struck by the unanimity and intensity of African feeling against the Internal Settlement and the sending of congressional observers.

When the subcommittee marked up the Carney resolution, Solarz and his liberal colleagues voted against it. But so did centrist Democrat Floyd Fithian who suggested that an escorted tour would be of doubtful value and tend to identify the United States with an unpopular regime. Among the Republicans, John Buchanan said his respect for McGovern as a political tactician was over-ridden by his fear that Congress could jeopardize a future U.S. "honest broker" role; Millicent Fenwick indicated she preferred completely private observers "to avoid any U.S. identification with the Internal Settlement; and William Goodling was also opposed.[10] The Subcommittee's unanimous action assured that the proposal would not be taken up by the full committee. And since Solarz had obtained McGovern's agreement that it would be a bad precedent for only one House to send observers, the subcommittee's action went far toward killing the proposal.

With little more than two weeks to go before the Rhodesian election, the only chance for congressional observers was for an amendment to be attached to other legislation being considered on the House floor. But, now, the stringent House "germaneness" rule, which prohibits amendments outside the scope of the legislation in question, came into play (Senate rules are more permissive). Conservative proponents of observers were unable to find a plausible occasion for a germane amendment for more than a week. Even then, the germaneness requirement prevented them from posing the question of congressional ob-servers pure and simple. Conservative leader Robert Bauman's germane amend-ment to the foreign assistance bill, authorized the President to appoint observers to report to Congress on elections in Southern Africa and provided $20 million from existing funds to an elected government resulting from the April election "which may be evaluated and reported on by observers".[11] Bauman acknowl-edged that it was too late for observers to go to the Rhodesian election, but said he hoped the House would at least have the opportunity to express itself on the issue.

Clothed for germaneness as part of the executive-administered foreign aid program, the observer proposal was more vulnerable to political attack. Liberal opponents pointed out that the Bauman Amendment went beyond lifting sanctions to offering aid, and that it did so even before elections had been held and observers had reported. Members of the Foreign Affairs Committee com-plained that the funds for Rhodesia would be taken from those already desig-nated for other, poorer Southern African Countries. And, as presidential emis-saries, Bauman's observers were depicted as aligning the United States with the

Internal Settlement. A Solarz Amendment to strike out the main clauses of the Bauman Amendment passed by 233 to 146 votes, attracting support from a number of congressmen who leaned toward lifting sanctions but could not support foreign aid as well. (Some even believed they were voting against an overall increase in foreign aid.) To solve this problem, Congressman John Rousselot introduced a new amendment which was identical with Bauman's stricken clauses except that it made the provision of aid optional. Bauman supported the revision wholeheartedly:

> This amendment simply puts us on the side of a new, freely elected black majority government in Africa and against the side of the terrorists, the bombers, those who shot down planes, those who make our assinine policy in the State Department and those who gather in the floor of the House to support that policy.[12]

But Solarz warned that if the amendment were adopted, "Every key figure in Africa [would] come to the conclusion that the U.S. House of Representatives had decided to throw its weight behind the Internal Settlement" and argued that the amendment still indicated "a willingness" to give aid "even if the elections were not free or fair."[13] During the debate, Solarz was strongly supported by Congressman Howard Wolpe of the Africa Subcommittee and Congressmen Andrew Maguire and Thomas Downey of the Ad Hoc Monitoring Group on Southern Africa (a liberal organization of 40 representatives and 2 senators which had formed in the wake of the murder of South African black leader Steve Biko in 1977). Even more than Solarz, they laid out the whole liberal case against the Internal Settlement and its upcoming election. Nevertheless, the Rousselot Amendment passed by 7 votes. In accordance with parliamentary procedure, the whole Bauman Amendment—Bauman's original preamble and Rousselot's new operative clauses—was now voted upon. Although the vote should have been identical to the previous one (apart from absences or new arrivals), Solarz and his associates now defeated the amendment by 10 votes. Solarz, Democratic Whip John Brademas (who had been approached previously by Solarz), and others had actively lobbied fellow Democrats with the result that 11 switched their votes.

Executive Influence: By assuming an ambivalent position toward the McGovern-Hayakawa Resolution instead of opposing it, the administration probably helped facilitate its overwhelming success in the Senate. But in the House, the administration's divided heart served the interests of conservatives who nearly passed legislation authorizing not only observers but also economic assistance. Such legislation would have given a strong psychological boost to the Internal Settlement and established a powerful precedent for the movement in the House to lift sanctions. By failing to either take a strong stand against congressional observers or anticipate and counteract the conservative maneuver on the foreign aid bill, the administration almost suffered an important defeat in the very chamber where it had the most allies.

The administration's stance raised some larger questions of political strategy as well. Many in and out of the executive branch were convinced that past appearances of partiality and inadequate efforts to explain Rhodesian policy had compromised the administration's credibility, and that a respectful attitude toward the observers proposal would ultimately pay off in political dividends. Yet, the very effort to display objectivity *on this particular question* could contribute to the notion that the elections themselves were crucial (despite the Constitution and the non-participation of the Patriotic Front) and that the observers could provide information critical to the development of U.S. policy. "Neutrality" also prevented the administration from educating senators and congressmen on such controversial questions as, "Are the guerilla leaders communists?"; "Who committed atrocities in the war?"; "Did Administration policy give the Patriotic Front a veto over peaceful change?"—lest it be accused of lacking objectivity. Yet, it was the very absence of such political education that had led McGovern to broach the observers tactic in the first place. Neutrality may also have fostered an impression that—unlike other foreign policy matters—Rhodesia was an area in which Congress could make decisions "on its own." As one involved State Department official complained, "By avoiding making a strong determination on the observers question, we set ourselves up to allow the Congress to make our decisions for us, as it turned out, not only on the observers question but also on the sanctions question."[14]

Lastly, the risks for U.S. sanctions inherent in sending congressional observers may have been more serious than the administration assumed. While McGovern occasionally observed that the team would also look at the Constitution and the electoral law, it was reasonably clear from both the language of the resolution and the legislative discussions that the primary emphasis would be on election mechanics. Also, to drop a politically hybrid team of lawyers and U.S. election officials lacking African expertise into an African election where political meanings were elusive and intimidation often subtle was to court a propaganda victory for the Internal Settlement.

Round Two: From the Rhodesian Election to the President's Case-Javits Determination

In mid-April the great majority of Rhodesians exercised their new right to vote. The winner of the election was Bishop Abel Muzorewa's United African Nationalist Council which took 51 of the 72 black seats at stake. Although Congress had not sent an observer delegation, approximately 250 foreign journalists and 70 international observers were there for the occasion. Most press and radio-television coverage in the United States focused on the five days of actual voting and sympathetically depicted the birth of a fledgling African democracy in the midst of a violent civil war. Conservative U.S. observer teams from the American Conservative Union, Institute of American Relations, and American Security Council pronounced the election free and fair. Perhaps more surprising, the respected liberal anticommunist group, Freedom House, whose observer team included veteran civil rights leaders Bayard Rustin and Allard Loewenstein (a former congressman), judged the election to be "a relatively free expression of the will of the people" and "a significant advance toward multiracial and majority rule. . . . Elections in most development countries are less free." As one administration observer commented, "The election tended to legitimate the Salisbury government in the mind of many."[15]

Senate Action: Even while Congress was considering the observers proposal, impatient conservatives in both houses had introduced resolutions expressing the "sense of the Congress" that the President should determine that the Rhodesian government had complied with Case-Javits by demonstrating willingness to attend an all-party conference and scheduling free elections, and that he should lift sanctions within ten days of the installation of the newly elected government. Now, with the elections completed, Senator Helms attempted to lift sanctions immediately without even waiting for the President's determination. The conservatives moved first in the Senate because of its looser germaneness rules.

On May 14th, Helms proposed a "non-germane" amendment to the State Department Authorization bill to prohibit the enforcement of sanctions against Rhodesia and eliminate penalties for violation of *any* executive order implementing U.N. sanctions. The administration, Senate Majority Leader Robert Byrd, and Senators Church, Javits, and McGovern agreed on a substitute amendment to be offered by the Majority Leader giving the President a fixed date—two weeks after the installation of the new government or June 30th whichever was earliest—by which to make his determination. This procedural rather than substantive response to Helms was consistent with the administration's continuing defensiveness about appearing to have "prejudged" the election and the Internal Settlement. Also, the administration's willingness to rely on Senator Robert Byrd to lead the charge reflected its inclination to limit its commitment on the issue.

During the floor debate on the Helms Amendment, Senators Helms, Hayakawa, Harry Byrd, and other conservatives emphasized that the President had already had three weeks to digest the reports of election observers and that the Rhodesian government clearly met the Case-Javits criteria for lifting sanctions. They quoted copiously from the Freedom House report as well as those of other observers and journalists. As for broader foreign policy considerations, Senator Harry Byrd commented:

The question presented is simple: Will the United States support Soviet-inspired terrorists by blockading a moderate pro-Western black government, or will the United States give democracy a change in Africa by permitting trade with a friendly and properly elected government.[16]

Two kinds of argument were put forth by those who wished to give the President more time. First, there was the legalistic, prudential reasoning of Robert Byrd, Javits, Church, and McGovern. By passing Case-Javits, the Congress had *itself* created the President's obligation to make a determination after installation of an elected government. If Congress did not like the determination, it could subsequently override it by law. Furthermore, as Javits explained, it was "no open and shut case" whether the election was free and fair:

We had wonderful observers from Freedom House who say that they were fair. Other observers [including journalists, Lord Chitnis's British All Party Parliamentary Group on Human Rights delegation, and the National Bar Association and Lawyers' Committee for Civil rights under Law whose opinions were solicited by McGovern, Kennedy, and others] say it was under a martial law situation, that masters of plantations took their workers to the polls, that there were soldiers around, and that it was not a fair election.

It would unnecessarily strain diplomatic relations with Britain and the Front Line states if we lifted sanctions before meeting with the new Conservative Party Government in Britain and allowing the Front Line "to cool off." Javits appealed to those on both sides of the issue who believed that "a little good sense and a little judgment and playing it cool may do it."[17]

Senator Tsongas was virtually alone is presenting a strong challenge to the basic conservative position. Rejecting the tendency to "consider the Case-Javits conditions in a vacuum," Tsongas stated that the criteria were "imprecise," inviting "subjective, personal interpretations. . . . I doubt whether Senator Helms and I could ever agree on what a fair and free election could be." Instead, Tsongas concentrated on the "larger implications of the vote today." He asserted that lifting sanctions would create a "de facto alliance" with the limited white-rule government of Bishop Muzorewa, "incur the wrath of key African allies such as oil-rich Nigeria," encourage neighboring states to accept Soviet and Cuban assistance, ignore the fact that "the change in government has not altered the long-term trend of guerilla advance and government retreat," and undermine the United Nations.[18]

Just as the agreed time for debate was expiring, Helms executed a deft parliamentary maneuver which prevented the administration's supporters from getting a vote on their substitute. Faced with an imminent vote on a new Helms' "perfecting" amendment to lift sanctions until June 1980, Majority Leader Byrd and his associates conferred in the cloakroom. Byrd indicated that his "head count" showed that Helms would win the upcoming vote. (Neither the Administration nor its supporters had done their own counts.) He then persuaded his colleagues to support, as a lesser evil; a Schweiker-Deconcini Amendment stating the "sense of the Congress" that Rhodesia had complied with Case-Javits and the President should lift sanctions within 10 days of the installation of the new government. (This Amendment could be considered ahead of Helms' because it was an "amendment to the bill" rather than "an amendment to an amendment" and it was the only other "non-germane" amendment the Senate had previously agreed to consider on Rhodesia.) Javits justified his support of this "compromise" because as a "sense of the Congress" exhortation it preserved the President's legal obligation to make a determination under Case-Javits. But Tsongas claimed that a majority or near-majority would have voted for the original Byrd substitute and that an overwhelming endorsement of Schweiker-Deconcini would send a misleading message to the House and to Africa about Senate preferences on Rhodesia. It appeared that Tsongas and many in the administration would have preferred to risk losing a close vote on a Helms Amendment actually lifting sanctions than to have the overwhelming 75-19 passage of the "sense of Congress" resolution that followed. In fact, both the U.S. press and the Rhodesian government interpreted the vote as one that foreshadowed an eventual lifting of sanctions in the Senate and probably in the House as well.

House Action: Largely because of the strict germaneness rule in the House, there were no further attempts to lift sanctions in the six weeks between the election and the President's Case-Javits determination. Yet, Solarz and other supporters of sanctions recognized that there would be a vote in the near future; and, in the aftermath of the election; it would be an uphill fight. Thus, Solarz took the initiative in creating a "Rhodesia Strategy Group" which included staff from the Africa Subcommittee, legislative assistants of members of the Black Caucus, the Ad Hoc Monitoring Group, and Members of Congress for Peace Through Law, representatives of Washington offices of church, labor, and liberal and civil rights groups (some of which were already active in effort led by the Washington Office on Africa and TRANSAFRICA), and observers from the Congressional Relations Bureau of the State Department. Over the next two months, the Strategy Group conducted a major campaign to influence both congressmen and the administration to act to maintain sanctions. (An attempt to involve Senate staffs was unsuccessful.) As many as 60 people were directly involved in the effort. Among their major activities were:

• encouraging a succession of "Dear Colleague" letters from one or more representatives to hundreds of their fellow representatives laying out the case against the freeness and fairness of the Rhodesian election and invoking the larger foreign policy considerations favoring the retention of sanctions.

Among the letter writers were Representatives Solarz, Fascell, McCloskey, Duncan, Pease, Erlenborn, and Edwards.

- encouraging letters from interest groups to congressmen. In addition to on-going lobbying by the Washington Office on Africa and TRANSAFRICA, the International Association of Machinists and Aerospace Workers, the United Steel Workers, the United Auto Workers, and the Methodist Office for the U.N. all communicated their concerns.

- encouraging letters to the President by congressmen and interest groups seeking an early and strong negative determination under Case-Javits. Those who responded included Congressmen Edwards (and 35 colleagues), McCloskey (with 9 cosigners), Rangel, as well as Americans for Democratic Action, the AFL-CIO, the National Conference of Black Mayors, the National Council of Churches, the United Auto Workers, and the Coalition of Black Trade Unionists.

- use a "swing list" of 93 apparently uncommited representatives as a focus for staff-to-staff and member-to-member lobbying. For instance, Solarz hosted a luncheon for the Foreign Minister of Botswana (a Front Line State) and five African Ambassadors. Approximately a dozen individuals on the swing list attended.

Meanwhile, the Subcommittees on Africa and International Organizations held new hearings on Rhodesia. Among those testifying were Allard Loewenstein of the Freedom House observer delegation and former Senator Clifford Case, the President of Freedom House. Both made it clear that Freedom House's positive remarks about the election did not commit the organization to the lifting of sanctions. Rather, they insisted upon further democratizing moves by the new Muzorewa government—new personnel, a commitment to allow blacks to vote on the Constitution, human rights advances—and consultations with the British and Africans as preconditions for lifting sanctions. Case emphasized that the Amendment he had co-authored with Javits did not set the only conditions for lifting sanctions, and suggested that the President could set new conditions even if he declared that the older ones had been met. Loewenstein, who had a vast acquaintanceship from his days on Capitol Hill, was extraordinarily active in explaining his position to dozens of congressmen.

In the first days of June, there were indications that the Rhodesia Strategy Group in-house lobby and various collateral efforts were bearing some fruit. First, John Erlenborn, a conservative Illinois Republican who was not even on the swing list, joined liberal Congressman Don Pease in a prosanctions "Dear Colleague" letter. (Erlenborn was increasingly sensitive to African concerns after participating in several international conferences on Africa.) Then a survey of 40 of the 61 "swing" list members most likely to vote to retain sanctions indicated that 11 leaned toward sanctions, 3 were undecided but had shifted from previous positions of leaning toward lifting, 23 either didn't have a position or were undecided, and only 3 were leaning toward lifting. This sounding suggested that, among those who had thought about the issue, the drift was strongly toward keeping sanctions. The poll also indicated the limited degree of public involvement in the issue: congressional mail was generally light, with the main sources being church and union groups on one side and individual conservatives on the other.

In contrast with the liberal Strategy Group, conservative interests were relatively inactive. In general, groups like the American Conservative Union and the American Security Council included material on Rhodesia in their regular newsletters but did not engage in special mailings or other lobbying efforts. Probably the most active conservative lobbyist was Ken Towsey of the Rhodesia Information Office (RIO), an agency of the Rhodesian government. Towsey provided information to key conservative leaders like Congressmen Bauman, Ichord, and Derwinski and Senators Helms, Harry Byrd, Hayakawa, and Schweiker. Operating on a budget of $17,000 a month, the RIO distributed numerous press statements and other materials to members of Congress, such as "Bishop Muzorewa's Message to Vice-President Mondale" and "Rhodesia's Election."

Executive Influence: Possibly, the administration's cautious strategy of not making a strong, early presidential determination and of trying to stave off its foes with procedural defenses would ultimately enable it to appear unbiased and more credible. But, for now, it meant that, in the Senate, a substantive case for maintaining sanctions was not being strongly made just as the policy was coming under strong attack from conservatives benefiting from media coverage of the Rhodesian election. Also, it appears that the administration's decision to permit Majority Leader Byrd to carry the ball contributed to a lopsided and important political defeat through the adoption of the Schweiker-Deconcini "sense of the Congress" amendment. In the House of Representatives, the administration's supporters had few illusions that a strategy of watchful waiting would pay off. Instead, they organized themselves into an ad hoc lobby, one task of which was to persuade the administration to strongly defend its own policy.

Round Three: Everyone Makes a Decision

On June 7th, President Carter announced his long awaited Case-Javits determination. While taking note of "some very encouraging progress" in "Zimbabwe-Rhodesia" and acknowledging that "the actual voting in the April elections appears to have been administered in a reasonably fair way under the circumstances," he held that the elections were "neither free nor fair" because the Constitution was approved by whites only and preserved "extraordinary power" for the white minority and the internal representatives of the Patriotic Front were barred from the election. He also observed that the government had not met the other Case-Javits criterion: it had been willing to attend an all-parties conference but not to negotiate "all relevant issues."

At the same time, the President promised to keep the question of sanctions "under review" in order to encourage the newly-elected government of Bishop Muzorewa to "progress toward a wider political process and more legitimate and genuine majority rule."[19] Thus, for the first time, the administration admitted the theoretical possibility of the Internal Settlement's reforming itself sufficiently to obtain U.S. support. Undoubtedly, some calculation of the political costs of a completely negative statement had influenced this new tone. Finally, in maintaining sanctions, the President also referred to the broader U.S. diplomatic interests which his policy served.

Having presumably recaptured its reputation for objectivity through its quiet course of the last few months, the administration swung strongly into action behind the President. A substantial group of influential House and Senate members was invited to the President's announcement of his determination and participated in the ensuing discussion. The following morning, Assistant Secretary Moose and State Department Director of Policy Planning Anthony Lake briefed 40 representatives of nongovernmental organizations and sought their support. At the same time, U.N. Ambassador Andrew Young, National Security Council Director Zbigniew Brzezinski, and Moose telephoned more than a dozen union officials for assistance in "the coming fight in Congress."[20] The AFL-CIO and the American Bar Association among others, responded rapidly to these appeals with letters to congressmen and senators. Ambassador Young also wrote 517 elected black officials, asking them to communicate their views to Congress and the White House. Secretary of State Cyrus Vance testified before the congressional Foreign Affairs Committees that it was "quite likely" the President would veto any bill lifting sanctions.[21]

Senate Action: The first legislative test came in the Senate only 5 days after the President's determination. Included in the Defense Department Authorization bill was a Harry Byrd Amendment lifting sanctions on the import of strategic materials and all other trade. Javits, Church, and others introduced a substitute amendment, which had been approved by the Foreign Relations Committee and the administration, to lift sanctions on December 1st unless the President certified that the national interest required them to be continued and so reported to Congress.

In defending this new version of Case-Javits, Senators Javits and Church employed a more circumspect rationale than the President had. In their view, the arguments for and against sanctions were closely balanced. The new Zimbabwe-Rhodesia government was flawed due to its Constitution but, given African experience, the new black government would probably change the Constitution. The absence of a political settlement with the Patriotic Front could lead to increased Soviet and Cuban influence, but the maintenance of sanctions seemed to give the communist-aided front no incentive to seek a peaceful resolution. The United States should be sensitive to African opinion, but it ought not to allow the Afro-Asian bloc at the United Nations to dictate American policy. Moreover, it was most important to defer to our British ally which had not yet lifted sanctions but might do so by mid-November when parliamentary sanctions had to be renewed. Given these considerations, Church and Javits concluded that the United States should maintain sanctions for a few more months to give Muzorewa a chance to demonstrate internal progress and the Patriotic Front added incentive to negotiate; and, at the same time, work closely with Britain, avoiding any *unilateral* American action that could harm U.S. interests in Africa. They asked for presidential "maneuvering room" within the framework of ultimate "congressional control."[22] Supportive speeches by Senators Tsongas, Metzenbaum, Bradley, and Kennedy were closer to the spirit of the President's determination as they castigated the Rhodesian Constitution, warned of African retaliation to any U.S. lifting (especially by Nigeria, America's second largest oil supplier), and expressed skepticism about Muzorewa's commitment to internal change. But most of the administration's supporters adopted the more balanced line of Javits and Church.

In the eyes of Helms, Harry Byrd, and their followers, the Javits-Church compromise was flawed because it permitted a "subjective" administration to make a new determination which was unlikely to be any less prejudiced than its previous one. Moreover, they argued, the President had proved that he was unresponsive to congressional opinion by ignoring the Schweiker-Deconcini "sense of the Congress" amendment. They urged lifting sanctions forthwith rather than leaving a new multiracial democracy to "slowly dangle in the breeze."[23]

When the decisive vote was taken, the Javits-Church substitute failed by 52–41. Thus, the Senate lifted sanctions and, in so doing, it rejected President Carter's Case-Javits determination.

House Action: Following the President's determination, Solarz took stock of the parliamentary situation in the House. In the next few days and weeks, there appeared to be at least three legislative opportunities for opponents of sanctions to act germanely and effectively from the House floor. Instead of responding to such quick jabs from the floor, Solarz decided to take the initiative with his own "compromise" bill to be constructed around a wide and politically viable consensus. While such a bill would never be passed by the Senate, it would establish a clear House position which could be used against moves to lift sanctions from the floor and in future House-Senate Conferences on the State and Defense Department bills containing the Schweiker-Deconcini and Byrd Amendments.

Solarz, therefore, launched a series of consensus-seeking meetings among key congressmen who had been active in various ways in efforts to maintain sanctions. The major pincipals were Representatives Solarz, Wolpe, Gray, Diggs, and Fenwick (from the Africa Subcommittee and, in the case of Gray and Diggs, the

Black Caucus as well); Representative Bonker (from the Subcommittee on International Organizations); and Representatives Maguire, Downey, McCloskey, and Pease (from the Ad Hoc Monitoring Group on Southern Africa). On June 13th, they agreed on a bill which clearly aspired to the consensus that Javits and Church had failed to attain in the Senate. HR 4439 declared the finding of Congress that the April election constituted "a significant step" toward multiracial democracy, that the United States had a foreign policy interest in "continued progress toward majority rule" and a "peaceful resolution" of the war, and that Britain "which retains responsibility for Zimbabwe-Rhodesia under international law" had not yet recognized the legality of the new government. Therefore, the President was directed to continue efforts to promote an end to the conflict, terminate sanctions "when the actions of the government of Zimbabwe-Rhodesia convincingly demonstrate the exercise of genuine majority rule," and make a determination, and report to Congress by December 31st.[24]

The following day, Solarz met with Chairman Zablocki of the Foreign Affairs Committee, a traditional administration loyalist, and Congressman Paul Findley, a leading opponent of the President's policy. Zablocki agreed to back HR 4439 if the criterion for lifting sanctions was changed from a convincing demonstration of majority rule to the more flexible "national interest" phraseology which had been acceptable to the administration in the Senate. Surprisingly, Findley also agreed to support the bill if the date of the determination were changed from December 31st to October 15th. Findley's apparent *volte-face* seems to have reflected Secretary Vance's threat to veto bills lifting sanctions, Findley's expectation that the British conservative Government would move quickly after its August Commonwealth Conference to lift sanctions, and a quick vote count by House conservatives that was not very encouraging.

The long, intense, and cooperative involvement of various House members and staffs in the campaign to maintain sanctions undoubtedly facilitated rapid agreement by Solarz's coalition on the new changes. Thus, on June 15th, eight days after the President's determination, the House Foreign Affairs Committee voted 33 to 0 to report HR 4439 to the floor. (Congressman Findley's switch spurred bipartisanship, but several Republicans who voted the bill out would subsequently oppose it on the floor.) With the completion of committee action, the House Democratic leadership cooperated with committee leaders in postponing other legislation which could result in a premature vote on sanctions.

The administration now weighed in heavily. Moose, Lake, and others made calls to individual representatives and their staffs in behalf of the Solarz bill. Vice-President Mondale hosted a breakfast for 100 congressmen which included a briefing by Deputy Secretary of State Warren Christopher, Moose, and Lake. The White House committed itself to "30+ calls once Panama is out of the way."[25] And it continued to work with interest groups; for instance, congressmen received strong letters supporting the bill from the United Steelworkers Union and letters and calls from the American Bar Association.

As in the Senate, those who spoke during the floor debate in favor of maintaining sanctions emphasized the danger of hasty action for U.S. relations with Africa and Great Britain and the desirability of continued leverage on Muzorewa to make further democratic progress. But less compromising statements were much more abundant than they had been in the Senate, reflecting the intense commitment of many liberal members. Thus, Cardiss Collins, the Chairperson of the Black Caucus, declared that, under the Zimbabwe-Rhodesia Constitution:

> Aside from the introduction of more black faces in the legislative assembly, life in Rhodesia would go on much the same as it has since the British colonialist Cecil Rhodes introduced the first white settlers to the privileged life of white supremacy at the end of the last century. . . . Black Americans are very much aware of the interdependence of domestic and foreign policy. Our African heritage is a reality and the determination of our African brothers to secure their freedom has been a constant source of inspiration to black Americans in the securing of those rights which have been elusive to us in our quest for economic and political parity.[26]

The opposition, led by Congressmen William Broomfield, Edward Derwinski, Bauman, and Ichord also echoed the Senate debate in praising "the only true multiracial, multiparty, constitutionally democratic society in Southern Africa," warning of the threat of pro-Soviet Marxist terrorists, and asserting that the President was "prepositioned" especially in an election year to not be objective in making a national interest determination. Unlike their Senate counterparts, who insisted on the immediate lifting of sanctions, the House conservatives pleaded for a lifting by December 1st without a presidential determination.[27]

The critical vote favored the administration by 242 to 147. It was largely a partisan verdict with the Democrats supporting the administration 217 to 30 and the Republicans opposing it 117 to 25. Of the 93 congressmen who had been on the Strategy Group swing list, 84 were present; 64 of the 66 Democrats favored the administration but only 7 of the 18 Republicans did.

Executive Influence: It is difficult to discern the influence of the administration on the Senate vote lifting sanctions. A comparison with the previous June 1978 vote on a Helms Amendment lifting sanctions, which the administration won by six votes, shows that the White House had picked up three former opponents but lost seven former allies—a net loss of four. Also, out of 20 new senators, eight voted differently from their predecessors, and the administration lost seven of them—a net loss of six; however, most of this latter group consisted of "unwinnable," strong conservatives. Perhaps the administration's strategy of not addressing the substantive issues till a few days before the climactic vote had reassured some Senators who were concerned about evidence of presidential prejudice. But it is also quite possible that the months of hesitation had served most the cause of Helms and his determined group of sanctions-lifters.

Heavy administration lobbying probably had a significant impact upon the final results in the House. Shortly before the President issued his Case-Javits determination, the Strategy Group had discovered that most swing congressmen were undecided. But, when the House voted a few weeks later, the overwhelming majority of the swing list—especially Democrats—supported the President. It is likely that the principal achievement of the Strategy Group was to help keep a large number of congressmen undecided and uncommitted during the Rhodesian election-Senate sanctions lifting period until they could be recuperated by a newly mobilized administration. But, had the Strategy Group not emerged and persisted, the administration's cautious approach might well have harvested a defeat.

Round Four: Two Conferences

By summer, then, there had been the following progression of legislative action. The House had been silent on Rhodesia in the State Department bill but the Senate had attached an amendment stating the "sense of the Congress" that the President should lift sanctions. The Senate had adopted an actual sanctions-lifting provision in the Defense Department bill; but the House had passed HR 4439 to maintain sanctions until October 15th when the President would make a new national interest determination, and it was now about to pass its own Defense bill without any language on Rhodesia. Therefore, the fate of the sanctions would be decided at the House-Senate Conferences on the State and Defense Department bills.

The conferees on the State Department bill, who assembled in July, were members of the House and Senate Foreign Affairs Committees, both of which favored sanctions. When the issue of Rhodesia was raised, Solarz tried to substitute his own bill's language for that of Schweiker-Deconcini, but Helms strongly resisted. Javits then intervened with a new compromise: there would be a presidential determination on November 15th to give the British time to make up their minds, but Congress could override the determination not by passing a law (which could be vetoed) but by a "veto-proof" concurrent resolution which needed only a majority in each house. Such a resolution would have to be passed within 30 days of the President's determination but would be considered under the "expedited procedures" in both Houses that were already being applied to presidential arms sales proposals. All of the conferees pronounced themselves satisfied with this compromise. But Helms and Javits appeared to be unaware that even the expedited procedures in the orderly House were such that the Foreign Affairs Committee and the Democratic leadership could probably bottle up an adverse concurrent resolution until the 30 days were up. In the Senate, however, the expedited procedures permitted any member to move to have his concurrent resolution considered if the relevant committee hadn't reported it favorably within 10 days. On August 15th, the President signed the State Department bill into law, although he objected to this new "legislative veto" as a violation of the principle of separation of powers.

By the fall, the British had succeeded in convoking a peace conference of the opposing Rhodesian parties in London to consider British proposals for ending the war. Around the same time, the conferees on the Defense bill also gathered. Despite the State Department compromise, the administration and its supporters were in a weak position. Only three of the ten Senate and three of the thirteen House conferees had voted to maintain sanctions. Moreover, the Conference Committee included some of the most effective proponents of lifting sanction—Ichord and Harry Byrd—and none of the leading opponents. The President would incur some political costs in vetoing a multibillion dollar defense bill, especially at a moment when the administration was stressing military preparedness in connection with its efforts to win Senate approval of the SALT treaty.

Solarz wrote to each House conferee reminding him of previous House votes, the State Department compromise, ongoing British responsibility for Rhodesia, and the danger that repeal of sanctions "at this time" could undercut British diplomacy and cause the collapse of the London peace conference.[28] Solarz and 92 other congressmen sent a similar letter to Congressman Melvin Price and Senator John Stennis who were leading the Conference as Chairmen of the Armed Services Committees. It was implied that the group would attempt to defeat an adverse Conference Report on the House floor. On the Senate side, there was less activity, but Senator Tsongas joined Solarz in an appeal to the President to make a strong public statement on the issue. Both felt that a public threat by the President to veto the bill would be the most effective way he could influence the conferees.

At the beginning of the Conference, high administration figures (including Secretary of Defense Harold Brown and Assistant Secretary Moose) urged Stennis and Price to reject the Senate provision on Rhodesia. In a letter released to the public, President Carter informed Stennis of his "firm opposition" to the Senate language and warned that its retention would "disrupt the negotiating process."[29] Carter also met with the chairmen privately to tell them he would definitely veto the bill if it contained the offending provision. However, the President did not answer directly when asked if he would once again veto the bill if it contained a new nuclear carrier—a favorite project of the conferees which was included in the House bill. Carter, therefore, left the chairmen with the impression that cooperation with the President on Rhodesia might increase the chances that he would not veto the carrier. Reluctant to spend scarce political resources unnecessarily on Rhodesia, the President hoped that a private veto threat relayed to the other conferees would be credible enough to carry the day. Both Price and Stennis, who had a vested interest in smooth passage of the bill (already delayed beyond the beginning of the fiscal year) and who were inclined to follow presidential leadership, promised Carter their support.

The accumulation of pressures on the conferees was ultimately decisive. Unfazed by an initial vote by the House conferees to yield to the Senate position and lift sanctions, Chairman Price, Congressman Nedzi, and Congressman Bennett argued persistently that Solarz had the votes to defeat the bill on the floor, further delaying the $41 billion military procurement measure. They also used the leverage provided by the President's ambiguity on the nuclear carrier: if the conferees gave in on Rhodesia, the President would probably give in on the carrier. Eventually, the House conferees agreed by just a single vote to resist the Senate. Pressed by the House conferees and Chairman Stennis, and themselves anxious to have the carrier, the Senate conferees finally yielded. Instead of lifting sanctions, the Conference adopted innocuous "compromise" language expressing the "sense of Congress" that the United States should have unlimited access to strategic and critical materials vital to its defense and that every effort should be made to remove artificial impediments against the importation of such materials into the United States from Zimbabwe-Rhodesia."[30]

Executive Influence: President Carter's skillful use of the veto threat played a major role in assuring a favorable outcome for the administration at the Defense bill conference. But his narrow victory—by one vote among the House conferees—underlined the administration's problem in prevailing on a second-ranking issue where it was unwilling to spend the political resource of a public veto threat.

Round Five: At Last, Consensus

Under the reigning State Department compromise, the President determined on November 14th that it would not be in the national interest to lift sanctions. The accompanying justification noted encouraging progress in the British-led peace conference and pleaded that "a termination of sanctions at this stage could lead all the parties to harden their positions," jeopardizing the chances for a settlement. It also pointed out that the British had permitted their parliamentary sanctions to expire but had retained most economic sanctions under executive orders. The President would lift sanctions "when a British Governor assumes authority in Salisbury and a process leading to impartial elections has begun. Our policy will continue to be that no party should have a veto over fair settlement proposals." This implied that if the British lifted sanctions and resumed authority in Rhodesia after a successful conference, or an unsuccessful one where the United States judged that the Patriotic Front rejected fair proposals, the United States would then lift sanctions too. Carter promised to keep the issue under continuous review and to "notify" Congress when conditions warranted the lifting of sanctions.[31]

But the Senate Foreign Relations Committee quickly indicated that it was unwilling to leave the future course of sanctions in the President's hands alone.

Helms presented a concurrent resolution to lift sanctions. Following Javits' lead, the committee responded with still another compromise bill which, again, set a date for removal of sanctions (after the arrival of the British Governor in Rhodesia or January 31, 1980, whichever was earlier), included a presidential national interest determination, and provided for a 30-day congressional override. In return for Helms' acquiescence, the administration provided him with a letter unconditionally pledging to lift sanctions within one month of the arrival of the Governor following a successful peace conference, and to consult with Congress if there were no agreement. In the latter case, it was reasonably clear that, if the British sent a Governor out even without an agreement, the United States would be prepared to lift sanctions. This was the import of Assistant Secretary Moose's favorable remarks about the impartiality and justice of the British peace proposals which Muzorewa had already accepted. Helms, who said he had received private assurances that the British would soon send the Governor, clearly believed that the lifting of sanctions was imminent. But to make sure that the President did not slip away, he threatened to bring up his resolution to lift sanctions immediately unless the House acted quickly to pass the Senate bill with its associated administration commitments. Helms' threat was a considerable one. While a similar concurrent resolution could be bottled up in the House, the very introduction of the Helms one in the Senate might send the wrong signal to the delicate negotiations in London which were in their final stages. For this reason, the House Foreign Affairs Committee overwhelmingly endorsed the Senate bill and scheduled it for the floor. But, in the process, two Black Caucus members voted no and three other liberals expressed "reservations" about the United States possibly lifting sanctions prematurely without consulting African countries and the United Nations.

On December 11, the day the House Committee acted, the British sent their Governor to Salisbury without waiting for final agreement by the Patriotic Front to disputed details of the last remaining issue: the cease-fire. The following day, Britain lifted sanctions. On December 15th, President Carter announced that he too was lifting sanctions. On December 17th, the Patriotic Front reached a final agreement with the British, hastened no doubt by the Anglo-American nudge.

CONCLUSION

In the end, the administration achieved one of its few clear foreign policy successes in Rhodesia. It managed to maintain sanctions until the British were able to mediate the Lancaster House Agreement which included a Constitution along the lines of the previous Anglo-American Plan and a British and Commonwealth-supervised election. The election, which took place in February 1980, resulted in a peaceful transfer of power to the Patriotic Front led by ZANU's

Robert Mugabe. Armed with both internal and international legitimacy, the former guerilla leader moved to reassure both the white minority and the West that the government of independent "Zimbabwe" would follow an evolutionary African socialism and maintain friendly relations with capitalist countries. Although the course of future relations with Zimbabwe would depend upon the way in which that government handled domestic pressures for reform and the responsiveness of the United States and other Western countries to its requests for economic assistance, as well as future developments in Southern Africa, it was clear to most observers that U.S. policy had helped achieve a peaceful settlement and left a residue of appreciation in the region.

Several factors accounted for the President's ability to maintain congressional support for his sanctions policy. Most important was the existence in the House of an effective liberal leader and a core of deeply committed supporters, many of whom were on the strategic Africa Subcommittee. It was this group which helped defeat an observer proposal which might have ultimately locked the administration into a favorable view of the Rhodesian election, helped mobilize friendly interest groups behind an effective-in-house lobbying effort, and assembled a politically viable coalition behind legislation to maintain sanctions, and actively preserved its gains at the time of the State and Defense bill conferences. In the Senate, the most active supporters of sanctions—Senator Tsongas, in particular—were not members of the Foreign Relations Committee. And the strongest supporter of the President on the committee, Senator McGovern, was inclined to move carefully. The overwhelming majority of committee members, led by Senators Javits and Church, were disposed to defend sanctions on legalistic or prudential grounds rather than out of a clear and compelling vision of the defects of the Internal Settlement or U.S. interests in Africa.

More stringent House rules also aided the opponents of lifting sanctions. The "germaneness" rule prevented conservatives from getting a timely vote on the attractive observer proposal, and discouraged efforts to lift sanctions in the immediate aftermath of the Rhodesian election. The orderly procedure for the consideration of 30-day concurrent resolutions effectively blocked their utilization by sanctions lifters. On the other hand, the Senate moved twice toward the lifting of sanctions through amendments which would have been largely nongermane in the House. And Senator Helms exploited the Senate's freer procedure for bringing concurrent resolutions on Rhodesia to the floor to force the House to accept a Foreign Relations Committee compromise bill.

At various times, the executive also intervened effectively in the legislative process. By threatening to veto bills lifting sanctions, President Carter helped move Congressman Findley, a key conservative, behind the Solarz bill. By skillfully wielding the veto as both a carrot and a stick, Carter helped persuade reluctant Defense bill conferees that they might obtain a desired nuclear carrier by yielding on Rhodesia. Furthermore, once the executive begain to exploit its considerable political potential—its superior organizational resources and credibility and clout with members of its congressional party and allied interest groups—it was able to rouse up the troops behind the Solarz bill and enlist key leaders in the Defense bill conference.

Yet, the administration's defensiveness and caution on Rhodesia often seemed to weaken its own case in Congress. Its ambivalence toward the observer proposal helped facilitate not only Senate passage, but also the near-adoption of a much more damaging version of the idea in the House. Its decision to forego an early Case-Javits determination after the Rhodesian election and fight a delaying action on procedural grounds helped create a political vacuum on its side of the issue. Its reliance on the Majority Leader as a surrogate for the administration produced a lopsided defeat that gave strong psychological sustenance to its congressional critics. Although the President's policy finally prevailed, there were many occasions when, by dint of insufficient effort, it almost lost. What if the Congress had sent observers and their report was as favorable to the election as Freedom House's? What if the administration's House supporters had not persisted in the Rhodesia Strategy Group due to discouragement? What if the House Defense conferees had not followed their chairman by a single vote? Had Congress passed legislation lifting sanctions, the President could have vetoed it, but the vote itself could have adversely affected the prospects for a peaceful settlement by hardening the Rhodesian adversaries' positions or discouraging British mediation. Ultimately, the President, who had been forced to acknowledge the possibility of dealing directly with Muzorewa in June, might have been forced further down this line.

The basic justification for the administration's caution was that of brushing up its past image of partiality. However, it is difficult to determine whether this strategy had any positive effects, and it ended up yielding considerable political ground to those who were irrevocably opposed to the President's policy. Whatever benefits may have been reaped in the Senate, it was hard to see any in the House where, as it turned out, the administration had the best chance of maintaining its policy.

Another reason for administration delicacy was the fear of having "too full a plate"—too many big foreign policy issues to work on with too little organizational and political capacity. Yet, given the relatively modest scope of the opposition, the administration could probably have maintained a more significant lobbying effort with minimal organizational and political costs. And it was the very failure to make such an effort that created the need for larger and larger efforts to maintain sanctions.

Lastly, whatever judgment one comes to on the administration's overall strategy, its implementation was sometimes faulty: as in the failure to adequately anticipate and counteract the possibility of an unfavorable observers' report, the parliamentary maneuvers of Bauman and Helms, and the wavering commitment of Majority Leader Byrd.

NOTES

1. U.S. Congress, *International Security Assistance Act of 1978*, Section 27.
2. U.S. Congress, House of Representatives, Committee on Foreign Affairs, Subcommittee on Africa, *Hearings on United States Policy Towards Rhodesia*, 96th Congress, 1st Session, March 22, 27 and 29, April 2, 1979, pp. 122–30.
3. *Congressional Record*, March 1, 1979, pp. S 1975–76; U.S. Congress, Senate, Committee on Foreign Relations, *Hearings on Rhodesia*, 96th Congress, 1st Session, March 5 and 7, 1979, pp. 6–9.
4. *Congressional Record*, March 1, 1979, pp. S 1975–76.
5. Senate Foreign Relations Committee, *Rhodesia*, p. 57.
6. Ibid., p. 40.
7. Ibid., p. 77–84.
8. Ibid., pp. 97–103, 121–23.
9. Washington Office on Africa (Washington, D.C.), "Notes on Meeting of Senate Foreign Relations Committee on McGovern-Hayakawa Resolution," March 14, 1979.
10. House Subcommittee on Africa, *United States Policy Towards Rhodesia*, pp. 233–40.
11. *Congressional Record*, April 9, 1979, p. H 2086.
12. Ibid., p. H2095.
13. Ibid., p. H2096.
14. "Memorandum: Re Analysis of Senate Vote on Rhodesia", May 1979.
15. *Washington Post*, April 20, 1979, p. A-13.
16. *Congressional Record*, May 15, 1979, p. S 5884.
17. Ibid., p. S 5889.
18. Ibid., S. 5875.
19. U.S. Department of State, Bureau of Public Affairs, *Sanctions: Zimbabwe-Rhodesia Decision Explained* (Washington, D.C., June 1979).
20. Frances D. Cook to Ambassador Young, Mr. Moose, "Memorandum: President's Statement on Rhodesia, Calls to Make This Morning To Union Leaders," June 8, 1979.
21. U.S. Congress, Senate, Committee on Foreign Relations, *Hearing on Trade Sanctions Against Rhodesia*, 96th Congress, 1st Session, June 12, 1979, p. 24; similar testimony was given to the House Foreign Affairs Committee by Vance the same day.
22. *Congressional Record*, June 12, 1979, pp. S 7379-81, 7398-7400.
23. Ibid., S 7384-86, 7392-96.
24. H.R. 4439, introduced in the House of Representatives June 13, 1979, 96th Congress, 1st Session.
25. Douglas J. Bennett Jr. to the Secretary of State, "Memorandum: House Consideration of Rhodesia," June 20, 1979.
26. *Congressional Record*, June 28, 1979, pp. H 5360-61.
27. Ibid., pp. H 5354-82.
28. Letter from Stephen J. Solarz to House Conferrees on Defense Authorization Bill for Fiscal Year 1980, September 20, 1979.

29. Letter from Jimmy Carter to Chairman John Stennis, September 25, 1979.
30. U.S. Congress, House of Representatives, Committee on Armed Services, *Conference Report: Department of Defense Authorization Act, Fiscal Year 1980*, 96th Congress, 1st Session, October 23, 1979, p. 52.
31. Presidential Determination No. 80-6 and accompanying Justification, November 14, 1979.

REFERENCES

A large portion of this essay is based upon material gathered through participant-observation by the authors. Also, we interviewed several informed officials and legislative staffs who played major roles in the events described. Those interviewed were given assurances of anonymity in order to maximize candor. In addition, the following publications were particularly useful:

Bach, Stanley. *The Amending Process in the Senate*. Congressional Research Service, Library of Congress. March 7, 1980.

Congressional Record, June 28, 1978, S9976-9989.

——, July 26, 1979, S 11783-11806.

——, March 28, 1979, S3582-3597.

——, April 9, 1979, H 2086-2098.

——, May 15, 1979, S 5858-5910.

——, June 12, 1979, S 7376-7402.

——, June 28, 1979, H 5354-5383.

——, July 11, 1979, H 5129-5133.

Deutsch, Richard. "Carter's Congressional Rift," *Africa Report* XXIII (November–December 1978): 46–49.

—— "Rhodesia's Scramble for Senate Votes," *Africa Report* XXIII (September–October 1978): 39–42.

Lake, Anthony. *The "Tar Baby" Option: American Policy Toward Southern Rhodesia*. New York: Columbia University Press, 1976.

Rhodesia: Proposals for a Settlement. London: Her Majesty's Stationery Office, September 1977.

"The Rhodesian Constitution." *Southern Africa* XII (March 1979), 11ff.

U.S. Congress. Senate. Committee on Foreign Relations. *Rhodesia*. 96th Congress, 1st session, March 5, 7, 1979.

—— *Rhodesia*. 96th Congress, 1st session, November 27, 29, 30, and December 3, 1979.

—— *Trade Sanctions Against Rhodesia*. 96th Congress, 1st session, June 12, 1979.

—— *U.S. Policy Toward Africa*. 95th Congress, 1st session, May 12, 1978.

U.S. Congress. Senate. Report 96-448. *Concurrent Resolution to Terminate Sanctions Against Zimbabwe-Rhodesia*, 96th Congress, 1st session. December 4, 1979.

—— . Report 96-41. *Impartial Observers of the Forthcoming Election in Rhodesia*. 96th Congress, 1st session, March 21, 1979.

U.S. Congress. House of Representatives. *Conference Report* 96-546 (Department of Defense Authorization Act 1980). 96th Congress, 1st session, Oct. 23, 1979.

———. *Conference Report* 96-399 (Department of State Authorization Act 1980, 1981). 96th Congress, 1st session, July 31, 1979.

———. Report 96-238. *Zimbabwe-Rhodesia: The Issue of Sanctions.* 96th Congress, 1st session, June 18, 1979.

———. Subcommittee on Africa. Committee on Foreign Affairs. *United States Policy Towards Rhodesia.* 96th Congress, 1st session, March 22, 27, 29, and April 21, 1979.

———. Subcommittees on Africa and International Organizations. Committee on Foreign Affairs. *Economic Sanctions Against Rhodesia.* 96th Congress, 1st session, April 2, May 14, 16 and 21, 1979.

———. *Rhodesian Sanctions: Should the United States Lift Them?* 96th Congress, 1st session, December 5, 11, 1979.

U.S. Department of Justice. *Supplemental Statement* (Pursuant to Section 2, Foreign Agents Registration Act of 1938, as Amended). Rhodesian Information Office (# 1958), January 30, 1979, July 30, 1979.

Chapter 7
Energy Policy
Mark E. Rushefsky

The President ought to be a strong leader. . . . The nation is best served by a strong, independent and aggressive President, working with a strong and independent Congress, in harmony for a change, with mutual respect, in the open.
. . . The President is the only person who can speak with a clear voice to the American people and set a standard of ethics and morality, excellence, greatness. He can call on the American people to make a sacrifice and explain the purpose of the sacrifice.[1]

No nation which lacks a sure supply of liquid fuel can hope to maintain a position of leadership among the peoples of the world. It follows that if the United States is to hold the place it now occupies on the world stage as an effective leader in elevating the standard of living for people, it must develop a national petroleum policy which will make certain that we shall not become dependent upon any other country for our supply of liquid fuel.[2]

Almost half of the last month's troubling increase in inflation is directly traceable to rising energy prices. The message, therefore, should be clear: the energy and inflation problems are inseparably bound. No one is going to solve the inflation problem without first solving the energy problem. . . . That is a stark but simple fact, which must impress itself on the President and the entire political system.[3]

INTRODUCTION

In 1966, Aaron Wildavsky wrote that the United States had two presidencies, a domestic one and a foreign one.[4] Presidents, early in their administration,

161

realized that they had much greater capacity and flexibility to act in foreign affairs, where there were few domestic actors concerned or affected by the course of our foreign policy, compared to domestic affairs where Congress played a key role, and affected interest groups swarmed over Washington lobbying both the legislative and executive branches. Thus, Presidents spent considerably more time on foreign than on domestic policy; the payoffs were simply higher there.

Eight years later, Donald Peppers critiqued the Wildavsky argument and said that times had changed and the distinction between foreign and domestic policy was now a blurred one.[5]

> there is likely to be an increasing emphasis on *nondefense* foreign policy issues, most of which will have a great impact on *domestic* politics and great attraction for domestic interest groups. Problems with the monetary system, trade deficits and surpluses, energy policy, and the import or export of things such as inflation, unemployment, technology, and pollution will consume more and more of the foreign policy effort. This will occur, not merely because the prominence of security issues may be declining relatively with the evolution of detente, but because these nondefense issues will have a larger absolute impact on American society. . . . As post-Vietnam foreign policy becomes more oriented to nonsecurity affairs, the President's choices will become more constrained; on the one hand, by independent foreign actors he will not be able to outmaneuver, such as economic institutions and foreign governments' economic policies, and on the other hand, by the fact that his decisions will have real domestic impact. . . . Indeed, the seamlessness of the distinction between foreign economic and domestic economic policy may simply extend the President's weakness in domestic policy to foreign policy as well.[6]

Peppers may well have understated his case. What we have seen since 1973 and are seeing now (in the case of energy policy) is the impact of foreign security policy on domestic life and our attempts to deal with a domestic issue affecting our security policy. Thus, it is too simple to distinguish between foreign and domestic policy and politics; rather we must now ponder "intermestic" policy.

Consider for a moment the impact which the fall of a king in a faraway and little understood country had on domestic politics in the United States. Iran was a major supplier of oil to the United States as well as an important ally in the strategically vital and politically unstable Persian Gulf region. Indeed, the Shah had been returned to his throne via a coup and covert action by the Central Intelligence Agency, and Iran had been designated as the regional policeman under the Nixon Doctrine. In November 1978, a revolution began against the Shah, led by the Ayatollah Khomeini, and culminated in 1979 with the fleeing of the Shah and the installation of an Islamic republic.

The fallout of that event could hardly be more dramatic. The revolution caused a cessation of all oil imports for several months (and then a resumption at lower levels). The cessation caused a tightening of the world supply of oil; the world market was short some 5.5 million barrels of oil a day (mbd); the U.S. market was short some 500,000 barrels a day. The shortfall permitted the members of the Organization of Petroleum Exporting Countries (OPEC) to significantly raise the price of oil. The shortfall in the United States led to gas lines, relaxation of air pollution standards, higher gas prices, and truck strikes. The higher price of oil (from approximately $14 a barrel in December 1978, to approximately $30 a barrel by December 1979) aggravated the already high inflation rate. By the end of 1979, the inflation rate was 13.3 percent; by March 1980, the rate had jumped to 18 percent. The increased inflation rate, combined with the exigencies of a presidential election, led President Carter to announce in March 1980 a new anti-inflation policy including a balanced budget for fiscal year (FY) 1981 (i.e., budget cuts), tightened credit controls, and an oil import tax.[7]

Further developments in the Persian Gulf area also affected the United States. Perhaps the major one was the Soviet invasion of Afghanistan in December 1979. The invasion heightened concern about Soviet intentions in this area. This act, combined with Soviet efforts in Ethiopia and South Yemen, raised the possibility of a pincers drive directed at this strategic oil supply region. The impact within the United States again was pronounced: the withdrawal of the SALT II treaty (and possibly eliminating any possibility of passage of an already beleagured effort); a beefing up of the defense budget (5 percent a year over inflation for the next five years), and calls for reinstatement of draft registration (and possibly of the draft itself). When the March 1980 budget cuts were announced, the problem of what to cut was compounded by the commitment to increase the defense appropriations. Why had all this occurred?

Few in 1960 could have predicted that by 1973 the United States would be faced with an energy crisis. We were the largest producer of oil in the world and we had ample supplies of natural gas. We had (and have) the largest reserves of coal in the world, and nuclear power generation was just beginning—its promise seemed strong. Beyond these sources were the breeder reactor with its potential for enormously expanding the supply of nuclear fuel; large reserves of oil shale; and, in the more distant future, the promise of fusion and solar energy.

By 1970, the situation had changed. We were no longer the largest producer of oil, indeed, domestic oil production peaked that year; domestic natural gas production would peak three years later. Opposition to nuclear power, combined with technical difficulties and increasing costs, led to a slowdown of construction of nuclear power plants.[8] In 1970, OPEC, previously ineffectual, began to flex its muscles and make demands on the oil companies.

As all this was occurring, the demand for energy increased markedly during the 1960s at an average annual rate of just over 6 percent. By 1977, the situation had changed so as to provide the impetus for the creation of a national energy policy. The United States was highly dependent primarily on two fuel sources, petroleum and natural gas, as it has been before to meet her energy needs. Oil contributed almost 48 percent of our energy needs, and natural gas about 25 percent. But U.S. oil and gas production had declined (see table 7.1) and the removal in 1973 of oil import quotas demonstrated our increased dependence on foreign oil. In 1970, we were importing only 12.1 percent (1324 thousand barrels per day) of our crude oil needs; by 1973, that figure had risen to 26 percent (3,244 thousand barrels per day). When Jimmy Carter became President in 1977, we were importing approximately 45 percent of our crude oil needs (6,548 thousand barrels per day) (see table 7.2). Most of our imports originate with the eleven members of OPEC (89.4 percent). The Arab OPEC members supplied us with 46.4 percent of our imports, and those OPEC members in the Persian Gulf area (i.e., Iran and Saudi Arabia) with 34 percent.[9]

The decline of domestic production combined with the increased reliance on other nations made the United States susceptible to actions by those nations. In 1973, the Arab OPEC nations began an embargo of the Western industrialized nations, especially the United States in response to the October Arab-Israeli war. While the effectiveness of the embargo was questionable, it did create significant disruptions within this country. Similarly, the Iranian revolution and the overthrow of the Shah led to more disruptions in 1979 and the eventual embargo of Iranian oil imports to this country by the President. The interruptions in supply combined with continual price increases (four in 1979) and tightened world markets to create havoc with the American economy.

Table 7.1. U.S. Oil and Natural Gas Production.

	Oil (thousands of barrels per day)	Natural Gas (million cubic feet per day)
1970	9,637	60,057
1971	9,463	61,625
1972	9,477	61,562
1973	9,208	62,048
1974	8,764	59,180
1975	8,375	55,092
1976	8,119	54,515
1977	8,179	54,863
1978	8,701	54,723
1979	8,550	53,795

Source: *Oil and Gas Journal*, January 28, 1980, pp. 119, 124.

Table 7.2. U.S. Crude Petroleum Imports.
(thousands of barrels per day)

1970	1,324
1971	1,681
1972	2,222
1973	3,244
1974	3,477
1975	4,105
1976	5,287
1977	6,548
1978	6,071
1979	6,348

Source: *Oil & Gas Journal*, January 28, 1980, p. 124.

The impact of these problems was three-fold. First, OPEC nations used their possession of this valuable resource as a means of advancing their foreign policy goals. This was by no means limited to the Arab nations. Nigeria was employing oil as a leverage to obtain a satisfactory solution to the Zimbabwe-Rhodesia situation. Mexico was utilizing its newly found but yet undeveloped resources to bargain with the United States over the illegal alien issue and quotas in imports of Mexican vegetables.[10]

Second, and related to the first impact, was the potential for supply disruptions. The dislocations caused by tightened markets and supply cutoffs were significant. Gas lines appeared, workers were laid off, factories were shut down, inflation soared and the economy was into full or near recessions.

The third impact of these developments was on the economy. The price of imported oil rose dramatically, particularly as a result of the Arab oil embargo (1973) and the Iranian revolution (1978) (see table 7.3). Those price increases were reflected in the price of gasoline and especially heating oil (see table 7.4), and also in overall prices as seen in the consumer price index (see

Table 7.3. Crude Oil Refiner Acquisition Costs–1974–1979.
($ per barrel)

	Domestic	Imported	Composite
1974 (av)	$ 7.18	$12.52	$ 9.07
1975 (av)	$ 8.39	$13.93	$10.38
1976 (av)	$ 8.84	$13.48	$10.89
1977 (av)	$ 9.55	$14.53	$11.96
1978 (av)	$10.61	$14.57	$12.46
1979 (av)	$14.27	$21.67	$17.72
Dec. 1979	$18.84	$28.91	$23.63

Source: U.S. Department of Energy, *Monthly Energy Review*, various issues.

Table 7.4. Average (Leaded Regular) Gasoline and Heating Prices, Plus Consumption.

	Gasoline		Heating Oil	
	Price (cents per gallon)	Consumption (thousand bbls. daily)	Price (cents per gallon)	Consumption (thousand bbls. daily)
1973	39.0	6,674	28.7	3,092
1974	52.8	6,537	34.7	2,948
1975	56.2	6,675	37.7	2,851
1976	55.2	6,978	40.6	3,133
1977	58.2	7,177	46.0	3,352
1978	59.8	7,412	49.4	3,432
1979	88.0	7,030	65.6	3,308

Source: U.S. Department of Energy, *Monthly Energy Review*, various issues.

Table 7.5) and compounded because of the importance of oil and other energy sources to the economy. Further, the increased oil import bill led to increased trade deficits which further contributed to inflation and weakened the dollar on the international market (see table 7.6).

One can see the impact of all this via one example: the domestic auto industry. Because the industry was slow to produce more fuel efficient cars, foreign manufacturers (especially Japanese), despite their higher prices, were capturing more of the American market; this resulted in high inventories of

Table 7.5. Consumer Price Index.

1970	116.3
1971	121.3
1972	125.3
1973	133.1
1974	147.7
1975	161.2
1976	170.5
1977	186.1
1978	202.9
1979	229.9

Note: 1967 = 100

Source: Department of Commerce, Bureau of the Census, *Statistical Abstract of the U.S. 1978* (Washington, D.C., Government Printing Office, 1978), p. 478; U.S. Department of Labor, Bureau of Labor Statistics, *Consumer Price Index Detailed Report*, (Washington, D.C., Government Printing Office, January, 1980).

Table 7.6. U.S. Trade Balance. (In Mil. $)

	Exports	Imports	Net	Petroleum Imports
1970	43,224.0	39,951.6	3,272.4	2,764.3
1971	44,129.9	45,562.7	−1,432.8	3,323.3
1972	49,758.5	55,582.8	−5,824.3	4,299.6
1973	71,388.8	69,457.7	1,931.1	7,614.2
1974	98,507.2	100,251.0	−1,743.8	24,269.5
1975	107,591.6	96,116.0	11,475.6	24,814.3
1976	114,992.4	120,677.6	−5,685.2	31,794.5
1977	121,212.3	147,685.0	−26,472.7	41,526.1
1978	143,659.9	172,025.5	−28,365.6	39,108.9
1979	181,801.6	206,326.5	−24,524.9	56,046.0

Source: *Survey of Current Business,* Department of Commerce, Bureau of Economic Analysis.

the domestic companies and layoffs of workers. As a result, talk appeared about limiting imports and/or motivating Japanese companies to begin production here.[11] Thus, the results of increased dependence were manifold: higher energy prices, higher overall prices, an uncertain economy, smaller cars, and a potential change in life-styles.

The events of late 1979 demonstrated the critical importance of our reliance on imported oil. The seizure of the American Embassy in Teheran on November 4 and the extended holding of over 50 American hostages led to tense relations between the United States and the revolutionary government in Iran. One product of that situation was the embargo of Iranian oil shipments to the United States by the Carter administration. A second critical event was the seizure, in late November, of the mosque in Mecca by some 700 people, in a country (Saudi Arabia) that was presumably stable. The third event was the December meeting in Caracas of the OPEC ministers, a meeting which had two results. The first was the failure for the first time to agree on a pricing structure; the second was the fourth increase in OPEC prices in 1979. Saudi Arabia, for example, in an attempt to head off large price increases, raised its prices from $18 to $24 a barrel. The final critical event was the Soviet invasion, in late December, of Afghanistan. Whatever the intentions of the Soviet Union, the effect was to move Soviet troops close to the Iranian border and closer to important oil shipping lanes of the Persian Gulf, especially the Straits of Hormuz. The immediate impact of the Soviet invasion was an increase in the U.S. defense budget and a call for the reintroduction of draft registration.

There were also some indications that oil was having a destabilizing impact on the Middle East countries. Because of the enormous increase in OPEC revenues (see table 7.7), economic development was taking place rapidly in

Table 7.7. Organization of Petroleum Exporting Countries' Revenues, 1970-1978,
(in millions of U.S. dollars)

1970	$ 7,729
1971	11,979
1972	14,374
1973	22,510
1974	90,500
1975	93,350
1976	115,000
1977	127,800
1978	118,300

Source: *The Middle: U.S. Policy, Israel, Oil and the Arabs,* 4th ed. (Washington, D.C.: Congressional Quarterly, 1979), p. 76. Reprinted by permission of the publisher.

Note: The dramatic increase in oil revenues is heightened when one considers that OPEC's 1978 total production was a bit less than her 1973 production level. Anthony J. Parisi, "OPEC Learns to Supply Less and Demand More," *New York Times,* December 16, 1975.

traditional societies, with those societies attempting to control the direction of that development (i.e., Saudi Arabia, Iran). Further, the lower Persian Gulf countries (Saudi Arabia, Kuwait, etc.) with small populations were becoming more dependent on foreign labor (Palestinian, Egyptian) which could prove to be an unsettling influence.[12]

As Stobaugh and Yergin[13] point out, the United States had become dependent on a critical resource from countries that were either hostile to its interests (Iraq, Algeria, Libya) or susceptible to supply disruptions (Iran). The outbreak of war, in September 1980, between the socialist government in Iraq and the revolutionary government in Iran further demonstrated the fragility of our dependence on imported oil. Though the U.S. did import oil from either country, fears were expressed that the war could spread to other Persian Gulf countries, that the important Straits of Hormuz would be blockaded, or that the Soviet Union would either intervene in Iran or gain significant influence in the region. These events required that the United States develop and implement a policy to decrease our vulnerability—thus, the rationale for a national energy policy with a coherent strategy.

The world market also created tensions within the Western industrialized nations. Though the United States depended on imported oil to a much lesser extent than the Western European nations and Japan, the U.S. consumed much greater amounts of oil (see table 7.8). Further, the countries' economies are closely tied. Trade balances, inflation rates in various countries, and growth of the various countries were external as well as internal policy concerns; the countries were economically as well as politically interrelated. Thus, many of our allies felt that it was incumbent upon the United States to decrease her oil consumption, given the greater alternative energy resources available to her and the little that had been done in the way of energy policy.[14]

Table 7.8. Oil Consumption and Imports for United States, Western Europe
and Japan, 1979.
(thousands of barrels per day)

	Consumption	Imports from Middle East	Imports from Africa	Middle East and African Oil as Percent of Consumption
Western Europe	14,870	8,685	2,880	77.8%
Japan	5,495	4,155	15	75.9%
United States	18,434	2,680	3,198	31.9%

Source: *Basic Petroleum Data Book* (Washington, D.C.: American Petroleum Institute, 1980), Section IX, Table 1 and Section X, Table 5. U.S. import figures were derived from tables.

The question to be addressed was what the response to all these developments ought to be. The early responses by Presidents Nixon and Ford were both symbolic and weak. The development of a national energy policy would take time and proceed slowly. The Nixon response was Project Independence, with the goal of making this country independent of imports by 1980, and a system to allocate available oil in the wake of the 1973 embargo.[15] The Ford response was to propose a strategic petroleum reserve, a tariff on oil imports, a floor on imported oil prices, and the decontrol of the price of domestic oil and natural gas.[16] The proposals were controversial, and the result of congressional deliberations was the passage of legislation in 1975, whose major accomplishment was the setting of mandatory automobile fuel efficiency standards, and legislation in 1976 that was quite mild.[17]

While the federal government—both the President and Congress—had provided neither the overall energy leadership nor the policymaking framework needed to adequately deal with the problem of energy as a whole, this early period (1973 to 1976) was important because it placed on the policy agenda those items that would eventually become part of President Carter's various energy proposals (see table 7.9). President Ford proposed a windfall profits tax and backed Senate passage of a loan guarantee program for synthetic fuels research. The questions of controls on oil and natural gas would recur during the Carter administration; and the natural gas issue, in particular, would be a major factor in delaying passage of a National Energy Act.

When Carter became President, he ordered his staff to develop an energy plan within ninety days. The result was the National Energy Plan, which was assembled via a process described by the *New York Times* as "conceived in secrecy by technicians, challenged in haste by economists, and altered belatedly by politicians,"[18] and presented to Congress and the nation in April 1977. It was a complex proposal (113 separate parts) which relied heavily

Table 7.9. Carter Energy Proposals

April 20, 1977

Gasoline tax—five cents per gallon for each of ten years
Gas Guzzler tax—tax on cars burning more fuel than standards and rebates for cars burning less than standards (new car purchases only)
Conservation—tax credits for conservation, utility loans, appliance standards
Crude oil equalization tax—to bring crude oil prices up to world levels and rebate revenues to public
Natural gas pricing—high prices and federal control of intrastate supplies
Coal conversion—mandatory conversion of existing industrial and utility facilities and ban on new facilities burning oil or natural gas; oil and gas users tax
National Energy Act passes Congress—October 15, 1978

February 27, 1979

Maintain thermostats in nonresidential settings within specified levels
Restrict sale of gasoline on weekends
Prohibit most commercial advertising lighting
Gasoline rationing

April 5, 1979

Phased decontrol of domestic oil prices
Windfall profits tax
Energy Security Fund
Conservation efforts

July 15, 1979

Synthetic fuels program
Energy Mobilization Board
Limit on oil imports (quota)
Energy Security Corporation
Requirement that utilities cut oil use 50 percent by 1990

Gasoline rationing passes Congress—October 23, 1979
Congress approves windfall profits tax—March 27, 1980
Congress defeats oil import fee—June 6, 1980
Congress approves synthetic fuels program—June 26, 1980
House defeats Energy Mobilization Board—June 27, 1980

---

on tax and regulatory mechanisms to suppress demand for oil and gas and induce a switch to coal and nuclear power. Congress deliberated on the plan for eighteen months and the result was considerably different from what the President had recommended. The centerpiece of the President's program, the crude oil equalization tax (COET), was rejected; the centerpiece of the 1978 legislation was the phased decontrol of the price of "new" natural gas, not even requested by Carter. Similarly, the impact of congressional action was considerably milder than was originally envisioned in the National Energy Plan.

In April 1979 and again in July 1979, Carter announced further energy policies, partially in response to new international developments, primarily the turmoil in Iran and increased prices for OPEC oil. The April proposals included the phased decontrol of oil prices, a windfall profits tax, an energy securiy fund, and (though not announced with the April address) gas rationing. The July message contained additional proposals including a massive synthetic fuels program to be directed by an Energy Security Corporation, an import quota program, and an Energy Mobilization Board. By February 1980, Congress had passed limited authority for gas rationing and a small synthetic fuels program. The administration, in early 1980, announced a gas rationing proposal and an eight point strategy, including limitations on use of automobiles, in the event of a serious supply disruption. Additional proposals from the administration in early 1980 were directed at increased production of gasohol (in response to the grain embargo of the Soviet Union) and a program to aid utilities in their conversion to coal.

The end result of these proposals and deliberations was the product of a number of forces. There was and is a lack of consensus, reflected in Congress, as to the nature of the energy problem and appropriate mechanisms to resolve that problem. There were questions, quite legitimate, about the merits of many of the President's proposals. There were questions related to the effectiveness of lobbying efforts by the administration to aid passage of its programs and the way the programs, particularly the National Energy Plan, were put together. Because the energy proposals had such wide implications on American life, they were the object of heavy interest group lobbying.

Then, of course, there is Congress. If the energy "crisis" pointed to the need for a coherent national energy policy, then it also tested the ability of Congress to respond to that need. There are a number of factors that both aided and hindered Congress' ability to make energy policy. First was the extreme fragmentation of Congress into committees and subcommittees, each one having jurisdiction over a piece of energy policy, but no one committee having overall responsibility. This problem is not, of course, limited to energy policy; but it is certainly a factor in energy policymaking. The House responded by creating an Ad Hoc Energy Committee fueled by the influence of the Speaker. The Senate was unable to create such a committee and, because its rules were flexible, most of the delay over the National Energy Plan was the product of the Senate. Then, too, energy policy seemed to be affected by dominant personalities with the power to reshape legislation to fit their own perceptions. Given the modest impact of energy legislation passed to date, the question must be raised as to the capacity of our political institutions, particularly the legislative branch, to respond rapidly and appropriately in vital areas.

ISSUES

Basically, there are three substantive issues that surround the makeup of energy legislation.[19] First, there is the question of how much oil and natural gas is left. The question is important because the United States depends so heavily on these two fuels. There are two aspects of this broad and technical issue: the potential domestic reserves of the fuels; and the speed with which they could be developed.

The second issue is the appropriate strategy to respond to the energy problem. This centers around whether we should employ a supply strategy by creating incentives for increased exploration and development of domestic energy resources, or whether we should employ a demand strategy and limit use of oil and gas, or some combination of the two.

The third issue is the perennial government issue; whether government should employ the tax mechanisms as well as regulatory procedures to induce desired changes, or whether the private market through the price system should be primarily relied upon was a question that marked the energy debates.

These issues are captured by the concept of energy ideology, essentially broad frameworks for understanding the role of the federal government in energy policymaking.[20] One ideology is the market approach which suggests that the private market, the price mechanism, and the laws of supply and demand should play major roles in energy development with government having, at most, only a supportive role. The central planning or regulatory ideology would look toward government through tax and regulatory powers to control the development of energy resources. The third ideology, the decentralist approach, would place primary reliance on conservation and renewable resources. Most of the policy debates have been between the first two approaches. The advocates of the first approach have, in general, a supply orientation; there are, these advocates state, bountiful energy resources available if only government would not interfere with the private market. Indeed, they lay the blame for much of the internal dislocations due to energy cutbacks to government regulation. The advocates of the central planning ideology, on the other hand, believe that there is insufficient time to develop other energy resources and that a massive conservation and conversion effort (i.e., to coal) is needed, prodded by government power. Their orientation is one of demand. While any of these approaches, or combinations of approaches, might lead to a resolution of our energy problems, the political task was to choose one approach and follow it. But because each approach implied short-term hardships, and because there were disagreements over the appropriate approach, the decision has not yet been made.

The Carter administration position was clear, though it underwent some change. The National Energy Plan (NEP) opted for a conservation approach, reducing demand through tax mechanisms. Thus, Carter proposed a crude oil equilization tax that would raise the price of old domestic oil to world prices, and an oil and gas user's tax which would force higher energy prices on industries and utilities that did not convert to coal. NEP also contained provisions for rebates to consumers to ease the burden of higher prices rather than allow oil and gas companies to reap the rewards from already developed oil and gas supplies. The 1979 proposals were marked by more of a supply and price orientation, with the phased decontrol of oil and the synthetic fuels program. Even here, there was an attempt to prevent energy companies from realizing the full extent of higher prices through the windfall profits tax. Indeed, the windfall profits tax was a version of the original crude oil equilization tax with the revenues to be used for programs such as synthetic fuels, solar energy, and aid to low income purchasers of heating oil.

Underlying all the Carter proposals were two beliefs. One was that the danger of the energy crisis would appear in the mid-1980s, too soon to develop alternative energy sources; hence the original emphasis on conservation. Second was a distrust of the oil companies, epitomized by the view that those companies would not spend the increased revenues from higher oil prices on new exploration—hence the crude oil equalization and windfall profits taxes.

Congress was of divided opinion. There were, of course, the liberal versus conservative views. The liberal view was typified by Senators Metzenbaum (D.-Ohio), Abourezk (D.-S.D.), and Kennedy (D.-Mass.). They were consumer, rather than producer, oriented, and favored governmental, rather than private, mechanisms. This was especially true of northern Democratic liberals. On the opposite side was the classic grouping of conservative Democrats, many southern, and most of the Republicans.

There were also differences between the two congressional houses. The House of Representatives was much more supportive of the President's early proposals (NEP) than the Senate; this was abetted by the disciplined manner in which the House operated, the support of the proposals by the House leadership, and the use of the Democratic party. Later proposals, such as gas rationing, and jurisdictional disputes—over the mobilization board for example—and fragmentation would slow the process in the House. There were reasons why the House was more supportive of the 1977 proposals than of the 1979 proposals. The National Energy Plan was consumer and urban oriented; it attempted to ease the impact of higher energy prices through devices such as the crude oil equilization tax whose revenues would be rebated to consumers. The later proposals, such as gas rationing and decontrol of domestic crude oil prices, promised supply dislocations (in the case of rationing) and higher prices (in the case of decontrol). The perceived impact of the 1979 proposals on constituents was higher. Thus, the House Democratic caucus went on record against decontrol; indeed, Speaker O'Neill opposed decontrol.[21] House members viewed the proposals from the parochial stance of how it would affect their constituents, when what was needed was the more heroic and difficult stance of what was in the national interest. On the whole, the Senate was more producer- and market-oriented than the House or the President. This was compounded by the relative looseness of Senate rules, the relative lack of support for the President's proposals by the Senate leadership, and dominance of a few individuals in powerful positions, such as Russell Long (D.-LA).

ACTORS

One of the major impacts of the 1973 Arab oil embargo was to change the nature of energy politics. Prior to 1973, policy decisions were made in each of the separate energy areas (and the emphasis was on the production aspect of energy) with no attempt to integrate the separate policies into an energy *policy*. Indeed, we had, and still do to a great extent, *quasi-policies* that aggregate into an energy policy.[22]

But the embargo changed that. Energy, as one writer has stated, had become a disorganizing concept and energy politics was changed.[23] It was changed in the sense that the arena in which politics took place was expanded to include more people than just those directly concerned with the production of energy. Indeed, more people were directly concerned because of the impact and potential impact of energy developments on the economy and life-styles; the issues had changed from distributive to redistributive issues.[24] The scope had been expanded and more people, groups, and politicians became involved in the making of energy policy; the result of this would inevitably be a moderating of the pace of policymaking.[25]

One example of this was the central role that the President played in energy policy, apparent during the Nixon and Ford administrations and patently obvious during the Carter administration. Just prior to the inauguration, Carter had set down the general outlines of what his energy policy should look like. He considered energy policy as one of his top—if not *the* top—priorities. He proposed three sets of policies and engaged in considerable effort to gain their passage. He addressed the nation on energy on a number of occasions, spoke out at press conferences, and made other speeches in an attempt to gain public support for his proposals. Similarly, he engaged in lobbying efforts directed at Congress.

The President was, of course, assisted in his efforts by the resources of the Executive Office of the White House and the various executive agencies. For most of this period, his chief energy advisor was James Schlesinger, first as energy advisor and then as the first Secretary of the new Department of Energy (itself an indication of the centralization of energy policy). Schlesinger brought with him his aides, such as John J. O'Leary, first as head of the Federal Energy Administration and then as Deputy Secretary of Energy. A third important figure was Stuart Eizenstat, Assistant to the President for Domestic Affairs and Policy. Other executive branch personnel involved included Michael Blumenthal, Secretary of the Treasury; and Brock Adams, Secretary of Transportation. By 1979, some administration figures in energy policy had changed. Charles Duncan became the new Secretary of Energy; and Eliot Cutler, Associate Director of the Office of Management and Budget, was assigned the public relations aspects of the energy policy campaign. Other important figures included Gael Sullivan, coordinating congressional support; and Katherine P. Schirmer of the Domestic

Policy staff. Other involved agencies included Health, Education and Welfare; Housing and Urban Development; and the Environmental Protection Agency. While there were a large number of agencies and people involved in formulating and lobbying for energy policy, the decision-making structure was centered in the White House. Such centralization did not occur in Congress. Because the National Energy Plan was so complex, there were five major committees in each house plus subcommittees that had jurisdiction over some aspect of energy policy. In a sense, then, one of the actors was the organizational structure of Congress. The post-Watergate, post-Vietnam changes in Congress made it more difficult for Congress to act as a body.[26] The "subcommittee bill of rights" gave more power to subcommittee chairmen, and it seemed as if every member of Congress chaired some subcommittee. The further disintegration of political parties in Congress and the greater independence of members of Congress compounded the problem, particularly in the House. Chairmen could no longer guarantee that their committee would follow their guidance. There were, of course, institutional rivalries between the two houses and the need to pass identical legislation or resolve differences in Congress. Conference committees, as we see in the natural gas pricing and windfall profits tax issues, could further delay passage of legislation. In the House, the two major committees were the Ways and Means Committee, with jurisdiction over the tax portions of the energy proposals; and the Commerce Committee, with jurisdiction over the major nontax provisions. In the Senate, the comparable committees were the Finance Committee (tax portion) and the relatively new Energy and Natural Resources Committee. Thus, the members of those committees, especially the chairmen and subcommittee chairmen, would automatically be important players.

On the Ways and Means Committee this would include the chairman, Al Ullman (D.-Ore.), and many of the liberal members of that committee. On the Interior and Foreign Commerce Committee, there were essentially three major figures: John Dingell (D.-Mich.), chairman of the Energy and Power subcommittee; Clarence Brown (R.-Ohio), ranking Republican on the subcommittee; and Bob Krueger (D.-Tex.), also on the subcommittee and one of the leading advocates of natural gas deregulation.

An important and unique committee was one approved by the House just prior to Carter's April 1977 energy address: the Ad Hoc Select Energy Committee, chaired by Thomas Ashley (D.-Ohio) and stacked with Democratic party loyalists. The purpose of the ad hoc committee was to provide a central location of authority for passage of the National Energy Plan. Finally, one of the most important actors in energy policy was the Speaker of the House, Thomas O'Neill (D.-Mass.), who prodded the House and oversaw energy policymaking.

In the Senate there was a major figure, that of Russell Long (D.-La), chairman of the Senate Finance Committee. A strong advocate for private enterprise, a spokesman for the oil companies and a representative from an oil state, Long was able to guide his committee in completely removing or drastically modifying the tax portions of the energy proposals, and was quite capable of delaying conference meetings on the tax portions of the legislation until the natural gas pricing question had been resolved. The other major Senate committee, Energy and Natural Resources, was chaired by Henry Jackson (D.-Wash). Other important members of that committee included Bennett Johnston (D.-La), chairman of the Energy Conservation and Regulation subcommittee with jurisdiction over natural gas pricing, and Senators Abourezk and Metzenbaum, leaders of the fight against deregulation. Two other Senators were prominent in the energy deliberations. One was Senator Kennedy. Kennedy was originally supportive of the Carter policies until the April 1979 energy message which contained the oil decontrol proposal. Since that time, and especially since Kennedy's fall 1979 announcement of his candidacy for the presidency, the Senator has been critical of the Carter policies. The other important Senator was the Majority Leader, Robert Byrd (D.-W.Va.). However, both because of his disposition and the greater leeway allowed in the Senate, he was not nearly as strong an advocate of the President's proposals as was Speaker O'Neill. Byrd's major concern seemed to be institutional—that the Senate not be bogged down.[27]

Because the National Energy Plan and the subsequent proposals affected so many different interests, it would be surprising if there were a dearth of interest group activity. All the major interests were represented and vigorously advocated their positions.[28] There were, of course, the energy companies (e.g., Exxon and Mobil) and their trade associations (e.g., the American Petroleum Institute, the Independent Petroleum Association of America, and the Natural Gas Supply Committee). Other interest groups included the coal companies and their trade association, the National Coal Association; the nuclear generator producers and their trade association, the Atomic Industrial Forum; and the utility companies and their trade association, the Edison Electric Institute. All these groups were directly affected by the proposals which, with a few exceptions, they opposed. For example, though NEP called for the increased use of coal, the coal interests were unhappy because the strip mining and pollution control issues were not resolved. Other industry groups were likewise directly affected such as the automobile companies.

Labor was also represented by the United Mine Workers, the United Auto Workers, and the AFL-CIO. Public interest groups also participated in energy politics: groups such as Common Cause, the Sierra Club, the Consumer Federation of America, and the Solar Lobby. Additionally, there was at least one ad hoc political interest group that attempted to affect energy policy—the National Citizens Coalition for a Windfall Profits Tax.[29] Finally, there were organizations of government officials; the strongest were the various gubernatorial associations. The governors were concerned with how various proposals affected their regions and states, and lobbied for control over conservation programs.

STAKES

The energy interest stakes were obvious. Natural gas producers wanted deregulation, but the Carter 1977 plan called for increased regulation, particularly for intrastate gas. The oil companies were faced with continued and more complicated price regulations embodied in NEP, and later with decisions that would affect revenues generated from oil decontrol (the windfall profits tax issue). The public interest groups were consumer and environmentally oriented, and with the 1979 proposals, for example, were concerned about the environmental impact of synthetic fuels development and the possibility of overriding other legislation inherent in the energy mobilization board.

The financial stakes were enormous. Natural gas prices would rise from $1.42 per thousand cubic feet (mcf) for "new" natural gas to $1.99 per mcf in 1978 and $3.86 by 1985 when the new gas would be deregulated. In terms of dollars, the estimate was from $9 billion to $32 billion in additional revenues for natural gas producers between 1977 and 1985.[30] Obviously, it would be the consumer (including industry and utilities) that would be faced with higher prices.

For oil producers, the financial stakes and economic freedom aspects were even greater. Domestic crude oil prices had been controlled since 1970 with the institution of wage and price controls by the Nixon administration. Legislation provided for a complicated system of oil pricing for different categories of oil (e.g., old, new, stripper). The Carter National Energy Plan would have retained the pricing system but added a crude oil equalization tax that would have raised the price of domestic oil to world prices but rebated the revenues to consumers. The tax failed to pass Congress; and Carter, in his April 1979 message, proposed decontrol of crude oil prices. Accompanying the phased decontrol was a plan for collecting the new revenues, or a portion of them, accruing to the oil companies through a windfall profits tax. As the price of OPEC oil continued to rise in 1979, the amount of "windfall profits" dramatically increased (windfall profits defined as the difference between the controlled price of specific categories of oil and the world price). At $22 a barrel, the price of OPEC oil around June 1979, the incremental revenues amounted to $474 billion through 1990. At $30 a barrel (the OPEC price by January 1980) the incremental revenues increased to $938 billion through 1990.[31] Who would receive the money and how it was to be spent were divisive political issues. The Carter administration wanted the funds for energy development projects (i.e., synthetic fuels, solar energy); the oil companies wanted the funds as capital for further energy exploration and development. Later developments in the House-Senate conference committee earmarked most of the funds for tax reductions.[32] Thus, the windfall profits tax issue was one that would take a long time to resolve and saw great differences among all parties involved. Even those who favored the tax disagreed on how to spend it.[33]

THE PUBLIC

Where was the public in all this? The public stake was equally clear. The general public was faced with increased energy costs, whether via taxes or prices; possible disruptions when supplies decreased; and potential changes in life-style. Moreover, the Carter administration was heavily dependent on public opinion to support the President and his policies as a counterbalance to interest groups prepared to gut the proposals. Thus, considerable presidential activity was aimed at mobilizing public support.

Unfortunately for the President and his policies, the public was not supportive. The polls consistently showed four things.[34] First, many people lacked basic information about the extent of the energy problem. For example, a sizable portion of the public did not know that the United States imported oil or how much we imported. Second, except for periods of severe dislocations, such as the embargo in 1973 and the gas lines in 1979, the public has never seen energy as a high priority concern. The state of the economy, during much of the 1970s, was considered a much more important problem. Further, there was no significant change when the President addressed the nation over television or via press conferences, with the partial and temporary exception of the July 15, 1979 speech.

If the public had a view of the energy problem, it was that the crisis was essentially contrived by the oil companies as a means of obtaining higher prices. This belief was hardly dissuaded when, during periods of tight supply and OPEC price increases, the oil companies reported consistently high profits. Given such a view, the public was unwilling to make sacrifices because of energy shortages; they simply did not believe the shortages existed. Thus, Carter's pleas continually fell on deaf ears. Fourth, the ratings of Carter as President showed a consistent decline almost from the time of his inauguration. Because the President had not won the 1976 election by a large popular margin to begin with, the polls convinced congressmen that they had little to fear from the President. Indeed, the President's standing would rise only in the face of direct foreign policy problems (i.e., the hostage crisis in Iran, the Soviet invasion of Afghanistan) and the general acclaim with which Carter handled them. In the case of the Iranian situation, for the first time in almost three years of his administration, Carter would be lauded for his presidential leadership. But the phenomenon may have been only a "rally round the flag" syndrome and could dissipate rapidly. That the crises aided Carter's reelection campaign could not be denied. But an important element in the administration's energy strategy—public support—never materialized.

CONCLUSION

The decline of domestic production of oil and natural gas plus our increased reliance on imports of oil created the need for the United States to develop a coherent energy policy that would guide our transition to a postpetroleum economy. Some national leadership was necessary because of the foreign and domestic implications of imported oil, even if that leadership decided to decrease federal efforts and allow private markets and the pricing mechanism to operate. But, more than six years after the 1973 Arab oil embargo, the United States had not taken decisive action to resolve or even minimize the energy problem.[35] The energy problem has many dimensions, both short and long term, and the effectiveness of energy legislation in dealing with these problems is problematical. For example, a short-term aspect is the impact of oil supply disruptions. How well is the United States prepared to handle a cutoff, such as the one that occurred as the result of the Iranian revolution or the more serious one as the result of the 1973 Arab oil embargo. The gas rationing bill has a 20 percent trigger. If the petroleum shortage were less than 20 percent, the President would need approval of both houses of Congress to implement rationing; if the shortage were greater than 20 percent, then a one-house veto could block implementation.[36] The Iranian cutoff from October 1978 to March 1979 resulted in a 2 to 4 percent decrease in supply (and considerable supply problems as the lengthy gas lines in June attested), while the 1973 embargo resulted in a 13 percent shortfall.

To illustrate further the dependence of the United States on imported oil and the necessity to reduce that dependence, consider the case of the strategic petroleum reserve.[37] The 1975 Energy Policy and Conservation Act called for the creation of a 500 million barrel petroleum reserve that could be used in the event of a cutoff similar to the 1973 embargo. President Carter raised the target to one billion barrels. But by 1979, the program was far from meeting the goals. There were problems of implementation, such as the failure to install pumps to retrieve the oil. But there were also more serious problems.

The United States was purchasing the oil, not on a long-term contract basis as the oil companies were, but on the spot market; that is, they were bidding for oil that often cost $40 a barrel as compared to the high OPEC price in early 1979 of about $23 a barrel. Further, the purchases by the United States would have added demand to an already tight market, thus producing a further price increase. The reserve, therefore, was costing significantly more than planned. There were also indications that OPEC was displeased by the reserve and might reduce production by the amount earmarked for the reserve. Thus, OPEC was telling us whether or not we could be prepared in case of a cutoff of OPEC production.

Other long-term measures that have been taken are equally as ineffectual. The synthetic fuels program, for example, was originally designed to produce 2.5 million barrels a day by 1990. By the time Congress was through with its deliberations, that goal had been reduced to 1.5 million barrels a day by 1995. And this was a program that was, to a great extent, the centerpiece of Carter's July 1979 proposals.

Why had six years of deliberations produced so little in terms of substantive policy or a coherent policy framework? Basically, there are three major reasons: the administration, public opinion, and Congress. First, the administration. There were legitimate concerns raised about the merits of the President's proposals. For example, all four analytical agencies of Congress (the General Accounting Office, the Office of Technology Assessment, the Congressional Budget Office, and the Legislative Reference Service) issued reports criticizing the various energy proposals.[38] All four agreed, for instance, that the goals of the National Energy Plan were unlikely to be met.

Additionally, the way the proposals were put together hurt their chances for passage. The National Energy Plan was formulated in a rather secretive process that ignored not only other members of the administration but members of Congress also. The view of the President was that he would present Congress with a plan and they would accept it on its merits. The plans were also assembled so rapidly to meet deadlines that there were gaps and inconsistencies which, when pointed out, served to weaken the arguments for them. This was most true of the National Energy Plan, but was also the case with the July 1979 proposals.[39]

A constant theme, almost from the moment of inauguration, was the poor liaison work between the administration and Congress.[40] Representatives and senators were rarely consulted during the formulation stage, and lobbying efforts were inconsistent. For example, the President was quite effective in his lobbying efforts during the initial House consideration of the National Energy Plan, but failed to follow up in the Senate. Similarly, administration witnesses were seen as ineffective in defending the various proposals. As late as November 1979, an article appeared in the *New York Times* with the headline, *"Slow Improvement Is Seen in White House Relations with Congress."*[41]

The second major factor was public opinion. As discussed in the introduction, Carter was counting on the backing of public opinion for his energy proposals as a counter to heavy industry lobbying against them. But with the brief exception of the July 15, 1979 speech, little that Carter did seemed to make a difference. The theme of most of the proposals was sacrifice, which meant higher prices and scarcer supplies. But, as measured by a number of polls, the public consistently believed that the energy problems were contrived, either by the oil companies or by OPEC. Carter could not, therefore, count on public support for his policies.

Then there is Congress. Energy policy provides an excellent opportunity to examine the ability of Congress to make public policy. It is no surprise to observers of Congress that that institution proceeds cautiously. But energy policy seemed to have a different imperative. Energy policy has both domestic and foreign implications—it is "intermestic policy." The fact of U.S. dependence on foreign countries for a critical resource meant that our foreign policy independence was compromised. Wildavsky has written of the "Two Presidencies," the domestic and the foreign policy presidencies:

> The President's normal problem with domestic policy is to get congressional support for the program he prefers. In foreign affairs, in contrast, he can almost always get support for policies that he believes will protect the nation.[42]

But if the foreign policy was to decrease dependence on imports of oil for national security reasons, then that policy would have internal significance, and it would be viewed not only as to its impact on foreign policy but also as to how it would affect any number of domestic interests. Thus, the advantage that Presidents have in foreign and national security policy was missing. Congress would clearly be a factor.

There are a number of factors that explain the results of congressional deliberations on energy policy. First is a set of organizational and procedural components. The federal government was deliberately designed to impede action, particularly by the legislative branch. Thus, we have the two houses of Congress and the need to pass identical legislation or reconcile differences in conference. Then, Congress conducts most of its work in committees, but the committee structure is a fragmented one. For example, when the National Energy Plan was sent to Congress each house had five committees with some jurisdiction over the legislation. A foreign policy requires a unity of purpose—one reason why the President has been dominant in policy formulation and execution in this area. But, with a wide variety of committees and subcommittees having a "piece of the action" that unity never appeared. For example, the committees considering the synthetic fuels program were not the same committees deliberating over the windfall profits tax, the funds from which were to be used, at least partly, for synthetic fuels development. There were some attempts to overcome this fragmentation in the House with the employment of an ad hoc energy committee and the use of the Democratic Party and the leadership, especially of Speaker O'Neill. But the ad hoc committee, as its name indicated, was a temporary situation; and there were points at which the party and other leadership elements were ineffectual—gas rationing, for instance. There are also current attempts in the House to strengthen party leadership and resolve some of the jurisdictional disputes over energy policy, but the jurisdictional issue (changing committee structure) has bogged down because of the impact the changes would have on particular representatives (i.e., Dingell).[43] The Senate was not able to undertake such integrative action (though it did create a standing energy committee); and, indeed, the leadership of the Senate was not nearly as supportive or effective as the House leadership.

Another difference between the two branches was procedural. The House is a more tightly organized and disciplined body, primarily because of its size; there are limits on debates and amendments. The Senate is more loosely run; for example, ordinarily there are no limits on debate and the opportunity to filibuster can cause both delay and frustration. Natural gas pricing is a case in point.

Then there is the influence of dominant personalities in Congress, people in positions of power on critical committees. Senator Long, chairman of the Finance Committee; Senator Johnston, chairman of the Energy Conservation and Regulation Subcommittee; Representative Dingell, chairman of the Energy and Power Subcommittee; and Speaker O'Neill were very influential in congressional deliberations over energy policy. But—and this is a big but—they were influential in different directions. Long and Johnston were opposed to the President's policies, O'Neill and Dingell were supportive. Long especially, because of his position and political astuteness, was able to shape energy legislation, even legislation that did not come under his committee's jurisdiction. He was able, for example, to delay conference considerations of the tax portion of the National Energy Plan until the natural gas deregulation issue was resolved, presumably in the direction he favored. The action of the Finance Committee to weaken the windfall profits tax is another mark of Long's influence (though, of course, he was supported in his efforts by a majority of the committee).

None of these factors would matter were it not for the lack of a national consensus as to how to resolve the energy problem or even what the extent of the problem was. The lack of consensus was combined with the issue of institutional distrust between the legislative and executive branches. The energy issue is one that requires a long-term solution, though there are short-term measures that need to be taken. But many in Congress looked at the question from the short-term perspective of who would benefit and who would lose. Energy was viewed from a parochial rather than from a national perspective.

The historic distrust between the President and Congress was exacerbated during the Johnson and Nixon administrations. Indeed, one theme of the successful Carter presidential campaign was the restoration of trust in the presidency. But the distrust remains and shows up in the unwillingness, for example, to give the President gas rationing authority except under fairly rigid conditions. Similarly, the attempt at placing restrictions on the President's ability to impose quotas on imports is a further indication of this distrust. The impact is to make it more difficult for the President to impose control measures in the event of a disruption in oil supply.[44]

Then there are the divisions in Congress that are reinforced by the enormous implications of potential energy resource scarcity and the redistributive nature of the issues.[45] There are liberal versus conservative interests, consumer versus producer interests (with the House more consumer-oriented and the Senate more producer-oriented), urban (especially in the House) versus rural (Senate) interests, environmental versus industrial interests. Of course, politics played a role in two senses: one way was the expected situation of Democrats and Republicans often on opposite sides, although many of the interests overlapped; then, too, presidential electoral politics played a role, with disagreements between President Carter and Senator Kennedy. One must not forget the multitudinous interest groups that attempted to affect energy policy. Each group, each interest, was prepared to defend its status and avoid a sacrifice. By the time all these interests were through, it was hard to see where the greater national interest lay.[46] The spending of the revenues from the windfall profits tax is illustrative. By the time House-Senate conferees were through, they had allocated only 3 percent to synthetic fuels development, and 60 percent of the $227 billion for a general tax cut.

A major question raised by the energy crisis is the capacity of our political institutions to deal with the problem of scarcity.[47] The problem has profound implications. The United States has generally relied on economic growth as a means of effecting social change and upward mobility for previously deprived groups. Economic growth allows for increased income for all groups without delving into the politically contentious issue of income redistribution. To use a metaphor, we have increased the size of the pie without examining whether or not some received bigger slices than others. But what would happen if economic growth slowed or ceased altogether; what if the pie remained the same size? Then we, as a nation, would begin to examine the fairness of the distribution of economic resources. Politics as usual would come to a halt; compromise would be difficult if not impossible, because we would move from a nonzero-sum situation (where everyone wins) to a zero-sum situation (where one person's gain is another person's loss).

This is a major impact of the energy problem. Energy may well be necessary for continued economic growth (though we can apparently do more with less energy than had been thought possible). Until the transition to a postpetroleum economy is complete, continued economic growth, and thus upward mobility for many, is problematical. For example, inflation increased dramatically in late 1979 and early 1980. The result, especially with a presidential election, was a tightening of the federal budget with most cuts coming in social programs accompanied by restrictions on the availability of credit. That inflation had many causes; but either directly or indirectly, one major cause was high energy prices (and our declining domestic capacity to produce oil and natural gas). Thus, growth of the budget has been severely curtailed, and the budget cutting process will be a difficult one: who will bear the burden of the cuts? Increasing budgets are always an easier and happier experience.[48]

But with such politics of scarcity, the normal compromises and log-rolling that are characteristic of our politics become rancorous. Where scarcity is not a factor, we can afford the kind of politics where each actor or set of actors seeks to further his own interests and where the public interest emerges from the interplay of rival actors. Where scarcity is a factor, then something more than procedural democracy is needed; indeed, scarcity calls into question the viability of democratic, and especially decentralized, institutions. Thus, the fact that we have yet to adopt a strong, coherent energy policy may be reflective of the inability or unwillingness of democratic institutions to face up to this problem of scarcity (at least scarcity in the short run).

This is not to say that nothing has been accomplished. The Carter and pre-Carter legislation will have and is having some impact. There are indications that gasoline consumption may have peaked, and other indications that conservation efforts are working.[49] Certainly, increased prices are a major factor in the lessened demand for oil products seen in 1979. Even if the federal government were united in the creation of an energy policy, there is a limit to what government can do.[50] Many energy decisions are in other hands—the general public, industry, energy companies, OPEC. The impact of these individual, private decisions may have more to do with the transition to a postpetroleum society than anything government may do.

It seems clear, based on more than six years of attempts at energy policy-making, that the single most important factor in passage of effective energy legislation is a sense of urgency and crisis, one that will not dissipate rapidly. For, without it, government machinery will act, if at all, very slowly.

> The disarray in Iran is another reminder of the growing vulnerability of the West. Even a suspicion that Iranian oil production had stopped again caused oil prices to shoot up overnight. And Iran, which in October [1979] exported fewer than 3 million barrels a day, is not the only Persian Gulf nation upon which the West depends. . . .
>
> The tiniest of these nations can thus be critically important. And since the Iranian revolution, *every* government in the area has been troubled by domestic opposition. Most of them are also concerned about external threats. The sense of security that the United States and the Shah once provided is gone. . . .
>
> In sum, a few well-aimed bullets around the Persian Gulf could cause a massive leak of Western-bound oil. There is no real prospect, let alone guarantee, of stability. The region's tensions are rooted in political, religious, national, dynastic, and military rivalries only marginally related to the Arab-Israeli conflict and largely beyond American influence. No prudent nation would count on containing them. It would race to escape its dependence.[51]

NOTES

1. Jimmy Carter, 1976, quoted in Dom Bonafede, "Carter Moves Boldly to Save His Presidency," *National Journal* 11 (July 28, 1979): 1239.

2. *Investigation of Petroleum Resources in Relation to National Welfare,* final report of the U.S. Senate Special Committee Investigating Petroleum Resources, 1947, quoted in Stephen Klebanoff, *Middle East Oil and U.S. Foreign Policy with Special Reference to the U.S. Energy Crisis* (New York: Praeger, 1974), p. vi.

3. "Energy is Still the Problem: Inflation is Merely the Mirror," *New York Times* (editorial), (July, 1979), p. 29.
4. Aaron Wildavsky, "The Two Presidencies," in *Perspectives on the Presidency*, edited by Aaron Wildavsky (Boston: Little, Brown, 1975), pp. 448-61.
5. Donald A. Peppers, "'The Two Presidencies': Eight Years Later," in *Perspectives on the Presidency*, pp. 462-71.
6. Ibid., pp. 463-64, 469.
7. Stephen R. Weisman, "Carter to Trim Budget $13 Billion and Curb Credit to Cut Inflation," *New York Times*, March 14, 1980.
8. The slowdown in orders and construction predated the accident in 1979 at Three Mile Island. For an account of the problems of the nuclear industry, see Richard Corrigan, William J. Lanouette and Robert J. Samuelson et al., "Energy Industry and the Government," *National Journal* 10 (June 10, 1978): 918-21.
9. Figures derived from Robert J. Beck, "Production Flat; Demand, Imports Off," *Oil and Gas Journal* 78 (January 28, 1980): 124.
10. See "Mexican Gas Deal Hinges on Tomatoes," *Gainesville Sun*, June 23, 1979; and Steven Rattner, "Oil Guns Get a Bigger Bang for the Buck," *New York Times*, July 15, 1979.
11. See, for example, Robert J. Samuelson, "A Troubled Future for the Automobile," *National Journal* 12 (March 15, 1980): 427-31.
12. See Youssef M. Ibrahim, "Persian Gulf May be 'Losing Control,'" *Gainesville Sun*, January 28, 1980.
13. Robert Stobaugh and Daniel Yergin, "Energy: An Emergency Telescoped," *Foreign Affairs* 58 (1980): 563-95.
14. See, for example, Paul Lewis, "Pinched Industrial Nations Getting Their Act Together," *New York Times* June 24, 1979, p. 24.
15. For an examination of energy policymaking in this early period, see T. H. Tietenburg, *Energy Planning and Policy: The Political Economy of Project Independence* (Lexington, MA: Lexington Books, 1976); and David Howard Davis, *Energy Politics*, 2nd ed. (New York: St. Martin's Press, 1978), pp. 92-105.
16. See *Energy Policy* (Washington, D.C.: Congressional Quarterly, 1979), pp. 35-A-86-A.
17. Energy Policy and Conservation Act, PL 94-163, December 1975; and Energy Conservation and Production Act, PL 94-385, August 1976.
18. James M. Naughton, "Carter Shaped Energy Plan With Disregard for Politics," *New York Times*, April 14, 1977.
19. See Frances Anderson Gulick, "Energy-Related Legislation Highlights of the 93rd Congress and a Comparison of Three Energy Plans Before the 94th Congress," *Public Administration Review* 35 (July/August 1975): 346-54.
20. See Terry D. Edgmon, "Energy as a Disorganizing Concept in Policy and Administration," *Policy Studies Journal* 7 (Autumn 1978): 64-65; and David W. Orr, "U.S. Energy Policy and the Political Economy of Participation," *Journal of Politics* 41 (November 1979): 1027-56.
21. Ann Pelham, "House Democrats Back Oil Price Controls," *Congressional Quarterly* 37 (May 26, 1979): 997-98, 1035.

22. Anthony King, "On Studying the Impacts of Public Policies: The Role of the Political Scientist," in *What Government Does,* edited by Matthew Holden, Jr., and Dennis L. Dresang (Beverly Hills: Sage Publications, 1975), pp. 301–02.

23. Edgmon, "Energy as a Disorganizing Concept."

24. See Theodore J. Lowi, "American Business, Public Policy, Case-Studies, and Political Theory," *World Politics* 16 (July, 1964): 677–715; Randall B. Ripley and Grace A. Franklin, *Congress, the Bureaucracy and Public Policy,* rev. ed. (Homewood, Ill.: The Dorsey Press, 1980); and Michael T. Hayes, "The Semi-Sovereign Pressure Groups: A Critique of Current Theory and an Alternative Typology," *Journal of Politics* 40 (Feb. 1978): 134–161.

25. See E. E. Schattschneider, *The Semi-Sovereign People* (New York: Holt, Rinehart and Winston, 1960); and Roger W. Cobb and Charles D. Elder, *Participation in American Politics: The Dynamics of Agenda Building* (Boston: Allyn and Bacon, 1972).

26. See Lawrence C. Dodd and Bruce I. Oppenheimer (eds.), *Congress Reconsidered* (New York: Praeger Publishers, 1977).

27. Byrd's viewpoint is demonstrated by his role in ending the Metzenbaum-Abourezk filibuster over natural gas price decontrol (Bob Rankin, "Senate Continues Dismantling Energy Plan," *Congressional Quarterly* 35, Oct. 8, 1977: 2122, 2136–38); and in prodding the Senate on the windfall profits tax ("Byrd Warns Oil Industry to Back 'Fair' Tax," *Gainesville Sun,* December 9, 1979).

28. See James E. Anderson, David W. Brady, and Charles Bullock III, *Public Policy and Politics in America* (North Scituate, Mass: Duxbury Press, 1978), pp. 52–55; and "Energy Establishment," *Washington Post,* April 23, 1977.

29. Richard Corrigan, "Scrambling For a Share of 'Windfall Profits,'" *National Journal* 11 (November 10, 1979): 1885–1888.

30. Richard Corrigan, "The Oil-Gas Price Gap is Widening," *National Journal* 12 (February 16, 1980): 282.

31. Corrigan, "Scrambling For a Share of 'Windfall Profits.'"

32. Ann Pelham, "Conferees Agree on Windfall Tax Bill," *Congressional Quarterly* 38 (March 1, 1980): 591–93.

33. Corrigan, "Scrambling For a Share of 'Windfall Profits.'"

34. See Walter A. Rosenbaum, *Coal and Crisis: The Political Dilemmas of Energy Management* (New York: Praeger, 1978), pp. 8–12. This section is based on a number of public opinion polls, including the Gallup Poll and the *New York Times*/CBS Poll. See, for example, Anthony J. Parisi, "Poll Shows Doubts Over Energy Shortage," *New York Times,* November 6, 1979.

35. The actual process of energy policymaking is extremely complex. It features twists and turns, stalemates and sudden parries. To enable the reader to have an understanding of the difficulties of policymaking without getting bogged down into detail, we have provided a chronology of important events in table 7.9. The reader should rapidly observe the length of time required to effect passage of energy legislation.

36. Ann Pelham, "New Standby Gas Rationing Powers Voted," *Congressional Quarterly* 37 (October 27, 1979): 2411-13.
37. See, for example, H. Josef Hebert, "U.S. Oil Storage Program Just an Embarrassment," *Gainesville Sun*, Sept. 10, 1979. The synthetic fuels bill, passed by Congress on June 26, 1980, contained a mandate to recommence filling the reserve. See Ann Pelham, "Synthetic Fuels Bill Nearly Ready for Carter," Congressional Quarterly 38 (June 21, 1980): 1695.
38. See, for example, General Accounting Office, *An Evaluation of the National Energy Plan* (Washington, D.C.: Government Printing Office, 1977); Office of Technology Assessment, *Analysis of the Proposed National Energy Plan* (Washington, D.C.: Government Printing Office, 1977); and Steven Rattner, "Carter Plan Gets Pumped: Will It Pump More Oil?" *New York Times,* April 27, 1979.
39. Bob Rankin, "Carter's Rush Led to Confusion," *Congressional Quarterly* 35 (June 18, 1977); and Steven Rattner, "Casting Out the Energy Package Has Barely Begun," *New York Times,* July 22, 1979.
40. Dom Bonafede, "Carter's Relationship With Congress—Making a Mountain Out of a 'Moorehill,'" *National Journal* 9 (March 26, 1977): 456-63.
41. Martin Tolchin, "Slow Improvement is Seen in White House Relations With Congress," *New York Times,* November 19, 1979.
42. Wildavsky, "The Two Presidencies," p. 448.
43. See Martin Tolchin, "House Democrats Seek a Return to Strong Leadership," *New York Times,* October 24, 1979; Warren Weaver, Jr., "House Acts to Spur Energy-Issue Moves," *New York Times,* November 4, 1979; and Irwin B. Arieff, "House Rejects Proposal For New Energy Committee," *Congressional Quarterly* 38 (March 29, 1980): 886. Indeed, the only change was to add the word "energy" to the title of the House Commerce Committee.
44. Steven V. Roberts, "Carter and Congress: Doubt and Distrust Prevail," *New York Times,* August 5, 1979; and Terence Smith, "Carter and Congress: The Last Picture Show," *New York Times,* September 9, 1979.
45. Warren Weaver, "Completing Energy Program Creates Smoke, Little Fire," *New York Times,* September 30, 1979.
46. John Herbers, "Carving Up the National Goals Leaves Very Little," *New York Times,* July 23, 1979.
47. William Ophuls, *Ecology and the Politics of Scarcity* (San Francisco: W. H. Freeman, 1977),
48. Aaron Wildavsky, *The Politics of the Budgetary Process,* 3rd ed. (Boston: Little, Brown, 1979).
49. Anthony J. Parisi, "Electricity Use No Longer Soaring; Nation Expected to Benefit in 80's," *New York Times,* April 6, 1980; Michael Knight, "Sharp Decline in Sales of Home Heating Oil is Reported by Dealers," *New York Times,* November 22, 1979; Richard D. Lyons, "Big Drops in Oil Use Spur Hope," *New York Times,* Nov. 21, 1979; Anthony J. Parisi, "The End of an Era: Gas Consumption Peaking," *New York Times,* September 16, 1979; and Anthony J. Parisi, "Slower Oil Price Rises Expected," *New York Times,* April 3, 1980.

50. The Energy Information Administration conducted a survey which concluded that federal energy policies since 1973 have had and will have only limited impact on energy supply, consumption, prices and imports. See "Little Impact on Fuels Seen for U. S. Moves," *New York Times,* August 13, 1980.

51. "How Fragile the Oil Machine," editorial, *New York Times,* November 8, 1979.

Chapter 8
Congress and the Presidency: The Dilemmas of Policy-Making in a Democracy
Joseph L. Nogee

The seven case studies considered here involve some of the most difficult foreign policy issues which faced the United States during the 1970s. Each study describes a struggle between the legislative and executive branches of government to determine the direction American foreign policy would take. With the exception of the chapter on energy policy, these case studies focus on a specific conflict between the United States and a foreign country. Mark Rushefsky's essay on energy publicy fits in, nevertheless, with the others because of the obvious linkage between domestic energy policy and United States relations with the Organization of Petroleum Exporting Countries (OPEC) and the Arab states of the Middle East in particular. Indeed, no single development during the 1970s had a more profound impact on American foreign policy than the dependency of the industrial democracies upon Middle Eastern oil.

The legislative-executive struggle described in these essays is one of the recurring themes of American constitutional history. American foreign policy has alternated between the pendulum swings of congressional versus presidential dominance in the formulation of policy, although the long-term trend has clearly favored the latter. That trend toward presidential power has been significantly reversed since the Vietnam War and the scandals of Watergate. We may be in what Thomas Franck and Edward Weisband describe as "a revolution that will not be unmade,"[1] a permanent shift of power toward Congress in the realm of foreign policy-making. While some, like Franck and Weisband, welcome this development, others have serious reservations. Even so ardent a critic of presidential power as J. William Fulbright admitted not long ago "I confess to increasingly serious misgivings about the ability of the Congress to play a constructive role in our foreign relations."[2] Which side is right? Should Congress or the President have the major voice in formulating foreign policy? What conclusions can we draw from the case studies presented here?

Any assessment of the proper role of the executive and legislative branches of government in the realm of foreign policy must begin with the Constitution. It is clear that the Founding Fathers intended that both branches of government be directly involved with foreign policy, for considerable powers are conferred on each. Under the Constitution, the President: (1) is empowered with the executive authority of the government; (2) is Commander-in-Chief of the Army and Navy; (3) can negotiate treaties; (4) appoints ambassadors, public ministers and consuls; and (5) receives ambassadors and other public ministers. Some of these prerogatives such as the treaty-making and appointive powers are subject to senatorial concurrence. Presumably the Founding Fathers saw these powers as the means by which the President would exercise the guiding hand in the conduct of the nation's foreign relations, for, in part, they called the Constitutional Convention into existence because of the mismanagement of foreign affairs by the Congress under the Articles of Confederation.[3]

That the Founding Fathers did not intend to create an "imperial presidency" is evident by the extensive powers given to the Congress in foreign affairs. Chief among them are the power to declare war, the power to authorize and appropriate funds, the power to raise and support an Army and Navy, the legislative power, the power of the Senate to advise and consent to treaties, and the power of the Senate to confirm executive appointments. Thus, the Constitution establishes a system of checks and balances with the potential for executive and legislative authority to develop in one of several different directions. The ambiguity of the constitutional mandate is well summed up in the oft-quoted observation of Edwin S. Corwin, the constitutional scholar, that the Constitution was "an invitation to struggle for the privilege of directing American foreign policy."[4]

Over the long haul the President has fared better than the Congress in that struggle because circumstances—both internal and external—have made the existence of a strong chief executive necessary for American security and prosperity. In other words, executive power reflects an adaptation of the American political system to meet the needs imposed by our domestic society, as well as those imposed by the international system. Foremost among the requisites for an effective foreign policy is the need for national leadership to provide for a coherent foreign policy, and it is here that Congress is at a distinct disadvantage.

THE PROBLEM OF LEADERSHIP

Never in American history has the problem of leadership been so linked with the security and well-being of the nation; rarely have the circumstances of domestic life made the creation of that leadership more difficult to obtain. The problem confronting American national political institutions is how to mobilize a fragmented public to support a coherent and sound foreign policy. In large part, the fragmentation of American political life is the product of a crisis of authority in American society. The institutions and values that have united Americans in the past no longer have the influence they once did. Increasingly American political activity is organized around an identification that stresses the separation of the individual from the larger society rather than his unity with it. Today these include political groups based upon racial, ethnic, sexual, generational, ideological, religious, professional, economic and other such identifications. We have "single issue," "special interest," and "political action" committees whose focus is on narrow issues rather than comprehensive programs. National political parties have steadily declined in appeal and importance. The number of voters who reject both major political parties has risen steadily in recent years to the point where independents now outnumber adherents to one of the two major political parties.

Inevitably, Congress also reflects the fragmentation of American political life. The decline in strength of the national political parties is reflected in the weakness of party authority in both houses of Congress. Not only party leaders but all the formal authorities of Congress—its officers and committee chairmen—are challenged today as never before. Seniority, which used to carry great weight, is now sharply reduced in importance. The new breed of congressman insists upon maintaining his or her independence. Until fairly recently, the practice was for committee recommendations to be accepted almost automatically by the full membership. This is no longer true, particularly in the area of foreign and defense policy. Ironically, a proportion of this new independence is the consequence of recent structural reforms intended to democratize the institution. For example, the availability of increased staff support now makes it possible for a congressman or senator to obtain his own supporting data and, thereby, to come to policy conclusions independently of the party of congressional leadership. Thus, Congress today is more decentralized than it ever has been. According to one recent study "The chief consequence of this structural disunity is to divide the congressional perspective, making the creation of an integrated and coherent legislation and policy almost impossible."[5]

The decentralized character of Congress is only part of its difficulty in formulating a coherent foreign policy program. There is in addition the problem of the lack of competence, interest, or purpose of the individual legislator. The vast majority of the members of the House of Representatives and, to a lesser degree, the Senate are motivated by a rather specialized set of concerns. Every congressman represents a specific constituency and is expected to support the interests of his or her district whether or not that coincides with the broader interests of the nation. Perhaps an extreme illustration is the story about the chairman of the House Naval Affairs Committee who, when asked whether the navy yard in his district was too small to accommodate the latest battleships, replied, "That is true, and that is the reason I have always been in favor of small ships."[6] As David Mayhew has noted in his study of Congress, the overriding goal of all members is to be re-elected.[7] Not unexpectedly, each congressman must promote the particular interest of his district. Of necessity he must be responsive to pressures from ethnic, racial, or religious minorities whose concerns may well be narrower and more parochial than those of the nation as a whole.

Foreign policy issues rarely have the support "back home" to induce a congressman to make them a major part of his legislative repertory. Indeed, as James Sundquist notes ". . . being national minded can be a positive hazard to a legislative career."[8] There are many congressmen ready to support defense appropriation because of sizable defense or defense-related industries in their districts. But who, for example, speaks for arms reduction or SALT? Apparently few. Alan Platt, in a recent study, found that:

> Perhaps most importantly, virtually no member of Congress felt compelling constituent pressure to play a more active role in the SALT process. . . . During the 1969–1976 years, there was little electoral incentive for any senator to be actively involved in the SALT policy process. On the contrary, almost all senators felt pressure to focus their attention on matters of higher political salience and more immediate urgency to their constituents. . . .[9]

Generally, foreign policy issues are further removed from the experience and knowledge of most congressmen. On domestic issues, members of Congress have the benefit of information (selected, of course) made available by constituency lobbies and special interests. They are more at home with domestic than foreign issues. As Congressman Les Aspin puts it, "Almost every Congressman feels that he is an expert on education, or economics or any number of domestic issues. But when it comes to defense, most Congressman lack confidence, and so they turn to 'experts.'"[10]

Further undermining the capacity of Congress in the foreign policy field is the process by which it does its business. An effective foreign policy must bring into balance a large number of diverse issues involving many different states. This is what is meant by coherence. The difficulty with the legislative process is that there is no one place in the institution where foreign policies are aggregated and synthesized. Every piece of legislation is examined independently in committee and acted upon in relative isolation from other related bills. Though principal responsibility falls upon the Foreign Relations Committee of the Senate and the Foreign Affairs Committee in the House, these are by no means the sole examining bodies of important foreign policy matters. According to one account, issues involving national security matters are dealt with by 16 Senate and 19 House committees and an even larger number of sub-committees.[11]

It is not uncommon for the same matter to be considered by two or more committees. Sometimes, committees only peripherally connected with foreign policy must act upon important foreign policy issues, such as the post office and civil service and judiciary committees which considered the bill for the Panama Canal treaty implementation in the House of Representatives.[12] The effect is to isolate issues that are very much connected in the real world. It is difficult, if not impossible, in most cases for Congress to make the necessary trade-offs, bargains, and compromises which are called for in an effective foreign policy. Thus, George Kennan observed that:

> Congress can act upon foreign policy only fitfully, in great ponderous lurches which establish its direction, and the limits within which it can vary, for often prolonged periods into the future. This may well have a certain negative value, as an insurance against Executive folly; but it greatly limits, of course, flexibility of reaction on the part of the Executive, where it does not rule it out entirely. It makes it impossible for the Executive branch to react sensitively and effectively to changes in the objective situation that were not foreseen and could not have been foreseen (and the course of international affairs is replete with such changes) at the time when the respective congressional norm was laid down.
>
> Congressional participation in the policy-making process, in short, not only reduces privacy of decision but inflicts upon that process a high degree of cumbersomeness and inflexibility; and these conditions, in combination, deprive the policy-maker of the possibility of initiative, the advantages of surprise, and the capacity for sensitive response to the unexpected.[13]

THE INTERNATIONAL ENVIRONMENT

Political power, then, has shifted away from the legislature to the executive, in part because the presidency is better structured than Congress to provide national leadership. The fragmentation of American politics and the diffusion of public authority are reflected in a decentralized Congress which cannot provide the leadership which a strong foreign policy requires.

We turn now to the reason why the United States more than ever must have a strong and coherent foreign policy. That reason has to do with the nature of the international system and the character of international politics.[14]

Since World War II, the international system has undergone considerable change. We are now in the midst of continuing change which makes it difficult to discern clearly all of the directions of global system change so as to know with any degree of certainty what kind of a world we are confronting. However, certain basic features seem to be clearly evident. The nation-state remains the dominant, though not the sole, political actor. The international system continues to be decentralized, that is, it lacks a universal, guiding mechanism or a world government. Nations are compelled to look to their own means for security and so engage in a continuous struggle for power. War and the use or threat of force remain among the maximum instruments for achieving national objectives. There is general agreement that a degree of interdependence exists among nations, particularly in the economic realm, but this interdependence does not limit political behavior in such a way as to keep nations from going to war against each other.

International politics today is characterized by a relatively high degree of tension and conflict. Currently, the major source of tension in the world is the East-West conflict. What keeps the leaders of the North Atlantic and Warsaw Pact alliances from going to war against each other is the nuclear arsenals possessed by the two superpowers. There are numerous other conflicts at the sub-nuclear level. Within the Third World, ethnic, racial, and nationalistic conflicts have frequently resulted in war. In addition, there is the non-violent but bitter hemispheric struggle between the industrialized "Northern" countries and the underdeveloped "Southern" nations for economic leverage and benefit.

Though international politics has always been characterized by a high degree of anarchy, there have been periods in the past when a greater degree of political consensus prevailed among the leading actors than exists today. For example, in the aftermath of World War II there was a more discernible commitment among the nations of the world against the use of force than there is today. Following the defeat of the Axis Powers the victorious Allied nations were determined to prevent another world war and toward that end created the United Nations as an instrument of collective security. The primary purpose of that organization, as stated in its Charter, was "To maintain international peace and security, and to that end: to take effective collective measures for the prevention and removal of threats to the peace, and for the suppression of acts of aggression or other breaches of the peace . . . ."[15] Many people looked upon the United Nations as a step in the direction of a world government. But the system of collective security established in the United Nations never came into operation and is now recognized as defunct. Perhaps of even greater significance has been the general decline in the commitment of nations to the renunciation of the use of force as an instrument of national policy. There is little doubt that the United Nations today is far less united than it was in the 1940s or that the prospects for world government are more remote than at any time since World War II. The idea of peace through collective security is a Western concept and as Western power has declined, so has Western political theory. In fact, many U.N. General Assembly declarations attest to the readiness of most of its members to resort to force to attain some political end.

What the disunity of world politics implies for the United States—and indeed, for all great powers—is the necessity of a strong, coherent, and rational foreign policy to guide the affairs of state in a world that regrettably must still be characterized as anarchical. The existence of nuclear weapons may indeed make war among the major powers more dangerous than ever, but the only guarantee that any superpower has that these weapons will not be used is the maintenance of a credible deterrent. And it is unrealistic not to anticipate that force and the threat of force at the non-nuclear level will continue to be a feature of international politics. The argument for a strong President rests in part on the contention that the United States must speak with one voice to other states; that the executive branch is better able than other branches of government to provide national leadership and mobilize the nation when United States interests are threatened; that the conduct of diplomacy often requires a government to act with speed and efficiency; and that the President still has access to vital sources of information which are unavailable to the Congress.

THE DILEMMA OF POLICY-MAKING

We turn now to the evidence of the case studies. Though, in part, these studies support the argument for presidential authority in foreign affairs, they do so only with qualifications and reservations. Perhaps the most basic conclusion to be drawn from them is that an effective foreign policy requires a partnership between the two branches of government, a partnership which the American political system makes difficult to attain. In each of the issues examined here the President and part of Congress took different positions on foreign policy issues because each was reflecting in different degrees the pressures of different constituencies. Four of the essays illustrate the impact on Congress of ethnic or religious groups whose objectives were narrower and more parochial than those of the administration. This was the case with Jewish groups in support of the Jackson-Vanik Amendment, the Israeli lobby on the sale of weapons to Arab governments, the Greek lobby in support of the Turkish embargo and the Black Caucus supporting sanctions against Rhodesia. In addition to ethnic and religious groups, Congress was pressured by economic interests as the oil companies (to influence energy policy), the AFL-CIO (for the Jackson-Vanik amendment) and the ferrochrome and stainless steel industries (over Rhodesian sanctions).

One cannot automatically assume that in every case the administration was right, and the Congress wrong, because the President was pursuing a "general" as opposed to a "special" interest, though several of the authors implicitly do come to that conclusion. But it is fairly evident that in several issues Congress made it difficult for the United States to pursue a coherent foreign policy. By a coherent policy we mean one that coordinates multiple objectives (some of them contradictory) with many nations (some of them adversary) in such a way as to maximize overall United States interests. For example, in the Middle East, Israeli security is an important United States objective, but so is the maintenance of United States influence among the Arab governments, particularly the pro-Western moderates. Kissinger's "shuttle diplomacy" following the 1973 war was designed to achieve both objectives. As John Roehm points out, Congress undermined that diplomacy by making it difficult for the United States to appear to be an honest broker and to influence the Israeli government toward flexibility in its negotiations with the Arabs. "Congressional activism," he concludes, " . . . clearly distorted the coherence of Kissinger's Middle East policy. . . ."[16]

Similarly, the Jackson-Vanik amendment distorted United States relations with the Soviet Union. The Nixon-Kissinger strategy was to use trade as one of the building blocks of detente. Presumably, the growth of Soviet-American economic ties would encourage the USSR to moderate its aggressive foreign policies. There is no guarantee that the tactic would have worked, but the idea is basically sound. As Dan Caldwell points out, had the trade patterns developed in the 1970s that were planned under the United States-Soviet Trade Agreement before the Jackson-Vanik Amendment, the United States today would have considerably more leverage than it does in confronting Soviet aggression in Afghanistan. The United States, he believes, "would have been in a far better position in the 1980s to influence Soviet foreign policy without the Jackson-Vanik Amendment than with it."[17] The point is that Congress, in pushing for a relatively limited though desirable objective, jeopardized a larger and more important policy. As it turned out Congress also set back the progress of Jewish emigration.

The Turkish embargo is a classic illustration of the disruptive effects of an ethnic minority—in this case the Greek lobby—operating upon Congress. Turkey posed a dilemma for the United States because it was both an aggressor and an ally. The larger goal, which was the concern of the Administration, was to keep Turkey as a viable member of NATO and retain United States bases on Turkish territory. A glance at a map will reveal the critical geo-strategic position of Turkey. It not only borders on the Soviet Union (and Iran) but it controls the narrow waters (the Bosporus and the Dardanelles) through which every Soviet vessel from the Black Sea must pass. Cyprus does not compare in importance. As Keith Legg points out, Congress' action was counterproductive. Instead of encouraging Greek-Turkish negotiations over Cyprus, the embargo only made Turkey more adamant. "The major consequence," Legg concludes, "was a re-examination by Turkey of its ties to the United States."[18]

Rhodesia-Zimbabwe also involved the issue of coherence in American foreign policy. This was a case where diplomacy, to be effective, had to be subtle and quickly responsive to changing circumstances. Presidents Ford and Carter both wanted the authority to maintain sanctions against the government of Rhodesia in order to use it as a weapon against the white minority to pressure them to make more concessions to the black majority, and also against the Patriotic Front in order to induce it to accept a compromise settlement. Lifting sanctions would have undercut British diplomacy in London to get both sides to accept a constitution and supervised elections. It would certainly have been a major blow to United States influence in Africa and the Third World. In the end, the administration overcame the efforts of the Senate to force the lifting of sanctions with the result, according to Stephen Weissman and Johnnie Carson that "U.S. policy . . . helped achieve a peaceful settlement...."[19] Here was a case where policy coherence was maintained by the victory of the President and one house of Congress over the other house.

The case of energy is special because it involved essentially a domestic issue, but one with important implications for foreign policy. United States dependence on OPEC threatens American security on at least three counts: (1) An embargo such as occurred in 1973 could seriously disrupt the economy; (2) the spiralling cost of oil stimulates inflation, and by adding to trade deficits, undermines the soundness of the dollar; and (3) it makes the United States vulnerable to foreign policy demands of the Arab governments. Legislation to reduce American dependence failed in Congress because of the opposition of many interests: oil and coal companies, the nuclear industry, labor and public interest groups. "House members," noted Mark Rushefsky, "viewed the [administration's] proposals from the parochial stance of how it would affect their constituents, when what was needed was the more heroic and difficult stance of what was in the national interest."[20]

Congressional action on the Panama Canal and SALT II treaties illustrate in different ways the capacity of a minority of Senators to obstruct the President in the conduct of foreign policy. It is significant that even though Congress was involved in the formulation and negotiation of these treaties to an extraordinary degree, the Panama Canal treaties passed with a margin of only one vote to spare, while the SALT II treaty had to be withdrawn in the face of Senate opposition. Both treaties, in the view of the authors of the two case studies, fundamentally served the interests of the United States. The Panama Canal treaties normalized United States relations with Panama and improved relations with all of Latin America; also it contributed toward a more stable, secure, and trouble-free operation of the canal. While the Senate did ultimately consent to ratification, the bitter debate on ratification coupled with the determined efforts of the House of Representatives to scuttle the treaty did considerable damage to the prestige of the Carter administration and destroyed some of the good will produced by the treaty. Though President Carter did prevail, William Furlong believes that "The President's position in national and international leadership was . . . weakened by the whole process."[21]

Even before the election of Ronald Reagan, SALT II was a doomed treaty, in spite of the fact that President Carter, like his Republican predecessors, had made SALT the centerpiece of his policy toward the Soviet Union. The domestic political struggle over SALT according to Stephen Flanagan "caused many observers at home and abroad to question . . . whether Washington is capable of executing coherently its major foreign policy initiatives."[22] SALT II was conceived of as an important step toward the avoidance of nuclear war and the enhancement of crisis stability. It set quantitative limits on the strategic arms competition and extended the dialogue between Washington and Moscow which both sides consider vital so long as each possesses nuclear arsenals. Specifically, the Carter administration considered SALT II important because it would have initiated the reduction of Soviet stockpiles, halted development of certain Soviet weapons systems, set limits on the total number of nuclear warheads the USSR could throw against the United States' ICBM deterrent (thus reducing "Minuteman" vulnerability), and finally, it would have made easier American monitoring of Soviet weapons development.

The SALT II treaty was a victim not just of hardliners in the Senate but of powerful elements in the executive bureaucracy as well. Flanagan describes several power centers and coalitions that emerged in the SALT II debate. Often the Arms Control and Disarmament Agency and State Department were arraigned on one side of an issue against the Joint Chiefs of Staff, Defense Department and National Security Council, so that opponents and proponents of the treaty could find support in the executive branch as well as the Congress. Jimmy Carter was simply not able to build the consensus necessary to ratify SALT II. The vote was believed to be close in late 1979 when the issue was still before the Senate, but the Soviet invasion of Afghanistan killed whatever prospects SALT II might have had.

The preponderance of judgment in the case studies is that where the President and Congress differed on an issue, the position of the former served the larger interests of American foreign policy better than the latter. This would seem to support the argument for a reversal of the post-Vietnam trend toward enlarging the congressional role in foreign policy. But on close examination, these case studies reveal a more complicated picture, raising doubts that a stronger presidency alone can guarantee an effective foreign policy. For example, Congress can rarely be described as a unitary actor. Not infrequently the two houses were divided with one house supporting the President. We saw this to be the case with Rhodesian sanctions, where the House of Representatives resisted senatorial pressures and saved administration policy. In the case of the Panama Canal, the situation was reversed with the House of Representatives determined to subvert administration policy, which had been endorsed by the Senate. The early energy proposals of the Carter administration had more support in the House than the Senate, though the positions were reversed with the later Carter proposals. Thus, at least potentially, the Congress is capable of being an ally as well as an adversary. More thought needs to be given to examining the conditions under which an executive-legislative partnership can be built.

Another point brought out in some of the case studies is that policy may falter because of the inadequacies of the President or divisions within the executive bureaucracy. There is no guarantee that an unencumbered President will be effective.

The authors of the studies in this volume have amply documented mistakes committed by the Nixon, Ford, and Carter administrations. Mark Rushefsky, for example, puts part of the blame for the failure of Congress to enact a comprehensive energy program on inadequate executive planning and poor liaison between the White House and Capitol Hill. Dan Caldwell attributed the collapse of the United States-Soviet trade agreement partially to the failure of President Nixon to involve Congress in the negotiating process. Weissman and Carson, in their analysis of economic sanctions against Rhodesia, put some of the blame for the Byrd Amendment on the indifference of President Nixon and the ineffective leadership of the Carter administration. The overall record of the Carter administration attests to the fact that leadership may falter under any circumstances. Institutional reform, in other words, does not guarantee leadership. There is no substitute for a capable, determined, and knowledgeable President.

CONCLUSION

We return to the question posed at the beginning of this chapter: should Congress or the President have the major voice in formulating foreign policy? The thrust of this essay has been to favor the latter. The case for presidential predominance in foreign policy rests on two general grounds: first, national security necessitates a foreign policy that is adaptable and capable of rapid and, if necessary, strong action in order to operate in an anarchic international environment; and secondly, the difficulty of Congress to develop a coherent and flexible foreign policy. Henry Kissinger summed up the issue in arguing that:

> The Congress can set broad guidelines and decide basic policies. But the Congress does not have the organization, the information, or the responsibility for deciding the tactical questions that arise daily in the conduct of our foreign relations or for executing a coherent, consistent, comprehensive policy. The President has this responsibility and must be permitted to exercise it on behalf of the entire nation.[23]

It is unlikely, however, that this problem can be resolved with a simple formula. We have previously noted that a large range of foreign policy decisions are today closely interwoven with domestic issues as the term "intermestic" reminds us. American democracy has been confronted with a fundamental dilemma from its very inception, and that is the necessity of American institutions to protect domestic liberty while at the same time operating effectively in the international system. Democracy requires a strong Congress; security requires a strong President. Whichever side one takes in this debate, one must still come to grips with this dilemma.

NOTES

1. Thomas M. Franck and Edward Weisband, "Congress as a World Power," *Worldview*, October 1979, p. 6.

2. J. William Fulbright, "The Legislator as Educator," *Foreign Affairs, Spring* 1979, V. 57, No. 4, p. 719.

3. Cecil V. Crabb, Jr. and Pat M. Holt, *Invitation to Struggle: Congress, the President and Foreign Policy,* (Washington: Congressional Quarterly Press, 1980), p. 34.

4. Edwin S. Corwin, *The President: Office and Powers, 1787-1957.* (New York: New York University Press, 1957), p. 171.

5. Richard Haass, "Congressional Power: Implications for American Security Policy," *Adelphi Paper,* No. 153, London: The International Institution for Strategic Studies, p. 7.

6. This irresistible story was told by Henry Stimson and is recounted in James L. Sundquist, "Congress and the President: Enemies or Partners?" in *Congress Reconsidered,* ed. by Lawrence C. Dodd and Bruce I. Oppenheimer, (New York: Praeger Publishers, 1977), p. 230.

7. David Mayhew, *The Electoral Connection,* (New Haven: Yale University Press, 1974).

8. Sundquist, *Congress and the President,* p. 230.

9. Alan Platt, *The U.S. Senate and Strategic Arms Policy, 1969-1977, (Boulder: Westview Press,* 1978), p. 101.

10. Ibid., pp. 100-101.

11. Haass, *Congressional Power,* p. 7.

12. William L. Furlong, "Negotiation and Ratification of the Panama Canal Treaties," chapter 4.

13. George F. Kennan, *Cloud of Danger, Current Realities of American Foreign Policy.* (Boston: Little, Brown, 1977), p. 6.

14. There are many fine descriptions of international politics. One that comes readily to mind is John Spanier, *Games Nations Play,* (New York: Holt, Rinehart Winston).

15. Article 1, Section 1.

16. John F. Roehm Jr., "Congressional Participation in U.S. Middle East Policy, October 1973-1976: Congressional Activism vs. Policy Coherence," chapter 2.

17. Dan Caldwell, "The Jackson-Vanik Amendment," chapter 1.

18. Keith R. Legg, "Congress as Trojan Horse? The Turkish Embargo Problem 1974-1978," chapter 5.

19. Stephen R. Weissman and Johnnie Carson, "Economic Sanctions Against Rhodesia," chapter 6.

20. Mark E. Rushefsky, "Energy Policy," chapter 7.

21. Furlong, chapter 4.

22. Stephen J. Flanagan, "The Domestic Politics of SALT II: Implication for the Foreign Policy Process," chapter 3.

23. Speech made February 4, 1976, *The Department of State Bulletin,* Vol. LXXXIV No. 1914, March 1, 1976, p. 256.

Index

About the Contributors

John **Spanier**, born in Germany, received his B.A. and M.A. at Harvard University and Ph.D. at Yale University. He is Professor of Political Science at the University of Florida and has been Visiting Professor at Haverford College, University of Texas, and Merrill Chair Professor at Utah State University. Past President of International Studies Association, South, he has lectured widely at various universities and service academies in the United States. He has also been State Department lecturer in Poland and West Germany. Among his many books are *The Truman-McArthur Controversy and the Korean War, American Foreign Policy Since World War II, Games Nations Play, The Politics of Disarmament* (coauthored with Joseph Nogee), *World Politics in an Age of Revolution,* and *How American Foreign Policy is Made* (coauthor).

Joseph L. **Nogee**, Ph.D., Yale University, is Professor of Political Science at the University of Houston. He has held visiting positions at New York University, Vanderbilt, and the Strategic Studies Institute of the Army War College. He is a former member of the Council of the American Political Science Association, a past President of the Southwestern Political Science Association, and a member of the editorial board of the *American Political Science Review.* His other books include *Soviet Policy Toward International Control of Atomic Energy, The Politics of Disarmament* (co-author), *Man, State and Society in the Soviet Union* (editor), and *Soviet Foreign Policy since World War II* (co-author).

Dan Caldwell is Associate Professor of Political Science at Pepperdine University, Malibu, California. He is the author of *American-Soviet Relations: From 1947 to the Nixon-Kissinger Grand Design.*

Johnnie Carson is a U.S. Foreign Service Officer, currently on leave as Staff Director of the Subcommittee on Africa of the U.S. House of Representatives' Foreign Affairs Committee. He holds an M.A. in International Relations from the London School of Economics. He has served abroad in the American Embassies in Lagos, Nigeria, and Maputo, Mozambique. As Deputy Chief of Mission in Mozambique during the mid-1970s, he was in contact with leaders of the Zimbabwe African National Union—including current Zimbabwe President Robert Mugabe—who were based in Mozambique during that period.

Stephen J. Flanagan, A.B., Columbia; Ph.D., The Fletcher School, is a Professional Staff Member of the Select Committee on Intelligence, United States Senate. Dr. Flanagan has published several articles on SALT and European security. Much of the underlying research for this chapter was completed while he was a Warburg Fellow at the Center for Science and International Affairs, Harvard University.

William L. Furlong, Associate Professor of Political Science at Utah State University, has published articles on municiple administration, political development, and international problems in Latin America. His chapter on "Democratic Political Development and the Alliance for Progress" can be found in Howard Wiarda's *The Continuing Struggle for Democracy in Latin America.* He is now in the process of editing a book entitled *The 1977 Panama Canal Treaty: The Struggle for a New American Foreign Policy.*

Keith Legg, B.A., University of Minnesota, Ph.D., University of California at Berkeley, is Professor of Political Science at the University of Florida. He is the author of *Politics in Modern Greece,* and other articles and books on comparative and international politics.

John F. Roehm, Jr., is Advisor to the Adjutant General of the State of Colorado. A 1950 graduate of the U.S. Military Academy, he served in Korea, Europe, and Vietnam. He holds an M.A. in English Literature, Columbia University, an M.A. in International Relations, Boston University, and a Ph.D. in Political Science, University of Pittsburgh. He has been Visiting Professor of Military Science at the University of Pittsburgh.

Mark Rushefsky, B.A., Queens College, Ph.D., State University of New York at Binghamton, is Assistant Professor of Political Science at the University of Florida. He does research and writing on energy and health policy and has contributed articles to the *Policy Studies Journal* and the *Journal of Health Politics, Policy, and Law.*

Stephen R. Weissman is Staff Associate with the Subcommittee on Africa of the U.S. House of Representatives' Foreign Affairs Committee. He received his Ph.D. in Political Science from the University of Chicago where he was a Falk Fellow in American Politics. He is the author of *American Foreign Policy in the Congo 1960-1964,* and articles on various aspects of U.S. policy making towards Zaire and Angola, Western Sahara, and Africa generally in *Political Science Quarterly, Foreign Affairs, Jeune Afrique Annuaire,* and other publications.